Years of Change
European History
1890–1990

Third Edition

ROBERT WOLFSON
AND JOHN LAVER

Hodder Murray
A MEMBER OF THE HODDER HEADLINE GROUP

～ ACKNOWLEDGEMENTS ～

The Publishers would like to thank the following for permission to reproduce the following material in this book:

David Higham Associates Ltd, for an extract from *Studies in War & Peace* by Michael Howard (2000) used on page 121; Greenwood Publishing Group Inc., for an extract from *My Autobiography* by Benito Mussolini (2001) used on page 191; Harper Collins (Harper & Row), for an extract from *The End of European Primacy 1871–1945* by J.R. Western (2000) used on page 122; Harper Collins (Harper & Row), for an extract from *Economic Consequences of the Peace* by John Maynard Keynes (1920) used on page 154; Harper Collins (Harper Trade), for an extract from *Hitler: A Study in Tyranny* by Alan Bullock (1991) used on page 200; Hodder & Stoughton, for an extract from *From Bismarck to Hitler: Germany 1890–1933* by G. Layton (1995) used on page 47; John Terraine, for an extract from *The Mighty Continent: A View of Europe in the 20th Century* by John Terraine (1974) used on page 123; Oxford University Press, for an extract from *England 1870–1914* by Sir Robert C. Ensor (1975) used on page 121; Pearson Education Ltd, for an extract from *Gorbachev* by Martin McCauley (1998) used on page 379; Pearson Education Ltd, for extracts from *The Soviet Home Front 1941–1945* by J. Barber and M. Harrison (1991) used on pages 326 and 327; Penguin Books Ltd, for extracts from *The Kaiser and his Times* by M Balfour, used on pages 59 and110; Penguin Putnam Inc. (Coward-McCann & Geoghegan), for an extract from *From Vienna to Versailles* by L.C.B. Seaman (2001) used on page 123; Random House Inc., for an extract from *A People's Tragedy. The Russian Revolution 1891–1924* by Orlando Figes (1997) used on page 80; Routledge, for an extract from *The Great War 1914–1918* by M. Ferro (1986) used on pages 121–2; Simon Publications, for an extract from *The War Memoirs of David Lloyd George* by David Lloyd George (2001) used on page 118; Transaction Books, for an extract from *Nazism: A Historical and Comparative Analysis of National Socialism* by G. Mosse (1978) used on pages 177–8; WW Norton and Company, for an extract from *Germany's Aims in the First World War* by F. Fischer (1996) used on page 122; Yale University Press, for an extract from *The Unknown Lenin* by Richard Pipes (1996) used on page 254.

The Publishers would like to thank the following for permission to reproduce the following copyright illustrations in this book:

AKG Photo London pages 16 (above), 231; AP Photo/Libor Hajsky/CTK page 381; AP Photo/Worth page 359 (above); Berliner Mauer-Archiv (Hagen Koch) page 358; Bibliotheque Nationale de France (Paris) page 33; Bildarchiv Preussischer Kulturbesitz page 155 (below); © British Museum, Department of Prints & Drawings page 277 (below); Will Dyson, Daily Herald, 13th May 1919/Centre for the Study of Cartoons and Caricature, University of Kent, Canterbury page 156; Giancarlo Costa page 175; David King Collection pages 73, 94, 95 (left), 95 (right), 346; David Low, Evening Standard, 24th January 1921/Centre for the Study of cartoons and Caricature, University of Kent, Canterbury CT2 7NU, Kent © Atlantic Syndiaction page 155 (top); Edimedia page 104; © Hulton Deutsch pages 17, 117; Hulton-Deutsch Collection/Corbis pages 167, 352; © Hulton Getty pages 3, 16 (below),63, 143, 173, 209; © Imperial War Museum page 310; John Appleton, Solo Syndication/Centre for the Study of Cartoons and Caricature, University of Kent, Canterbury, page 108; Peter Leibling/Bildarchiv Preussischer Kulturbesitz page 359 (below); Punch Publications Limited, pages 56, 59; Ullstein Bild-Stary page 341; Weimar Archive page 49.

Every effort has been made to trace and acknowledge ownership of copyright. The publishers will be glad to make suitable arrangements with any copyright holders whom it has not been possible to contact.

Orders: please contact Bookpoint Ltd, 130 Milton Park, Abingdon, Oxon OX14 4SB. Telephone: (44) 01235 827720. Fax: (44) 01235 400454. Lines are open from 9.00–6.00, Monday to Saturday, with a 24 hour message answering service. Email address: orders@bookpoint.co.uk

British Library Cataloguing in Publication Data
A catalogue record for this title is available from the British Library

ISBN-10: 0 340 77526 2
ISBN-13: 978 0 340 77526 4

First published 2001
Impression number   10 9 8 7 6 5
Year   2007 2006

Cover photo shows 'The Big Three' at the Yalta Conference, 1945, The Art Archive.

Produced by Gray Publishing, Tunbridge Wells, Kent
Printed in Malta for Hodder Murray, a division of Hodder Headline, 338 Euston Road, London NW1 3BH

Contents

⤳ LIST OF TABLES ⤳

❧ LIST OF MAPS ❧

⤳ LIST OF DIAGRAMS ⤲

⤳ LIST OF ILLUSTRATIONS ⤲

⤳ LIST OF PROFILES ⤳

↶ LIST OF ANALYSES ↷

Introduction to the Revised Edition

∽ GENERAL ∽

The principal aim of this book is to provide a factual account, combined with some analysis, of the events of this crucial period in modern European history. Several chapters follow a 'country by country' approach, often divided into sections on political history, economic developments and foreign affairs. Where this division is adopted, it is of course an artificial one, but many students find this approach useful particularly when coming to a study of the subject for the first time. There are frequent cross-references alongside the main text, and these should help readers place developments in a broader context.

This considerably revised edition takes account of the changes in the English AS and A2 examinations introduced in 2000. The text is designed to be useful for AS students seeking a broadly narrative outline to particular topics; whilst students studying at a more advanced level will find the analytical sections useful. The bibliographies at the end of chapters provide suggestions for further reading. The exercises at the ends of chapters, including structured questions, essays and source-based exercises, supplemented by advice, are also designed to assist students with the requirements of various examination courses. However, this book has been written not just with the expectations of students following the English examination system in mind: it should be useful to any student in the 16–19 age group following a course in modern European history.

∽ THE STARTING DATE ∽

The starting point of 1890 has been chosen for specific reasons. Primarily, this is a book about the twentieth century. Since any student of history has to study the period immediately preceding his or her main focus, we have in many cases taken the narrative back to 1870. Had we chosen 1870 as our starting date, we would have been forced to examine the events of the 1850s and 1860s. This would have given the book too great an emphasis on the nineteenth rather than the twentieth century.

Secondly, the 1890s were, in a number of respects, a starting point for reigns and events that were to have a crucial bearing on the twentieth century: Bismarck resigned as Chancellor of Germany in 1890 and Nicholas II became Tsar of Russia in 1894. Similarly, many of the issues and disputes that came to a head in World War I had their foundations, though not their origins, in the 1890s.

There are only two chapters covering the period after the World War II, which finished in 1945. These two chapters between them take the history of Europe to 1991, and specifically the break-up of the Soviet Union and the ending of the Cold War. Space does not permit a detailed treatment of all European affairs after 1945. We have deliberately focused on themes relating to the Cold War, the origins of which can be traced back to the Russian Revolution of 1917 which brought the Communists to power, and have also taken account of the emergence of the USA on to the world stage. After 1945 Europe was seemingly no longer in charge of its own destiny. Whilst events such as the creation and development of the European Union were of great significance, we have not covered them in great depth, but have described and analysed some of the main events in Western and Eastern Europe. We have also detailed the impact of the USA and the USSR, the two post-war Superpowers, on Europe. We have knowingly focused on certain events at the expense of others. The justification for this focus might seem arbitrary: it is an attempt to pursue the legacy of the events and developments of the first half of the twentieth century through the crises of the Cold War and the particular ways in which Europe was affected by Superpower dominance. Students seeking a more wide-ranging approach to developments in specifically post-1945 European history, including those involving for example the European Union, will benefit from studying a companion volume in this series, *Years of Division: Europe Since 1945.*

STRUCTURED ANSWER SKILLS

Most history examinations, for example those designed for AS students in their first year of advanced study at post-16, require answers to structured questions. These will vary considerably in format, but will often be in two or three parts, and each part may require a different type of response. The 'lead-in' question may simply ask for an explanation of a term given in a source or stimulus material. For example, the question might ask, 'What do you understand by the term "Lateran Treaty"?' Such a question requires some background knowledge. A more demanding analytical question might be the next one: 'What was the significance of the 1929 Lateran Treaties in the context of relations between the papacy and Mussolini's Fascist state?' This requires a more sophisticated response. It is important to pay attention to the mark allocation for such questions. A question may carry only a few marks, for example 3 or 4, and should require no more than a short answer of a few lines or a short paragraph. Other structured questions will carry a higher mark tariff, say 7 or 15 marks, and will require a more substantial answer. Make sure that you follow the instructions: the question will almost certainly require you to introduce some 'own knowledge' into your answer, but it may also require you to make use of source material if this is provided. If this is the case make sure that you do both. However, these questions will rarely be 'full' essay answers in their own right: the time you are expected to devote to such questions may be no more than 20 minutes. You should adjust your answer accordingly: it is important to be concise and direct in your answer, and not become over-conscious of the need to structure it with an 'introduction' or 'conclusion' in the way you would with more substantial essay answer. In other words, whilst you should write in good English, you will be marked on substance and not style.

✐ ESSAY-WRITING SKILLS ✐

Essays, in the sense of one-part questions expecting an answer of some 45 minutes, require lengthier answers than those expected in response to structured questions. Such essays often fall into one of the following categories:

(i) 'List' questions require you to list, usually, causes and/or effects of a particular event or series of events. For example, they may ask you to 'account for' (list the *reasons*) the outbreak of war in 1914, 'explain' why there were revolutions in Russia in 1917 or identify the 'effects' or 'consequences' of Fascist rule in Italy. This type of question requires a series of paragraphs that put forward a number, or 'list', of the different reasons, effects, etc.

   A good answer requires more than just a list: you should also be able to demonstrate the skill of synthesis, that is, be able to show the connections between causes and/or effects, and to come to an overall judgement.

(ii) 'Yes/No' questions ask you to consider a particular judgement or point of view and decide whether or not you agree with it. They sometimes include the word 'Discuss', which is used as an alternative to 'Do you agree?'. For instance, you may be asked to 'discuss' the view that 'the rise of Hitler was primarily the result of the depression' or whether you 'agree' that 'Austria-Hungary was doomed by the nationalities problem'. These questions require you to consider all the arguments that support the view expressed (the 'Yes' arguments), and all those that refute it (the 'No' arguments) and then draw some conclusions. You might come down on one side or the other, or come to a 'balanced' judgement, or you might use the evidence you have assembled to argue a particular case.

(iii) 'Importance' questions: these ask you to consider the importance or significance of a particular event or person, and usually include one of these two words in the title, though they are also disguised as 'To what extent ...'. For example, you might be asked to consider the 'significance' of the Spanish Civil War in the international affairs of the 1930s, or the extent to which Hitler was responsible for the outbreak of World War II. (In these terms, they are very similar to Yes/No type questions.)

'Importance' questions require you not only to identify the ways in which the person/event *was* important, but also in what ways he/it was *not* important and, logically, *what else* was of importance. They therefore require a three-part answer, whereas the other types require one and two parts, respectively.

Obviously, this analysis does not cover all eventualities, but the vast majority of essay questions fall into one of these categories. Once they have been identified, you can write the answer appropriate to the particular type of question. Many of the essays included in the exercises in this book have been written with these categories in mind.

Whatever the type of essay question, a good answer is likely to display certain characteristics, and these are frequently referred to in examiners' reports. A good answer is always one which is *relevant*, that is, it answers the particular question set, not the one that the student necessarily wanted. Some students make the mistake of reproducing pre-prepared essays, which do not answer the actual question. You may earn some of the available marks for writing accurate narrative or description which falls within the subject matter of the question, but you will not achieve higher marks until you begin to answer the actual question. At this level that will require at least some analysis or argument. You are not required to be original, but a good answer should demonstrate some evidence of reading around the subject and an ability to produce supporting evidence to back up your arguments. You are not expected to know the arguments of the most recent historical writers on the issues, but it is no bad thing to acquaint yourselves with at least some of the past historiography of the subject.

↜ SOURCE-ANALYSIS SKILLS ↜

Many history exams require students to answer questions on sources and documentary extracts, both primary and secondary, in addition to writing structured answers or essays. Some of the skills are similar, since both sources questions and essays require you to respond in the form of extended writing, but there are particular skills involved in answering the former. You probably encountered sources questions when you were a younger history student, and you should build upon the skills you learned then, but at a more advanced level you need to be very aware of the types of question and the responses required.

It is very important not to make stock responses to sources questions. For example, a statement such as 'All sources are biased or subjective' may or may not be true, but such a comment will earn no credit in an examination. If you are asked to analyse sources, relate your answers to the *particular* sources you are given, rather than generalise. Also avoid generalisations which imply that one type of source is automatically of greater historical reliability or usefulness than another (for example, many students are still under the impression that primary evidence is always 'superior' to secondary evidence, although this is frequently not the case). When answering questions, use the mark allocations as a guide: a question carrying less than, say, 4 marks requires a short response, one carrying 6 or 7 marks probably requires one or two paragraphs, one carrying 9–12 marks requires a 'mini-essay'. Hence some of the skills involved are similar to those involved in answering structured essay questions. However, with source-based questions, make sure that you read the sources and the questions carefully before you answer the latter. This may seem obvious, but it is surprising how many students refer to the wrong sources in their answers, or miss obvious points. Sources usually carry their attribution, that is, information about when they were produced, who produced them, often for whom, plus sometimes other information. Use this information – it is part of the evidence and may help you answer some of the questions.

Sources questions usually fall into one of several categories:

(i)   There are often short introductory questions which ask you to **explain** a word, phrase or historical reference. Such questions lead you into the document, and are often just testing your recall, so you will probably know the answer or you won't, but the topic should not be an obscure one.

(ii) There will be questions relating to one particular source, asking you a variety of things – for example, **why** this source was significant in the history of a particular event; or you may be required to effectively **summarise** the contents. Your skill of **comprehension** will be tested (in other words, whether you understand what you have read or seen) and your ability to précis or summarise. The latter is a skill which requires practice: you should certainly avoid regurgitating the whole source or simply quoting chunks of it wholesale – a practice which annoys examiners and makes them suspect the student's ability.

(iii) Some questions will ask you to **compare** and/or **contrast** particular sources for a particular reason. Make sure that you do use all the sources to which the question refers, and in addition to commenting upon or describing each particular source, do try to draw some conclusions.

(iv) Some questions will ask you about the **reliability** of sources. You should always ask yourself 'reliable for what?', but relate your answer to *these* particular sources and events, not sources in general.

(v)   You may be asked about the **value**, or the **uses and limitations** of sources. This is not the same thing as reliability – we all know that an 'unreliable' source may be very useful to an historian, depending on the use which he or she makes of it. Consider both the uses *and* the limitations – it is amazing how many students do only one or the other, when asked to do both.

(vi) You will be asked some **synthesis** questions. These will be broad questions, sometimes asking you to query a particular statement, for example, and they usually carry several marks. They may require you to use *only* the sources, or the sources *and* your own knowledge. Make sure that you follow the instructions, or you will be penalised. If necessary, go through each source in turn, before you make your conclusion.

To re-emphasise a point made above, when answering source-based questions, you will use many of the skills that you use in writing essays –

it is just that instead of one long piece of extended essay writing, the questions are structured or broken down so that many of them will each be testing a particular skill. But this does not make them necessarily easier than essays, and good answers require the same careful thought, practice and preparation. There are many examples in this book of the various types of sources questions you are likely to encounter elsewhere.

Austria-Hungary 1890–1914

INTRODUCTION

For centuries, central Europe had been dominated by Austria-Hungary. Maps 1 and 2 illustrate the extent of this mighty Empire. Almost 50 million people lived under the rule of the Habsburg family. Yet while the other Great Powers prospered, Austria-Hungary struggled to survive, challenged as it was by the demands of minority national groups for more rights within the Empire. Also significant was the fact that Austria-Hungary bordered the Balkans. The Balkans included 'new' states such as Greece, Serbia and Bulgaria, all of which had gained

See Map 1 below and
Map 2 overleaf

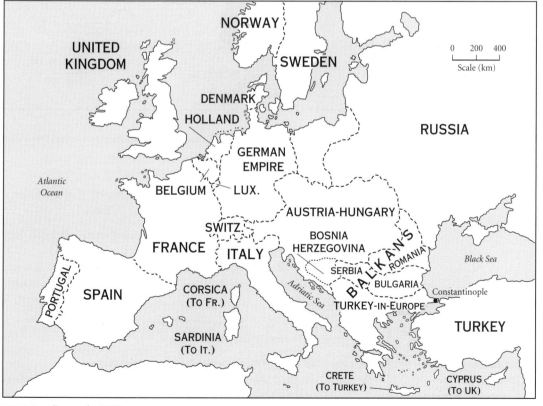

MAP 1   *Europe in 1890*

MAP 2   *Austria-Hungary*

their independence from Turkey during the nineteenth century. Austria-Hungary's rulers had two main concerns in the Balkans:

● they were determined to maintain and expand their influence there and to win a share of the Turkish Empire
● there was a danger that Serbia might try to expand northwards and seize parts of southern Austria-Hungary, an area which contained many Serbs.

Austria-Hungary faced two other problems shared in varying degrees by European Powers at this time:

● could the Empire's traditional monarchy survive?
● more acutely, it was faced by the problem of ruling many people of many nationalities.

KEY ISSUE

What factors threatened Austria-Hungary's position as a Great Power in the late nineteenth century?

1 ∽ THE CONSTITUTIONAL ORGANISATION OF AUSTRIA-HUNGARY

Under the 1867 *Ausgleich*, or Compromise, two separate but equal kingdoms of Austria and Hungary, known as the 'Dual Monarchy', were created. Map 2 illustrates this division of the Empire after 1867. Austria was to be ruled by an Emperor and Hungary by a King. They were the same person, Franz Josef.

The constitutional arrangements were complicated, to allow for Hungary's new autonomy while maintaining the ancient links. The old Empire was divided along the river Leitha and each half had its own ministers and parliament with control over all matters within its boundaries. In Austria universal manhood suffrage was introduced in 1907. Hungary received universal suffrage in 1908, but only those who could read and write Magyar, the Hungarian language, were entitled to vote. As a result, less than 7 per cent of the population had the right to vote, so the Magyars remained in control of the Parliament.

The Joint Ministers controlled foreign policy and war. The third Joint Ministry, finance, was only to administer the budgets required by the other two. There was no joint prime minister or cabinet, and so government was a complex affair.

Despite the concessions they had won, the Magyars remained dissatisfied. They disliked the common army whose German insignia and words of command were a reminder of Austrian domination. Equally, they feared Russia as their one-time conqueror and leading Slav power and felt that the common foreign policy was not sufficiently anti-Russian.

2 ∽ POLITICAL BACKGROUND

A *The Emperor*

Much depended on the ability of the Emperor to maintain stability and order both in and between his two kingdoms. Since becoming Emperor in 1848, Franz Josef had possessed an unshakeable belief in his divine right to rule, without obeying either of the parliaments. His powers were limited by the arrangements of 1867, but he still had the right to declare and conclude war, call and dismiss both parliaments and appoint government ministers.

Franz Josef's nephew, Franz Ferdinand, was heir to the throne. He was a distant and unpopular man. He was a supporter of the 'Trialist' solution to the Empire's problems – the creation of a third kingdom of the Slavs in the Southwest of the country. This meant that he had few supporters among the traditionally minded Germans and Magyars. He had married a Czech, Sophie Chotek, who was not considered sufficiently high born for their children to be heirs to the throne.

PICTURE 1 *Emperor Franz Josef and Empress Elizabeth*

B *The nationalities problem*

The nationalities problem dominated Habsburg politics after 1890. There was rivalry and hostility between the Austrians, who were racially German, and the Hungarians, who were Magyars. The Magyars were eager to form a completely independent country. However, the main feature of the nationalities problem was the number and variety of different national groups living in the Empire. Many Czechs and Poles wanted similar concessions to those won by the Magyars: at the very least, a measure of independence from the central government. For example, they wanted to have national universities and to be allowed to use their own language in local government. Other races, especially the Serbs, Croats and Slovenes, wanted not only civil rights but also the opportunity to join with another country, Serbia, to form a South Slav federation. Others still, particularly the Italians and Romanians, were, like the Serbs, minority groups with an existing state to which they could look for leadership.

In addition, many groups within the different races had different aims. While some Croats were contented citizens of the Habsburg Empire, others wanted to join with Serbia while others still wanted their own Croat state. The Emperor was therefore faced by a range of complex demands and problems. To complicate the issue further, many areas were of mixed population. In such areas, laws that could be seen as 'fair' to all the nationalities were impossible.

Austria and Hungary approached these problems differently. In Austria, the Germans were outnumbered about 2 to 1 by other nationalities. In the Austrian parliament or *Reichsrat*, representatives were usually chosen on the basis of nationality rather than political party. In the 1911 *Reichsrat*, after universal suffrage had been introduced, there were 185 Germans, 82 Czechs, 81 Social Democrats, 71 Poles, 37 Serbs and Croats, 30 Ruthenes, 16 Italians, five Romanians and nine others. Austrian ministries were usually coalitions. Count Taaffe, Prime Minister from 1879 until 1893, was German and had Czech and Polish support while Count Badeni, Prime Minister in the late 1890s, was a Pole with Czech and German support. Because of their numbers, the

<table>
<tr><td>**KEY ISSUE**</td></tr>
<tr><td>*How significant were the problems facing the Habsburg Empire, particularly those caused by nationality issues?*</td></tr>
</table>

Racial group	Austrian half	Hungarian half
Germans	9 950 266	2 037 435
Magyars	10 974	10 050 575
Czechs	6 435 983	
Poles	4 967 984	
Ruthenes	3 518 854	472 587
Italians	768 422	
Romanians	275 115	2 949 032
Slovaks	1 967 970	
Slovenes	1 252 940	
Serbs	783 334	1 106 471
Croats	1 833 162	
Others	469 255	
Approximate total	28 000 000	21 000 000

TABLE 1
Distribution of population of Austria-Hungary according to 1910 census

Czechs and Poles were usually represented in the Government and won concessions. For example, the Badeni Language Ordinance of 1897 gave equality between German and other languages. In turn, those races that were never represented in the Government, especially the Serbs and Croats, believed their interests to be neglected.

The Magyars had an altogether different policy. Despite laws guaranteeing language rights, the minority races were suppressed by the Magyars. At the turn of the century, they provided over 90 per cent of state officials, local government officers, doctors and judges, although they were in a minority in the whole population. In the *Diet* of 1910, they occupied 405 of the 413 seats in the House of Representatives. At the same time, a policy of 'Magyarisation' was undertaken to bring the minority races into line. Magyar was made compulsory in all schools in 1883, even if there were no Magyars among either staff or pupils. Outside schools, local traditions, festivals and costumes were forcibly suppressed. Whereas the Austrians allowed a degree of freedom and representation, the Magyars did not.

> **Diet** the word used for an elected parliament in several European countries

3 ⌁ POLITICAL HISTORY 1890–1918

The political history of this period is complex. At any time, there were two Prime Ministers and Governments as well as the Joint Ministries and the King-Emperor himself. He often chose not to replace ministers for some months, while in Hungary there were occasions when the King's appointee was opposed by a parliamentary leader. Although the constitutional arrangements give the appearance of democratic government, Austria-Hungary remained an **autocracy** in many respects. There was a large police force in Austria and the press, though not censored, was often bribed and bullied into loyalty. Personal freedoms, such as the right of association and the right to trial by jury, were limited. The *Reichsrat*'s power over ministers was minimal, since ministers owed their loyalty more to the Emperor than to a parliamentary majority. In any case, the restricted franchises ensured the pre-eminence of the aristocracy. The 1896 reforms in Austria added over five million voters to the register. However, the new, poorer, voters were represented by only 72 deputies while the other 1.7 million voters had 353 deputies.

> **autocracy** a system of government in which there is absolute or near-absolute rule by one person, usually a king or emperor

AUSTRIA

Austrian Governments were plagued by the constant rivalries between the nationalities. Until 1893, Count Taaffe maintained the support of German, Polish and Czech conservatives (the 'Iron Ring') by a series of minor concessions, such as additional language rights and local government posts. The radical Young Czechs, who wanted more rights, won 37 seats in the 1891 election. This led to demonstrations against Austrian rule and military law was declared in Prague in 1893. Taaffe considered extending the franchise, in the belief that the masses would be conservative, but the idea so alarmed his conservative supporters that Franz Josef dismissed him.

There followed two years of confusion. The Emperor decided not to appoint his own minister, but to allow Parliament to agree on a leader from its own ranks. This proved impossible as the different nationalities could not agree. In 1895 Franz Josef decided to choose his own man again. Count Badeni, the Polish governor of Galicia, became Prime Minister. Like Taaffe, he relied on the Poles, Germans and Czechs for support. In 1897 he decreed that from 1901 both Czech and German should be used in the Bohemian civil service. This would give the Czechs a virtual monopoly since most educated Czechs spoke both languages whereas few Germans spoke Czech. Moreover, the Slovenes demanded similar rights. The German Nationalist Party was furious and there was rioting in the streets. Badeni was dismissed and in 1899 his language laws dropped. Now the riots were in Czech areas in protest at the restrictions on their language.

Badeni's successor, Ernst von Körber, did not even attempt to rule through Parliament. Instead he ruled by decree (passing laws without referring to Parliament for approval) until 1907. In that year, universal suffrage was introduced. The Germans lost seats, and Ruthenes, Poles, Czechs and Slovenes all gained seats.

Two political parties stood out among the 28 that were now represented:

● after 1907 the Social Democratic party, a left-wing party founded in 1888, was the largest single party with over 80 seats in the *Reichsrat*. It was particularly popular in the north of the country, among the largest industrial centres. However, it proved difficult to uphold the idea of international brotherhood in a political climate dominated by nationalism. As early as 1910 the Czechs broke away to form their own party, which soon joined with other Czech deputies in creating the disturbances that led to the closure of the *Reichsrat* in the years before the Great War

● the Christian Socialists, the other leading party, had been founded in the 1890s by Karl Lüger, mayor of Vienna. They drew their support from Austria itself, were opposed to liberalism and Marxism, and were anti-Semitic. Christian Socialism was essentially an attempt by lower-middle-class Germans to put their case against the capitalists, the non-Catholics and the enemies of the Emperor. Nationality, however, remained the key difference between the deputies.

HUNGARY

In Hungary, three issues dominated internal politics:

● whether or not to permit civil marriage
● the policy of 'Magyarisation' – making sure that everyone could speak Magyar and that the Magyars dominated key positions in national and local government – was continued
● by far the most important problem, however, was the relationship with Austria. The Liberal party, led first by Count Koloman Tisza and then by his son Stephen, supported the 1867 Compromise, and sought to strengthen Hungary within it. The Independence Party, led

by Francis Kossuth, opposed the *Ausgleich* and sought greater autonomy. In 1903, this party refused to support an increase in the size and budget of the joint army unless Magyar insignia and words of command were authorised for Magyar regiments. This was tantamount to demanding a separate Hungarian army and was rejected outright by Franz Josef.

In the elections of 1905, the Independence Party won a majority. Since it still refused to approve an increase in the army, Franz Josef appointed his own Prime Minister, Baron Fejerváry, and sent troops to disperse the Hungarian Parliament. The Independents were unable to mobilise enough support to oppose this 'royal dictatorship'. Negotiations followed, in which the King threatened to introduce universal suffrage unless the Independents gave way. Since this would give the vote to millions of non-Magyars, and thus destroy the Magyar dominance, they surrendered and approved the army bill. Two years later, in 1908, universal suffrage was introduced, but it was based on Magyar literacy tests and so enabled the nobility to maintain its domination. Tisza once again became Prime Minister and in the years before the war the old relationship was restored.

The other issue in Hungary was the position of the Croats. They had been given more autonomy than any other minority in Hungary. Their position there was complicated by the fact that some of their number were in Austria, and by rivalry with the Serbs. While the Croats were Roman Catholics and looked to the West, the Serbs were Orthodox and in many respects almost eastern. In 1905 a conference demanded the unification of Croat provinces in the two halves of the Empire. When the Emperor dissolved the provincial *Diet* by decree, Croatian hostility was assured. Croats increasingly looked to Serbia for

KEY ISSUE

What domestic problems faced the Austrian and Hungarian Governments in the late nineteenth century?

1891	Renewal of Triple Alliance with Germany and Italy
	Gains in elections by Young Czech Party
1893	Resignation of Count Taaffe as Austrian Prime Minister
1896	Franchise reform in Austria
1897	Badeni's language laws, followed by demonstrations and Badeni's resignation
	Agreement with Russia to maintain the status quo in the Balkans
1899	Repeal of Badeni's language reforms
1903–6	Parliamentary government proved impossible and decree laws passed. In Hungary, the refusal of the Independence Party to approve the military budget and their successes in the 1905 election led to the appointment of a non-parliamentary ministry and troops in Budapest.
1906	*Opening of 'Pig War' with Serbia*
1907	Universal suffrage introduced in Austria
1908	Universal suffrage, with literacy qualifications, introduced in Hungary
	Annexation of Bosnia and Herzegovina
	New commercial agreement with Serbia ended 'Pig War'
1912	*First Balkan War*
1913	*Second Balkan War*
1914	*Assassination of Franz Ferdinand at Sarajevo*
	Outbreak of World War I

TABLE 2
Date chart of chief events in Austria-Hungary 1891–1914. (Foreign affairs in italics)

See pages 111–14

annexation the taking over of land and its absorption by one country from another

leadership against the Empire, and in so doing gave some credence to the belief, widely held in the Austrian Government, that Serbia was plotting to seize Croatia. Following the **annexation** of Bosnia-Herzegovina in 1908, the idea of a South Slav kingdom was given extra impetus, and many Croats were prepared to settle their differences with the Serbs in exchange for freedom from Habsburg rule. By the time of the Balkan Wars, Croatian discontent had become a matter of international concern.

4 ~ THE END OF THE AUSTRO-HUNGARIAN EMPIRE

The outbreak of war in 1914 brought short-lived unity to the Empire. Despite some victories, for example against the Italians after 1915, Austria's military performance was not impressive. Franz Josef lost much of his power to the High Command. However, in 1916 the Austrians were forced to set up a Joint High Command with the Germans, who increasingly controlled the Habsburg forces. The inexperienced and indecisive Karl, who succeeded his great-uncle Franz Joseph as Emperor in 1916, was in no position to prevent this. Throughout the war the Habsburg war effort was dogged by poor preparation and planning, whilst subject nationalities were increasingly reluctant to fight for the Empire. National groups began to break away, and the Empire to dissolve, even before the end of the war in 1918. New states were to emerge from the ashes of the Empire, although its dissolution had never been a war aim of any of the Great Powers at the start of the war – and the subject nationalities of the Empire themselves at that stage would mostly have been more content with internal autonomy rather than with complete independence.

5 ~ ECONOMIC HISTORY

The economy of Austria-Hungary was dualist, Austria being industrial and Hungary agricultural. In such circumstances, the union of the two countries was advantageous, since it facilitated trade between the two sectors. However, the economic arrangements were reviewed every 10 years, giving each side an opportunity to press for more favourable terms of trade.

Industry developed rapidly in nineteenth-century Austria. Coal and iron ore were exploited in Bohemia. Almost a third of the population there was employed in industry in 1890 – the highest proportion for any area in the Empire. Further south, there were considerable cotton and textile industries. Timber resources were exploited throughout Austria. Vienna itself was a centre of light industry, such as small arms factories.

In contrast, Hungary was almost exclusively agricultural. In 1890, it was estimated that almost 95 per cent of Magyars derived their living from agriculture. Owners of large estates had little desire to develop new methods, and were united in their hostility to industrial develop-

KEY ISSUE

How strong was the Habsburg Empire economically?

ment, with the result that the vast majority of wage-earning peasants lived in terrible poverty. Illiteracy was the norm and infant mortality among the highest in Europe. The predominant crop was grain. In 1900, Hungary was the third largest exporter of grain in the world, behind only the USA and Russia.

There was also considerable agricultural activity in Austria and most people lived in the countryside. Equally, Hungary had some industry. In 1893 there were some 400 factories in Budapest (compared with 40 in 1846), where flour milling, distilling and shipbuilding were the chief industries. In 1906, half the equipment for London's Piccadilly Underground line came from Budapest, while Hungary was unchallenged as the world's leading manufacturer of electric milking machines.

Two important questions remain:

● how 'backward' was the economy at the turn of the century?
● how did the Empire's production levels relate to those of the rest of the world? Tables 3–5 provide some indications of Austria-Hungary's place in the world economy.

Austria-Hungary was not in the front rank of world producers, but it was in most respects ahead of the weakest European countries, Italy and Russia, although Russia was rapidly catching up by 1914. In 1901, there were over 36 000 kilometres of railway track in Austria-Hungary, compared with 49 000 in Russia, an area five times as large.

The economic differences between the two halves of the Empire only exacerbated their political differences. As far as the Austrians were concerned, the agricultural areas of Hungary were a burden on their resources. The regionalism of the economy also highlighted some of the nationalities' grievances. For example, the Czechs who formed the bulk of the population in industrial Bohemia could justifiably claim that they would be better off independent, since they could then take full advantage of their wealth.

USA	5.10
Great Britain	4.01
Germany	3.85
France	1.59
Austria-Hungary	**1.17**
Italy	0.35
Russia	0.32

TABLE 3
Coal production per head of population (tons) in 1913

USA	27.8
Germany	14.1
Great Britain	9.1
France	4.1
Russia	3.0
Austria-Hungary	**2.1**
Italy	0.6

TABLE 4
Pig iron consumption (millions of tons) in 1910

Agriculture:		
Wheat	39%	
Potatoes	47%	
Sugar beet	21% in Austria	
	180% in Hungary	
Industry:		
Soft coal	85%	
Iron	144%	
Steel	133%	
	(261% in Bohemia)	

TABLE 5
Percentage increases in production in Austria-Hungary 1893–1913

6 ∾ FOREIGN POLICY

A *The aims of Habsburg foreign policy*

The chief aim of Austro-Hungarian foreign policy was to ensure the influence of the Habsburgs in the Balkans and, simultaneously, minimise Russian influence there. This did not necessarily mean that Austria-Hungary intended actually to take land from the Turkish Empire, but rather to make sure that any new regimes established there were friendly towards it. If the opportunity to take land arose, so much the better. Since Russia's intentions were identical, a Great Power conflict was perhaps inevitable, although each endeavoured to conceal its intentions and in 1897 signed an agreement to maintain the **status quo** in the Balkans.

The Balkan problem was complicated by the rise of the Serbian state. Serbia represented the two things most feared by Austria-Hungary –

status quo keeping things as they are.

MAP 3 *The Balkans in 1912*

KEY ISSUE

What were the main foreign policy issues for the Habsburg Empire before 1914?

the possibility of Russian influence in the Balkans and Slav nationalism in the North Balkans, which included the southern part of the Empire. After 1903 Serbian support for Croats and Slovenes, as well as Serbs, in the Empire was growing, at least in the minds of Habsburg politicians.

To assist it in its opposition to Russian and Serbian influence, and to help it maintain its world power position, Austria-Hungary relied on the friendship of Germany. This was sealed by two treaties before 1890 – the *Dreikaiserbund* of 1873 with Germany and Russia and the Triple Alliance of 1882 with Germany and Italy. By the latter, Austria-Hungary and Germany agreed to come to each other's assistance in the event of a Russian attack on either of them. The balance of the German alliance changed considerably during the period. Whereas in the 1870s Germany was glad of the friendship of an established world Power, by 1914 Austria-Hungary was almost wholly dependent on the help of Europe's greatest military Power.

What of the Empire's relations with the other Powers? Italy, as a co-signatory of the Triple Alliance, should have been friendly. However, there was considerable disagreement over the treatment of Italians living in the Empire and over Austria-Hungary's control of the South Tyrol. Britain's attitude was dictated by two factors. As Germany's closest ally, Austria-Hungary was treated with some suspicion. Secondly, the Balkans might threaten European peace and therefore Britain was interested in Austrian actions there. France's attitude was similar, though its consistent hostility towards Germany made it less friendly.

In 1903 the pro-Russian Karadjordjević dynasty came to power in Serbia. This, combined with the threat of Serbia acting as the centre of South Slav opposition to the monarchy and the possibility of a victorious war bringing prestige to the Crown, led Austro-Hungarian politicians to adopt an aggressive attitude towards Serbia.

In 1906, the existing tariff arrangements between the two countries were not renewed. As Serbia's main export of pigs was excluded from the Empire, this was known as the 'Pig War'. This lasted until 1908 when a new commercial treaty was signed which committed Serbia to higher imports from the Empire.

B *The 1908 Bosnian crisis*

In 1906, Aehrenthal became Joint Foreign Minister. He was keen to annex the provinces of Bosnia and Herzegovina which had been occupied and governed by the Empire since 1878 but still technically belonged to Turkey. Annexation would enable Austria-Hungary to put down Slav opposition in the provinces more easily and pierce Serbian pride by ending Serbian hopes of winning them. If annexation led to war with Serbia, so much the better, since the Serbian army would be no match for Austria-Hungary, provided that Russia did not join the conflict. When Aehrenthal won Izvolsky's (the Russian Foreign Minister) approval for the annexation in return for a promise to support Russia's claim for its navy to be allowed to use the Straits of Constantinople, the stage was set for action.

See pages 111–14

On 5 October 1908 Aehrenthal announced the annexation of the provinces. This precipitated an international crisis, since it amounted to seizing the territory of another Power, Turkey. Moreover, the Russian Government denied Izvolsky's deal and threatened military support for Serbia. Germany's support for Austria-Hungary was therefore crucial. Its promise of military assistance made both Serbia and Russia unlikely to risk war, and both accepted Austria-Hungary's action. Turkey was paid compensation and the provinces became a part of the Empire.

KEY ISSUE

What was the significance of the 1908 Bosnian crisis for the Habsburg Empire?

The annexation did not have the desired effect of establishing Habsburg domination once and for all in the North Balkans. It served instead to bring the conflict with Russia into the open and make each Power more determined than ever to win 'the next round', when it came. To this end, Austria-Hungary signed a secret treaty with Bulgaria and war plans were drawn up. Russia was equally determined not to be pushed around by Germany and Austria-Hungary again. Even more importantly, Serbia openly supported South Slav opposition to the Habsburgs and did nothing to stop terrorist organisations forming in its towns to operate in the southern provinces of the Empire. The most famous of these was the Black Hand, founded in 1911 in Serbia for operations in Bosnia, where a number of imperial officials were assassinated.

Serbia's power and prestige grew with its victories in the First Balkan War. When Bulgaria attacked Serbia in the Second Balkan War, partly as a result of the encouragement of Austro-Hungarian diplomats, Serbia was again victorious and its prestige reached new heights. By 1914, almost all Austro-Hungarian politicians were convinced of the need for a war against Serbia to prevent its power and confidence increasing further.

See page 115

So when Gavrilo Princip assassinated Franz Ferdinand at Sarajevo in June 1914, the Austro-Hungarian Government had just the excuse it needed to take a hard line against Serbia. The rest, as they say, is history ... .

7 ↜ BIBLIOGRAPHY

The Decline and Fall of the Habsburg Empire 1815–1918 by A Sked (Longmans, 1989) offers useful interpretations of this period. Particularly useful for the student are *The Dissolution of the Austro-Hungarian Empire 1867–1918* by J Mason (Longmans Seminar Studies, 1986) and *The Habsburg Empire* by N Pelling (Hodder and Stoughton, Access to History, 1994). *Francis Joseph* by S Beller (Longman Profiles in Power, 1996) is a useful analysis of Habsburg history as well as a biography. *Austria-Hungary and the Origins of the First World War* by S Williamson (Macmillan, 1991) is detailed on Habsburg foreign policy.

8 ↜ STRUCTURED QUESTIONS AND ESSAYS

1. (a) Outline the main grievances of the nationalities of the Habsburg Empire before 1914; (10 marks)
    (b) Explain which of these grievances was the most serious to the Habsburg Government, and why; (15 marks)
2. (a) What were the main principles of Habsburg foreign policy before 1914? (10 marks)
    (b) How did the Balkan Wars affect Austria-Hungary's attitude to the Balkans? (15 marks)
3. To what extent was the Austro-Hungarian Empire 'ripe for dissolution' by 1914? (25 marks)

France
1890–1945

2

INTRODUCTION

Before 1914 the French economy did not match that of Germany or Britain, but in other respects, such as the size of its army and the expansion of its Empire, France remained in the forefront of world affairs. However, France's image was one of apparent weakness. This is partly due to the prominence of important scandals such as the Dreyfus affair, and partly due to the fact that France was severely weakened by World War I, despite being on the winning side, and was defeated early on in World War II.

1 ⌐ THE CONSTITUTIONAL ORGANISATION OF THE STATE

The Third Republic was born out of France's defeat by Prussia in the War of 1870–1. Following a civil war between the people of Paris, who formed a 'Commune' in 1871, and the army of the Government of the National Assembly at Versailles, a right-wing National Assembly was accepted as the governing body of the Third Republic. There was no formal written constitution by which the Republic was governed. A President was to be Head of State. He was to be chosen every seven years by the **legislature**, not by the general public. He was given the power to appoint and dismiss ministers, negotiate treaties, suggest laws to the legislature and, with the approval of the Upper House (Senate), dissolve the Lower House (Chamber). Although he did not have the right to **veto** legislation, his powers were considerable on paper, but in practice he was largely a figurehead. Other features of French government were:

legislature the body, usually parliament, which makes the laws of a country

veto the power to prevent something such as a law from being passed

- the legislature consisted of the Senate and the Chamber of Deputies. Members of the Senate were chosen by an electoral college
- the Chamber was elected by universal male suffrage
- government was to be carried out by a Council of Ministers, similar to the British Cabinet, and which needed the support of the Senate and Chamber to govern. There was no 'prime minister', but the President of the Council of Ministers was normally referred to as such. He was appointed by the President, who then chose the members of his council for himself.

2 ～ POLITICAL BACKGROUND: REPUBLICANS AGAINST MONARCHISTS

On 30 January 1875 the continued life of the Republic was determined when the National Assembly voted by a majority of only one in favour of an elected presidency. Many Frenchmen wanted to see a restoration of the monarchy instead. The Orleanist and Legitimist candidates proved ultimately unwilling to have their names put forward. Later monarchist hopes centred on anyone who might provide the firm, old-fashioned leadership that the royalists wanted.

THE BOULANGER CRISIS

In the 1880s the hopes of the monarchists reached a peak with General Georges Boulanger. Boulanger won fame initially in 1886 as a reforming Minister of War, and was therefore a Republican. During 1887 he seemed to be growing in power and prestige. His supporters put his name forward as a candidate for a by-election and he was elected a deputy in parliament. An aggressive stance towards Germany won him more support amongst right-wingers, who loved to antagonise Bismarck. Indeed, they saw Boulanger as a possible leader of a campaign to regain Alsace and Lorraine, taken by Germany in 1871. The Government decided Boulanger was becoming too popular, and sent him to a military command in the Auvergne, well away from the centre of events.

In December 1887 President Grévy and Prime Minister Rouvier were forced to resign following revelations that Grévy's son-in-law, Daniel Wilson, had been selling military honours and decorations. Many felt that a Republic allowed the 'wrong sort of people' into power – whereas someone like Boulanger would provide firm and honourable leadership. With the prestige of the Republic so low, Boulanger's chances of seizing power for himself or a monarchist claimant seemed better than ever. In March 1888 he resigned from the army and stood for election in several parliamentary constituencies simultaneously, as he was entitled to do. During 1888, Boulanger won four by-elections. In January 1889, he won in the Department of the Seine – Paris itself had voted for the nationalist/monarchist candidate, Boulanger. Many expected him to carry out a *coup*. He did not, possibly through a failure of nerve. Republicans rallied. Boulanger was later charged with endangering national security. He fled to Brussels, where he committed suicide in 1891.

> **KEY ISSUE**
>
> *How significant was the Boulanger crisis for the Third Republic?*

The Boulanger crisis illustrated a fundamental problem of the Republic. Any error or crisis aggravated anti-Republican feeling, the more so because the Republic seemed unable or unwilling to stand up to Germany, which had humiliated France in 1870–1. This weakness was exploited by anti-Republicans. However, in the wake of the Boulanger farce, many monarchists did turn to give their support to the Republic, in a movement known as *Ralliément*, on the basis that it was the duty of all citizens to 'rally' to support the Government. Many churchmen, traditionally opponents of Republicanism, supported this stand. Therefore Republicans could look to the 1890s with renewed confidence, until two major scandals shattered it again.

1871	Defeat by Prussia
	Paris Commune
	Treaty of Frankfurt
1875	Adoption of Republican Constitution
1881	*French occupation of Tunis*
1883	*Establishment of French protectorate over Indo-China*
1886	Beginning of Boulanger crisis
1889	Flight of Boulanger
1892	*Franco-Russian military convention*
	Panama scandal
1893	*Franco-Russian alliance*
1894	Assassination of President Carnot
	Conviction of Dreyfus
1898	*Fashoda crisis*
1899	Retrial of Dreyfus case. Eventual pardon
1900	*Secret Franco-Italian agreement*
1902	*Franco-Italian Entente*
1903	Dissolution of religious orders
1904	*Entente Cordiale with Britain*
1905	Separation of church and state
	Moroccan crisis
	Foundation of United Socialist Party
1906	*Algeçiras Conference*
1909–10	Major strikes
1911	*Agadir incident*
1912	*Morocco became French protectorate*
	Anglo-French naval convention
1913	Three-year military service introduced
1914	*Outbreak of World War I*
1919	*Signing of Versailles Treaty*
1920	Formation of French Communist Party
1921	*Franco-Polish alliance*
1923	*Occupation of the Ruhr*
1925	*Locarno Treaties*
1930	*Last part of Rhineland evacuated*
1935	*Franco-Russian Treaty*
1936	Victory of Popular Front in elections
1938	*France signed Munich Agreement*
1939	*Outbreak of World War II*
1940	*France signed armistice with Germany*

TABLE 6
Date chart of events in France 1870–1940 (foreign affairs in italics)

3 ⌒ POLITICAL HISTORY 1890–1914

A *The 1890s*

THE PANAMA SCANDAL

The French had established a Panama Canal Company to build a canal through the isthmus of Panama to link the Pacific and Atlantic oceans. The president of the company was Ferdinand de Lesseps, the architect of the Suez Canal. The Chamber of Deputies had given loans to the

PICTURE 2

From a French magazine of 1893. At the base of the picture, the deputies argue, while the female figure representing the Republic points to the danger of German and Austrian soldiers

KEY ISSUE

What was the significance of the Panama scandal?

PICTURE 3

Alfred Dreyfus

company and approved the issues of shares. By 1888 thousands of Frenchmen had invested in the company. However, the company had grossly underestimated the difficulties involved in building the canal and had spent many of its funds on a corrupt and inefficient administration. In 1889 the company was declared bankrupt and 830 000 investors lost their money. In 1892 it became clear that the company had been in difficulties in 1888 – *before* the Chamber had approved a bill for a further 600 million francs to be raised by the sale of shares. Why, therefore, had the deputies approved the bill, and why had the press been so keen on the idea? Rumours of bribery abounded, and it became known that two German Jews, Baron Jacques de Reinach and Cornelius Hertz, an American citizen, had been responsible for paying deputies and journalists to support the company. Reinach committed suicide, threatened with blackmail by Hertz.

A former Boulangist deputy claimed to have cheque stubs showing that 150 deputies had been paid, and demanded that they should be tried. Even the Finance Minister, Rouvier, was implicated and resigned, admitting he had received money but saying, 'What I have done all politicians worthy of the name have done before me.' Eventually, in February 1893, four directors, including de Lesseps, his son, the engineer Gustave Eiffel, and a former Minister of Public Works, were sentenced to pay large fines.

The old question arose – what kind of Republic was it that needed bribery to uphold its prestige?

THE DREYFUS AFFAIR

In 1894 an official at the Ministry of War realised that military secrets were being given to the Germans. Captain Alfred Dreyfus, the only Jew in the Ministry and personally unpopular with his colleagues, was found guilty of selling secrets. He was degraded and deported to Devil's Island for life. Press and politicians alike – both Republicans and their opponents – were delighted that the honour of the army had been preserved and justice done so swiftly.

Three years later, Major Georges Picquart, the new Chief of Intelligence in the French Army, was sent some new documents which convinced him that Dreyfus had been wrongly convicted and that the real agent was Major Count Walsin-Esterhazy, an ex-Austrian Army officer. When Picquart told his superiors of his suspicions he was told to keep them to himself.

Shortly afterwards Picquart was posted to a command in Tunis. Before going, though, he had passed his news on to a journalist, who in turn informed Scheurer-Kestner, the Vice-President of the Senate. By then, Scheurer-Kestner had already been told by Dreyfus' brother, Mathieu, and Bernard Lazare, a Jewish journalist, that the handwriting on the *bordereau*, the original document by which Dreyfus had been convicted, matched that of Esterhazy. Esterhazy himself urged that he should be put on trial. In January 1898 he was acquitted by a military tribunal, and Picquart was dismissed from the army.

Two days later the affair really came to life with the publication of the article 'J'Accuse' in *L'Aurore*, the paper edited by Clemenceau. The article was written by the leading novelist of the day, Emile Zola, and was an open letter to the President of the Republic, Felix Faure. In it, he accused five generals and two other officers of having known of Dreyfus' innocence and deliberately permitting his conviction. The article had a tremendous impact – 200 000 copies were sold in Paris alone – and suddenly the divisions in French political life were exposed again.

On one side were the Dreyfusards, who not only believed that Dreyfus was innocent but also that he should be shown to be innocent. On the other were the anti-Dreyfusards, who believed that even if Dreyfus were innocent, which to them was by no means certain, a retrial would be against the honour of the country. Zola's article led to a libel case in which he was found guilty and both fined and imprisoned for a year. Meanwhile the press continued the argument, the Dreyfusards, led by Clemenceau and Jaurès, presenting their handwriting experts, while the anti-Dreyfusards presented theirs.

In July 1898 Cavaignac, the new Minister of War, presented new evidence of Dreyfus' guilt – three papers, two initialled 'D' and the third signed 'Dreyfus'. These were held to be conclusive proof for the anti-Dreyfusards. Then Cavaignac's own handwriting expert admitted that he had been wrong, and that the writing was actually that of Colonel Henry, the new Chief of Intelligence. Henry admitted his guilt, and committed suicide before he was brought for trial, while General Boisdeffre, the Chief of the General Staff, resigned. The innocence of Dreyfus was all but proven, and was hardly the issue any longer. Clemenceau later said, 'From this moment the discussion ceased to be whether or not Dreyfus was guilty but began to turn on whether or not Jews were birds of ill-omen, whether it was bad for the country and the army that

KEY ISSUE

Why did the Dreyfus affair split France?

PICTURE 4
The law gives the army a kick in the face – a comment on the revision of the Dreyfus case, November 1898

a court martial might have been in error, and so forth. Arguments of that sort can drag on till the world itself comes to an end.'

The affair of Dreyfus' guilt was not yet over. A retrial was held in August 1899 and ludicrously found Dreyfus 'guilty with extenuating circumstances' but reduced his life sentence to 10 years. *If* he were guilty, which he obviously was not, then 10 years was hardly a fit punishment for treason. And if he were not, then why say he was? The new Prime Minister, Waldeck-Rousseau, tried to correct the judgement by having President Loubet pardon Dreyfus. Many Dreyfusards, like Jaurès, as well as Dreyfus' own family, were satisfied by this, for the Captain was now free, and the victory won in fact, if not in law. Some however insisted that Dreyfus should be *proved* innocent. Eventually, in July 1906, Dreyfus was declared innocent. He was decorated and promoted to Major, thus finally ending *L'Affaire* that had split France so fiercely at the turn of the century.

The case had divided France because it was a scandal involving the Republican Government in a most tender spot, the army. The army was crucial to many French people, since it alone would lead to France's recovery of Alsace and Lorraine from Germany. It had to be seen to be incorruptible – and the Dreyfus case showed that it was not. Traditionally, like the Church, the army was an upholder of the monarchy, with titled officers who favoured a strong, non-democratic central government. Could the army be trusted to support the Republic?

More important, however, was the division of Frenchmen into Dreyfusards and anti-Dreyfusards. The two sides had quite different ideas about government and the Republic. The Republic had been founded on the ideas of liberty and the Rights of Man. Men should be protected by a just legal system, and they should not be persecuted on grounds of class, race or religion. Dreyfus was a Jew and an 'outsider', particularly amongst army officers. To those who saw the Republic as the protector of individual freedom, the persecution of Dreyfus was an outrage.

On the other side were those who considered the greatness of France more important than the freedom of the individual. To such people, the army and its honour, as well as the national religion of Catholicism, were of paramount importance. Frenchmen in 1899 were very concerned about the nature of the Third Republic. Should it be a means of making France strong enough to defeat Germany, whatever the cost in individual freedom? Or a Republic based on the rights of man? It was for these issues that Frenchmen fought over Dreyfus' guilt. The arguments continued long after the actual Dreyfus affair was resolved in the courts.

The Dreyfus affair led to some reforms which reduced the power of the Catholic Church. The monastic orders, which had supported the case against Dreyfus, had their power and influence reduced. Other reforms led to greater religious toleration. The Chambers elected in 1902 and 1906 were more left wing and Dreyfusard, suggesting that the case had influenced political opinion, though the elections of 1910 and 1914 reversed this trend. On another level, the case perhaps resolved the true nature of the Third Republic. The freedom of the individual was to be more important than the honour of the state. Democracy was to be upheld and justice preserved. Historians may argue that in the long run this actually weakened France, since it meant that the Government never had the strength to enforce firm but unpopular measures – like rearmament or the extension of **conscription** – but equally it meant that France remained in the forefront of democracy.

> **conscription** the compulsory enlistment of a country's citizens into its armed forces

B *1900–14*

The Republic had other pre-occupations before World War I.

CHURCH AND STATE

The relationship between the Church and the State was of great importance. The Catholic Church had traditionally supported the monarchy and strong central government, and opposed the extension of democracy. Was it therefore right that, in a Republic whose ideals were essentially humanist rather than Christian, the Church should have such extensive influence in society? It controlled most aspects of education through the teaching and preaching of the religious orders, the Congregations, and had close connections to the State, through the appointment and payment of bishops and priests by the Government.

> **KEY ISSUE**
>
> *Why were the state and church separated?*

During the 1890s Church and State were on friendly terms. In 1892, Pope Leo XIII issued an **Encyclical** to try to persuade monarchists to accept Republican government rather than campaign for the restoration of the monarchy. It seemed that the Church notables had accepted the fact of the Republic and were prepared to work within it. However, the Dreyfus case reopened old wounds.

> **Encyclical** a papal decree

Following their victory in the elections of 1902, many Radicals saw the opportunity for reducing the power of the Church in the State:

- even before the Dreyfus Affair was over, the 1901 Associations Law forbade the formation of any congregation without a law defining its activities. All unauthorised congregations were to be dissolved. Some 3000 schools were closed until they applied for, and received, authorisation
- in 1904, all teaching by the congregations was forbidden and control of education was taken over by the State through the *Université*
- in 1905 the Law for the Separation of Church and State permitted complete liberty of conscience: no one *had* to belong to any church. All links between the Church and the State were ended so the Government would no longer appoint or pay any priests. All property belonging to the Church was to be confiscated.

The relationship as settled by the Concordat of 1801 was over. France became a lay State, so ending one of the debates that had divided France for 30 years.

THE DEVELOPMENT OF SOCIALISM

This period saw the rapid development of a Socialist movement, both inside and outside Parliament. However, the trade union movement remained independent of the political parties, as the result of a vote taken in 1905.

Many Socialist groups were formed in the 1890s, some more radical than others. In 1891 Government troops had fired on left-wing demonstrators, including women and children, some of whom had been killed. This 'massacre of Fourmies' did much to arouse Socialist hostility towards the Government, as did anarchist activity, which reached a peak in June 1894 when President Carnot was stabbed by an Italian anarchist.

The Socialist Alexandre Millerand caused a great stir by joining Waldeck-Rousseau's Cabinet in 1899 as Minister of Commerce. He thereby created a dilemma for Socialists. Should Socialists join in parliamentary governments, or should they work wholeheartedly for the overthrow of the bourgeois State and all that it stood for, including parliamentary government?

In 1901 the Socialists were reorganised into two parties, each led by one of the great Socialist leaders. Jules Guesde led the PSDF (*Parti Socialiste de France*) while his rival Jean Jaurès led the more moderate PSF (*Parti Socialiste Française*). The PSDF represented the revolutionary wing of the movement, while the PSF accepted the **reformist** view that participation in parliamentary government was necessary and desirable. However, when the Second International (of all Socialist parties throughout the world) voted against reformism *and* that the French Socialist parties should unite, Jaurès accepted the decision and agreed that the new united party – the SFIO (*Section Française de l'Internationale Ouvrière*) – should adopt a revolutionary programme. In fact, except during World War I, none of its members joined French Governments until 1936, although it did accept democracy to the extent of putting up candidates for election to the Chamber. By 1914 the SFIO was the second largest single party in the Chamber of Deputies.

Despite the ever-increasing representation of the Socialists in Parliament, there was little Socialist legislation. As Minister of Commerce, Millerand did introduce State-paid factory inspectors and the Ten-hour Act of 1900. However, although they were approved by the Chamber in 1906, old age pensions were not introduced until 1910, by which time the Senate had considerably altered their value and structure. Income tax, too, was approved by the Chamber, but opposition prevented its introduction until 1914, and then it was postponed on the outbreak of war.

However, many Socialists, and especially trade unionists, would have been proud of this record. For their campaign was for direct action against the bourgeois State, a policy approved by the 1905 Congress of the CGT (*Confédération Générale du Travail*) which voted that social legislation was insulting and that working men should use the general strike against the State. In so doing they were following the **syndicalist**

reformist belief in a gradual, parliamentary approach to reform

KEY ISSUE

How significant was the development of French Socialism before 1914?

syndicalist from syndicalism, a belief that radical political and social change can be achieved through industrial action such as strikes ideas of Georges Sorel, and a number of strikes were organised in the following years.

The Government always won these confrontations. Clemenceau's Government used troops to force the postal workers back, and had a law passed forbidding civil servants the right to strike. Briand, Prime Minister during the rail strike of 1910, called the strikers into the army as reservists, thus making them subject to military law, and so unable to strike. The effects of these strikes were to embitter the Socialists, who gained nothing, and force many middle-class people away from Socialism to the safe harbours of the Right, as the elections of 1910 demonstrated.

The importance of French Socialism at this time should not be exaggerated. Only half the trade unions were members of the CGT, and it has been estimated that there were only some 400 000 resolute syndicalists out of a population of 11 million working-class people. As long as the Socialist movement was split between unions and politicians, and, within each, between reformists and revolutionaries, it could never be as great a force as its German counterpart.

FRENCH POLITICS

French politics in the Third Republic were extremely complex. A study of the list of Prime Ministers and of the election results will show that Governments came and went with remarkable frequency. In addition, political parties were fragmentary, and became more so. However, there were few elections despite the frequent changes of government.

French Prime Ministers were rarely the representatives of the majority party in the Chamber. Instead, they were chosen by the President as the men most likely to command support in both Parliament and the country. Sometimes, the President found it difficult to find such a man. Often, as in the case of Clemenceau in 1909 who resigned over a report on the state of the navy, premiers resigned over trivial issues. Resignation did *not* lead to an election, but merely to the search for a new man. French Prime Ministers should not be equated with British ones as the leaders of the majority party in the parliament, nor with German Chancellors as the personal servants of the *Kaiser*. Rather they were

TABLE 7
Presidents of France 1870–1940

Dates	Name	
1871–3	A Thiers	resigned
1873–9	P MacMahon	resigned
1879–87	J Grévy	resigned over the Wilson scandal
1887–94	S Carnot	assassinated
1894–5	J Casimir-Périer	resigned
1895–9	F Faure	died in office, while entertaining his mistress
1899–1906	E Loubet	served full term
1906–13	A Fallières	served full term
1913–20	R Poincaré	served full term
1920	P Deschanel	insane – forced to resign
1920–4	A Millerand	forced to resign
1924–31	G Doumergue	served full term
1931–2	P Doumer	assassinated
1932–40	A Lebrun	served full term, re-elected, resigned July 1940

TABLE 8

Prime Ministers of France
1889–1940

Date of appointment	Name
February 1889	P Tirard
March 1890	C de Freycinet
February 1892	E Loubet
December 1892	A Ribot
March 1893	C Dupuy
December 1893	J Casimir-Périer
May 1894	C Dupuy
January 1895	A Ribot
October 1895	L Bourgeois
April 1896	J Méline
June 1898	H Brisson
October 1898	C Dupuy
June 1899	P Waldeck-Rousseau
June 1902	E Combes
January 1905	M Rouvier
March 1906	J Sarrien
October 1906	G Clemenceau
July 1909	A Briand
March 1911	E Monis
June 1911	J Caillaux
January 1912	R Poincaré
January 1913	A Briand
March 1913	L Barthou
December 1913	G Doumergue
June 1914	A Ribot
June 1914	R Viviani
October 1915	A Briand
March 1917	A Ribot
September 1917	P Painlevé
November 1917	G Clemenceau
January 1920	A Millerand
September 1920	G Leygnes
January 1921	A Briand
January 1922	R Poincaré
June 1924	E Herriot
April 1925	P Painlevé
November 1925	A Briand
June 1926	A Briand and J Caillaux
July 1926	E Herriot
July 1926	R Poincaré
July 1928	A Briand
November 1928	R Poincaré
November 1929	A Tardieu
February 1930	C Chautemps
March 1930	A Tardieu
December 1930	T Steeg
January 1931	P Laval
February 1932	A Tardieu
June 1932	E Herriot
December 1932	J P Boncour
January 1933	E Daladier
October 1933	A Sarraut
November 1933	C Chautemps
January 1934	E Daladier
February 1934	G Doumergue
November 1934	P Flandin

June 1935	F Buisson
June 1935	P Laval
January 1936	A Sarraut
June 1936	L Blum
June 1937	C Chautemps
March 1938	L Blum
April 1938	E Daladier
March 1940	P Reynaud
June 1940	H Pétain

leading members of a governmental team, and only in rare cases, such as Clemenceau in 1917–19, the real rulers of the country.

Similarly, French political parties should not be equated with other European ones. Many politicians were members of more than one party, and it is only possible to determine who belonged to what by the way they voted in the Chamber. Except for three or four very broad groupings – Republicans, Radicals and Socialists – political parties and labels had little relevance to French deputies. Deputies saw themselves not as representatives of a party, but as representatives of the area in which they lived. In the period 1870–1940, 90 per cent of deputies were elected in the *département* in which they lived, a very different situation from Britain. In the period 1898–1940, one-third of all French deputies were simultaneously local mayors while another third were members of their local councils. The deputy was seen as and acted as the representative of the people of his own area, and not as the member of a political party.

French Governments changed frequently and yet French politics remained apparently stable, because although Governments changed, the people in government did not. In the period 1870–1940, of 4892 deputies elected, more than two-thirds served only one or two terms (that is, four or eight years) but 496 were elected five or more times, and were therefore in the Chamber for anything up to and over 20 years, so providing a small but substantial group of really experienced deputies. The same pattern is seen with ministers – 120, out of a total of 561, were ministers five or more times. When it is also seen that three-quarters of ministers and over half the deputies were from the professions (lawyers, academics, doctors, journalists, engineers or civil servants), one important reason for the political stability of France is apparent. France was ruled by a small group of very experienced politicians from the professional classes.

KEY ISSUE

How stable was the political system of the Third Republic?

	1889	1893	1898	1902	1906	1910	1914
Right of Centre parties[1]	210	102	100	163	107	228	223
Republicans (also Known as Right Radicals)	350	279	235	175	119	105	96
Radicals	153	180	192	278	145	164	
Socialists[2]	31	55	45	71	100	103	

TABLE 9
Political representation in the French Chamber of Deputies 1889–1911. Since political groupings were fluid, the table is only an approximate guide

[1]This includes a range of parties, including Boulangists in 1889, *Rallies* in 1893 and 1898, Nationalists in 1902, Progressives and others.
[2]This includes some independent Socialists not affiliated to the SFIO.

difficult to exploit for economic gain. In addition, few resources of men and money were invested in the Empire: colonial investments accounted for only 10 per cent of France's total foreign investments. Far more went to Russia.

B *The French colonial empire after 1918*

Following World War I, France was eager to maintain its Empire, even though there were pressing problems closer to home. The French Government had to face opposition groups agitating for independence in several of its colonies, including Tunisia, Morocco and Algeria. The French also faced opposition in Syria, granted to France as a mandate following the War; and in French Indo-China. France's colonies in Africa other than those in the North were more peaceful, and a number of economic and administrative reforms were implemented there in the inter-war years.

C *European policy*

The overriding aim of French foreign policy was *Revanche* (or 'return match'), meaning the recapture of the provinces of Alsace and Lorraine, taken by Germany in 1871. Some sought commercial co-operation with Germany as a way to the peaceful reoccupation of the provinces; whilst those like Déroulède sought reconquest at the earliest moment.

Most Frenchmen realised that France would need allies against Germany. Agreement with Britain seemed unlikely. Interests in Africa brought the two into conflict, while the possibility of an Anglo-German agreement in the 1890s put a British alliance almost out of the question. Instead, Republican France turned to autocratic Russia. French diplomats saw this as a means of diverting Germany's attention. The Russians were less keen on such a commitment, but finally agreed to a treaty in January 1894. By it, each party agreed that if the other were attacked by Germany, it would attack Germany; or if the forces of the Triple Alliance – Germany, Italy and Austria-Hungary – mobilised, then both would **mobilise** their forces. In 1912 a naval convention was added, and in 1913 a military protocol by which both Powers would mobilise if either were attacked by Germany 'without there being need for preliminary agreement'. Despite their political differences, France and Russia recognised their common interest against Germany and built a firm alliance on this foundation.

France was also able to come to agreement with Italy, although, as a member of the Triple Alliance, it was ostensibly a potential enemy. In 1900 Italy recognised France's rights in Morocco in exchange for French recognition of Italian claims to Tripoli. Then, in 1902, Italy assured France that if it were attacked by one of Italy's allies, Italy would remain neutral. So although Italy remained a member of the Triple Alliance, it was actually in agreement with the chief enemy of that alliance, France.

mobilise The process whereby, at the outbreak of war, a country calls up its reservists into the armed services and generally prepares those armed forces for the first stages of the war

KEY ISSUE

How successful was France in escaping from international isolation before World War I?

Delcassé, France's long-serving Foreign Minister, remained convinced of the need for an alliance with Britain, as much to prevent an Anglo-German alliance as to use Britain against Germany. The first agreements with Britain were reached over Africa. France recognised Britain's 'privileged position' in Egypt and Britain in turn accepted French rights in Morocco. These agreements led to the *Entente Cordiale* of 1904 which reinforced the settlements over Africa.

France also surrendered its claim to the coast of Newfoundland in exchange for land near French Gambia. Disputes over Siam, Madagascar and the New Hebrides were settled.

Military discussions began in January 1906. Britain refused to promise support to France in the event of an attack by Germany but agreed to more general discussions on co-operation should they be needed, thereby creating the 'moral obligation' of Britain to France.

In 1905 and 1911 France was involved in two major crises with Germany over Morocco. France was determined to maintain its influence in Morocco, and, especially, to demonstrate its ability to stand up to Germany. France was not in a position to threaten war against Germany in 1905, and Delcassé was forced to resign when the rest of Rouvier's Cabinet realised this was the case. However, at the Algeçiras Conference of 1906, only Austria-Hungary stood by Germany and the French could be pleased with the outcome.

In the 1911 crisis, the Socialist-Radical Prime Minister, Caillaux, was prepared to meet Germany's demands for a part of the French Congo in exchange for recognising France's control over Morocco. The Chamber unwillingly agreed, but Caillaux was forced to resign over this 'sell-out'.

There followed a distinct revival in nationalist feeling and hostility towards Germany. Most French people did not actively seek war with Germany, but extensive preparations were made between 1912 and 1914. Conscription was extended from two to three years, despite the opposition of the Left. Raymond Poincaré, formerly Prime Minister and elected President in 1913, was largely responsible for these policies. Certainly at the outbreak of war in August 1914 France had never been more ready, though not for the type of war that followed. However, in the summer of 1914 French people were more interested in domestic issues: the debate over income tax, the trial of Madame Caillaux for the murder of a newspaper editor, and the assassination by a nationalist of the Socialist leader, Jean Jaurès.

> **entente** a friendly agreement, but falling short of a full military alliance

> See pages 54–6

> French foreign policy in the inter-war years is dealt with in Chapter 11

6 ∽ BIBLIOGRAPHY

A most useful introductory book, which follows the history of the Third Republic chronologically rather than thematically, and which includes a number of documents, is *The Third French Republic 1870–1940* by L Derfler (Van Nostrand, 1966). Students will also find *France: The Third Republic 1870–1914* by K Randell (Hodder and Stoughton, 1986), *The Third Republic From 1870 to 1914* by R Gildea (Longman

Seminar Studies in History, 1988), and *France 1870–1914* by R Anderson (Routledge and Kegan Paul, 1977) very useful. *France 1914–69: The Three Republics* by P Neville (Hodder and Stoughton, 1995) is useful on the post-1918 period. Foreign policy is dealt with in *France and the Origins of the First World War* by J Keiger (1983) and *The Foreign Policy of France from 1914 to 1945* by J Nere (Routledge, 1975).

7 ⌐ STRUCTURED QUESTIONS AND ESSAYS

1. (a) Briefly explain the circumstances in which the Third Republic was set up; (3 marks)
   (b) Outline the main features of the Constitution of the Third Republic; (7 marks)
   (c) How stable was the French political system between 1871 and 1914? (15 marks)
2. (a) Outline the main events of the Dreyfus Affair in France; (10 marks)
   (b) Why, and with what consequences, was France so deeply divided by the Dreyfus Affair? (15 marks)
3. To what extent was the Third French Republic under threat from both Left and Right throughout its history? (25 marks)
4. (a) Outline the main developments in the French economy **either** in the period 1870–1914 **or** 1918–40; (10 marks)
   (b) To what extent, in the period which you have selected, did France undergo an 'economic revolution?' (15 marks)
5. (a) What were the terms of the Franco-Russian alliance of 1893? (3 marks)
   (b) Explain the stages by which France reached agreement with Britain between 1898 and 1914; (7 marks)
   (c) To what extent had France regained its Great Power status by 1914? (15 marks)
6. 'French foreign policy was based on a false belief in France's continuing power and influence.' To what extent is this a valid interpretation of French foreign policy in the 25 years before 1914? (25 marks)

8 ⌐ SOURCE-BASED EXERCISE ON THE DREYFUS AFFAIR

Study the following sources relating to the Dreyfus Affair. Use the sources and your own knowledge to answer the questions which follow.

With such a collection of documents and facts no trace of doubt remained in our minds. Our certainty was pure, whole and serious, and we were convinced that it would be shared spontaneously by the whole universe, once the universe was informed of what we had learned ourselves . . . The Dreyfusards have been accused of engineering a treacherous plot to divide France and tear it apart. But they did not and I think could not have suspected that there would be a Dreyfus Affair. For them everything was clear, luminous, obvious, and they did not doubt that universal reason must be persuaded by this truth. For the moment, at the end of the holidays [of 1897] public opinion was calm and indifferent; it was unaware and expected nothing. Yet when the truth was revealed what a generous cry would be heard throughout France! The nation had abhorred the crime as one, and as one it would proclaim the error and set it right! . . . Those who had had the misfortune to be most closely concerned in the fateful proceedings, the judges of Dreyfus, his friends, his commanding officers, would be the first to make their confession and to express their remorse. We were enchanted by that prospect. The only painful, anxious feeling we had was one of impatience. For until he returned to France to be showered with flowers and good wishes, to be consoled by the commiseration of a whole country, the innocent was still far away, in chains on his torrid rock. He would be freed when the truth was made public, but when would that be? When would be the chosen moment? Feverishly we counted the days.

SOURCE A
*The recollections of Leon Blum
(from Leon Blum* Souvenirs
sur l'Affair, Gallimard, 1935)

I accuse Lieutenant-Colonel Du Paty de Clam of having been the diabolical worker of the judicial error, unconsciously, I would like to believe, and of afterwards having defended his unhappy work for three years, by the most irrelevant and blameworthy machinations. I accuse General Mercier of being an accomplice, at the very least by weakness of spirit, to one of the greatest inequities this century. I accuse General Billot of having had in his hands certain proofs of Dreyfus' innocence and having suppressed them . . . I accuse Generals Boisdeffre and Gonse of being accomplices to the same crime, one doubtless motivated by clerical passion, the other by that esprit de corps which makes the War Office an unassailable Holy Ark. I accuse General

Pellieux and Major Ravary of having conducted a wicked investigation … I accuse the three handwriting experts … of having made false and fraudulent reports, unless a medical report finds them stricken by diseased views and judgements. I accuse the War Office of having led an abominable press campaign, especially in the *Eclair* and in the *Echo de Paris*, to mislead public opinion and to conceal their blunder. I accuse, finally, the first Court Martial of having broken the law in condemning the accused on secret evidence, and I accuse the second Court Martial of having concealed this illegality, on orders, and committing, in turn, the juridicial crime of knowingly acquitting a guilty man. In making these accusations, I am aware that I put myself under the jurisdiction of articles 30 and 31 of the press law which punishes libel offences. I willingly expose myself to it. As for the people whom I have accused, I do not know them; I have never seen them, I bear them no hatred or bitterness. The act that I have accomplished here is only a revolutionary means to hasten the revelation of truth and justice. I have only one passion, enlightenment, in the name of humanity which has suffered so and has a right to happiness. My inflamed protest is only the cry of my soul. Let someone therefore indict me at the court of assizes and let the investigation take place in full daylight! I am waiting!

SOURCE B

The Zola letter 'J'accuse', 13 January 1898

SOURCE C

The opinion of an army officer: From a letter by Marchand, the French commander at Fashoda in 1898

I have only two lines to add. An hour after opening the French papers the ten officers were shaking and crying. We learned that the terrible Dreyfus Affair had been reopened by the horrible campaign of those vile people. For thirty-six hours we were incapable of saying anything to each other. Such feelings cannot be shared.

SOURCE D (PICTURE 5) *An anti-Dreyfusard cartoon*

1. *What evidence is there in each of the four sources of the strength of feeling generated in France by the Dreyfus Affair? (8 marks)*
2. *Comment upon the techniques used by the authors of Sources B and D to put across their messages. Which do you find most effective, and why? (6 marks)*
3. *What motives does Zola attribute to the participants in the affair in Source B? Was he accurate? (6 marks)*
4. *'The object of political dispute rather than of political consensus.' To what extent does the evidence of these four sources support this conclusion by the historian James Joll on the Dreyfus Affair? (10 marks)*

The questions above could be equally useful both to prompt a class or group discussion, or as a written exercise.

Germany
1890–1918

3

INTRODUCTION

Of all the European Powers, Germany's power increased the most in the period after 1890. The country had been united only 20 years before, but by 1900 had become one of the three great economic Powers in the world, causing great concern to contemporaries. Could a highly modernised economy be directed by an almost autocratic form of government? What effect did Germany's strength have on the balance of power in Europe? Political, economic and military factors were closely linked.

1 ⌐ THE CONSTITUTIONAL ORGANISATION OF THE STATE

Diagram 1 outlines the organisation of the German Empire according to the Constitution of 1871. The German Empire technically consisted of four kingdoms, six grand-duchies, five duchies, seven principalities, three free cities and the imperial territory of Alsace-Lorraine, captured from France in 1871. The Empire was **federal**, so some local powers remained in the hands of the individual states.

The states' power in the central Government was maintained through the *Bundesrat*. This contained 58 members, one from each of the 26 states, except for the larger ones which had more – Bavaria had six and Prussia 17. The voting system was such that the Prussian

federal A federal state is a country like the USA in which the power of central government is limited, with individual states within the country retaining certain powers.

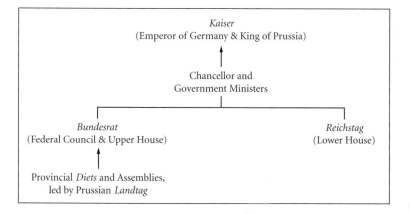

DIAGRAM 1
The constitutional organisation of Germany

members had a veto over legislation. The members of the *Bundesrat* were representatives of their state legislatures and thus bound by their instructions. The provincial *diets* and assemblies were therefore important. Franchise systems varied between states: Prussia had a three-class voting system that assured the nobility of a majority. In the 1908 *Landtag* elections, 600 000 votes elected six Social Democrats while 418 000 votes secured 212 Conservative seats.

The *Bundesrat* and the *Reichstag* jointly made laws. Members of the *Reichstag* were elected by constituency every five years by all men over the age of 25. However, its legislative power was limited. Many revenues were permanent rather than annual, so the *Reichstag* could not control individual ministers by threatening to limit their budgets. The *Reichstag* could be, and was, dissolved by the *Kaiser* with the consent of the *Bundesrat*. So the *Reichstag* criticised and amended legislation that was proposed by others as much as it put forward its own laws. Its relationship with the *Bundesrat* and the *Kaiser* became critical in the period before the Great War.

The Chancellor and ministers were responsible only to the *Kaiser*, not to the *Bundesrat* or *Reichstag*. He appointed and dismissed them, and, as events demonstrated, it was very difficult for them to pursue policies with which he was not in complete agreement. Since the *Kaiser* also had the power to dissolve the *Reichstag*, his control over politics was considerable. As Prussia dominated the *Bundesrat* and the *Kaiser* was also King of Prussia, he could rely on loyal support there. *Kaiser* Wilhelm II intended to maintain his power: in 1895 he stated, 'It is my wish to uphold undiminished the Right and Fullness of Power founded on history and the constitution.' Wilhelm probably had greater control over the course of events than any other ruler in Europe.

> ### KEY ISSUE
>
> *How democratic was the system of government in the Second Empire?*

See pages 40–5

2 ⤸ POLITICAL BACKGROUND

A *The Kaiser, the Junkers and the army*

The nobility and the army dominated politics and society in Germany. Between 1898 and 1918, 56 per cent of army officers were titled. The nobles, the *Junkers*, owned enormous estates in the East. The Prussian voting system and the prominence of *Junkers* in bodies like the Colonial League and the Agrarian League, as well as through their personal positions and contacts with the *Kaiser*, ensured that they influenced policy.

The army took an oath of loyalty personally to the *Kaiser* rather than the State, and money for the army was voted by the *Reichstag* only every seven years. This enabled the officer corps to avoid civilian control. These officers had great influence in the *Kaiser*'s circle. Count Philip Eulenburg, himself a member of that circle, wrote of Wilhelm II that he 'sucked in like an infant at the breast the tradition that every Prussian officer is not only the quintessence of honour, but of all good breeding, all culture and all intellectual endowment. How a man so

See page 52

clear-sighted as Wilhelm II could have attributed the last two qualities to *everyone* in guard's uniform has always been a puzzle to me. We will call it a combination of military Hohenzollernism and self-hypnotism.'

B *Political parties*

There were two main right-wing groups in Germany:

- the Conservatives represented the views of the landowning classes and of Prussia. They generally supported authority and military discipline and a nationalist foreign policy. As the political party of the *Junker* class, they were loyal supporters of the *Kaiser*
- the Independent, or Free, Conservatives had similar views and also favoured protectionist economic policies. They were less oriented towards Prussia and farming and more likely to win the votes of wealthy commercial and professional people.

(a) Kaisers

1871–9 March 1888	Wilhelm I
9 March–15 June 1888	Frederick III
15 June 1888–9 November 1918	Wilhelm II

(b) Chancellors

1871–18 March 1890	Prince Otto von Bismarck
1890–26 October 1894	General Georg Leo von Caprivi
1894–16 October 1900	Prince Chlodwig zu Hohenlohe-Schillingfurst
1900–14 July 1909	Prince Bernhard von Bülow
1909–14 July 1917	Dr Theobald von Bethmann-Hollweg

TABLE 15 *Political rulers of Germany 1890–1914*

	1884	1887	1890	1893	1898	1903	1907	1912
Conservatives	78	80	73	72	56	54	60	43
Independent Cons	28	41	20	28	23	21	24	14
National Liberals	51	99	42	53	46	51	54	45
Liberal Progressives	67	32	66	37	41	31	42	42
German People's Party	7	—	10	11	7	9	7	—
Centre Party	99	98	106	96	102	100	105	91
Social Democrats	24	11	35	44	56	81	43	110
Nationalities: Poles, Danes, Hanoverians and Alsatians	38	35	34	32	29	33		
Others	7	21	41	22	33	19		

TABLE 16 *State of the parties in the Reichstag 1884–1914*

1871	Proclamation of Wilhelm I as German Kaiser *Treaty of Frankfurt with France*
1875	Formation of Social Democratic Party Kulturkampf against Catholics at its height
1876	Laws passed against SDP
1879	*Dual Alliance with Austria-Hungary*
1882	*Triple Alliance with Austria-Hungary and Italy*
1884	*German occupation of Southwest Africa, Togoland and Cameroons*
1885	*German protectorates over Tanganyika and Zanzibar*
1887	*Reinsurance Treaty with Russia*
1888	Accession of Wilhelm II
1890	Resignation of Bismarck as Chancellor
1892	Schlieffen Plan devised
1893	Foundation of Agrarian League
1898	Foundation of Navy League Navy Bill passed
1899	End of repressive laws against Socialism
1900	Second Navy Bill passed
1905	*Moroccan crisis*
1908	*'Daily Telegraph' affair*
1911	*Agadir incident*
1913	Army enlarged Zabern affair
1914	Outbreak of World War I
1918	Revolution in Germany

TABLE 14

Date chart of main events in Germany 1871–1918 (foreign affairs in italics)

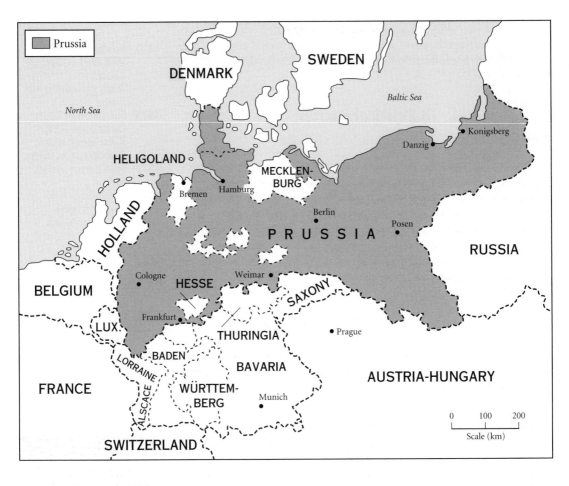

MAP 5   *Germany in 1890*

There were also two main 'liberal' parties and a third, smaller, one – the German People's Party. These were not 'liberal' by modern standards in that they were generally nationalist and opposed to the rise of the Socialist party. The National Liberals had been the leading party in the 1870s and had supported Bismarck's policy of *Kulturkampf* aimed at reducing the power and influence of the Church. By 1890, both they and the Liberal Progressives were losing votes, and were forced to ally with the more conservative parties in the *Reichstag* to maintain a majority for the Right.

German politics were complicated by the existence of the Centre Party, which represented the interests of the Catholic Church and its members. It was opposed to the domination of Prussia and, especially, to Bismarck, because of his **anti-clerical** policies in the 1870s. Equally, it was concerned by the rise of the parties of the Left. Consequently, it was almost always in the key position of balancing Left and Right in the *Reichstag*, particularly as, from 1874, it always had between 90 and 110 seats, making it one of the largest parties.

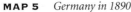

anti-clerical
anti-clericalism is a belief that religion or the institution of the Church should have no political influence in the state

C *The rise of the SPD*

The rise of the Social Democratic Party, or SPD, was the major political feature of the pre-war era, and was of great concern to Wilhelm II and his chancellors.

During the 1870s and 1880s the SPD was restricted by anti-Socialist laws, although some more moderate members won *Reichstag* seats. Ideological arguments between Marxists, reformists and anarchists divided the membership of the SPD in its early years. In 1891 the party voted to adopt the Erfurt programme, which was Marxist. Many members though supported the reformist argument put forward by Eduard Bernstein in 1898. He argued that, contrary to Marxist doctrine, capitalism was growing stronger. Consequently, the overthrow of the system was becoming harder and change could only be achieved by joining 'bourgeois' parliaments and governments rather than by total revolution. This revisionist argument was expressed in a motion to the 1900 Congress of the Second International:

> In a modern democratic state, the proletariat must not conquer power by coup, but rather through a long, patient organisation of proletarian activity in economic spheres, moral and physical regeneration of the working class, gradual conquest of municipal councils and legislative assemblies.

The motion was defeated, and the SPD rejected reformism. Nonetheless, many SPD members joined legislative assemblies. Consequently, the SPD won more and more votes and seats, especially as the anti-Socialist legislation was relaxed or ignored after 1890. By 1912 it was the largest single party in the *Reichstag* and had increased its proportion of the vote from 10 per cent in 1887 to 31.7 per cent in 1903.

KEY ISSUE

How significant was the growth of the SPD?

3 ↽ POLITICAL HISTORY 1890–1914

German history in this period was dominated by the expansion of the economy and by foreign affairs. However the rise of Socialism, which went hand-in-hand with the industrial expansion, was seen by the *Kaiser* as a problem. Other domestic issues were closely linked to foreign affairs, notably the size of the army and navy and the regulation of overseas trade.

A *Bismarck*

The new *Kaiser*'s enthusiasm to personally determine policy led to an inevitable clash with Bismarck who had, almost single-handed, dictated policy for over 20 years. Two issues in particular divided Bismarck and Wilhelm II:

See page 57

- Bismarck wanted to renew the Reinsurance Treaty with Russia in 1890; Wilhelm favoured a more obviously pro-Habsburg policy, and suggested the possibility of friendship with Britain
- in January 1890 the anti-Socialist legislation of the 1880s was due for renewal by the *Reichstag*. The *Reichstag* opposed the laws and the *Kaiser*, after initially supporting Bismarck's firmness against Socialism, agreed with the deputies. He suggested that an international conference on labour relations should be held. Bismarck regarded this as a concession to revolutionary elements.

Clearly co-operation was impossible when such fundamental issues divided them. Bismarck was ordered out of office in March 1890.

B *Caprivi*

Bismarck's successor, General Georg Caprivi, was a Prussian soldier with little political experience. He was expected to do as the *Kaiser* said. Wilhelm continued his conciliatory policy towards Socialism, in the

PROFILE

KAISER WILHELM II (1859–1941)

Wilhelm was a complex character who maintained a love–hate relationship with Britain throughout his reign. He was a grandson of Queen Victoria, and had a difficult relationship with his own parents. Dogged by feelings of insecurity and physical disability (he had a paralysed left arm), Wilhelm was prone to adopt aggressive attitudes. Although he did not experience active service, he loved military uniforms and took great pride in the army. Wilhelm was a strong believer in autocratic power and did not take criticism well, tending to forget that there were restrictions on his power.

There are broadly two schools of historical interpretation of Wilhelm's role in government. One tends to emphasise the personal nature of his rule, and the fact, for example, that he surrounded himself with favourites like Count Eulenburg. Others prefer to play down his role and emphasise instead the political and economic forces which were shaping Germany's destiny. It is difficult to establish exactly the significance of Wilhelm's influence. He was prone to change his mind on important issues such as attitudes towards the Socialists and protectionism. He also made blunders such as the 'Daily Telegraph' affair. One of his biographers, Michael Balfour, claimed that the decision to expand the Navy was the only major policy which can be directly attributed to Wilhelm. On the other hand, his bluster and tactlessness, witnessed for example in the Moroccan crises, were an unsettling influence in European diplomacy. In the last resort, in the war crisis of July 1914, the *Kaiser* allowed his own doubts to be pushed aside and he bowed to his generals' insistence that war was inevitable and that Germany had to go all the way – a fundamental abnegation of his own responsibility as ruler.

KEY ISSUE

How significant was Wilhelm II's role in shaping German policy?

hope that concessions would woo moderates away from extremist policies. A series of laws was approved to this end. In 1890 Sundays were made a compulsory rest-day and the employment of women and children was restricted. A system for the establishment of industrial courts to arbitrate wage claims was set up. The next year the system of factory inspection was tightened up and workers were permitted to elect committees to negotiate with employers on working conditions.

However, it was clear that the policy was doing little to win the new proletariat away from the SPD. In 1890 the party won 35 *Reichstag* seats and in 1893 it gained 44. The concessions were actually encouraging support for the SPD. Voters had taken the view that if so few deputies could win this much, how much more could more deputies win? When the French President Carnot was shot by an Italian anarchist in 1894, Wilhelm had second thoughts about Socialists, and proclaimed '. . . forward into battle for religion, for morality and for order against the parties of revolution'. Unfortunately, Caprivi was less co-operative and refused to draft a bill against subversion. Instead he resigned, retiring into obscurity.

See Table 16 on page 37

During his chancellorship, Caprivi had also made overtures to the Left by a series of commercial treaties. These were made with Austria-Hungary, Italy, Russia and a number of other countries. Each reduced tariffs between Germany and the country concerned. This facilitated the export of German industrial goods and reduced the cost of agricultural imports, which in turn lowered the price of food, which had reached a peak in 1891–2.

However, the policy infuriated the landowners who were forced to reduce their own prices to compete with the cheap imports. In 1893 they organised themselves into the *Bund der Landwirte* (Agrarian League) to campaign for the interests of German farmers. By 1900 the League had 250 000 members and had won considerable concessions on agricultural policy.

Caprivi was also responsible for increasing the size of the army. In 1891, Count Alfred von Schlieffen was appointed Chief of Staff. Like his predecessors, he was concerned by the possibility of a two-front war against both France and Russia simultaneously. The danger of this had increased with the *Kaiser*'s policy of friendship with Austria-Hungary rather than Russia. Schlieffen's solution reversed traditional German policy and aimed to attack France first in the event of war, on the assumption that the Germans could defeat the French Army before the more slowly-mobilising Russians could bring their forces into play.

The Schlieffen Plan necessitated an increase of 84 000 in the size of the army. This was initially rejected by the *Reichstag* and only after the *Kaiser* dissolved it in 1893 did a new *Reichstag* agree to the increase. Even then, considerable concessions were made, notably that the period of service for conscripts should be reduced from three years to two and that the *Reichstag* could debate the army's financial grant every five years instead of every seven. These concessions further infuriated the Right, whose opposition to Caprivi was influential in his resignation.

C *Hohenloe*

Caprivi's successor, the aged Hohenlohe, was not expected to oppose the *Kaiser's* policies, since he seemed to meet the requirements for chancellor that Philip Eulenberg claimed the *Kaiser* desired – 'neither conservative, nor liberal, neither ultramontane nor progressive, neither ritualist nor atheist . . .'. Hohenlohe pronounced that he was 'Imperial Chancellor, not an office boy' but in reality he had little influence over the *Kaiser*.

In 1894 he proposed the bill against subversion that the *Kaiser* wanted, but when it was rejected by the *Reichstag* the issue of Socialism was temporarily allowed to drop. Wilhelm made a lot of noise about the need for firmness, but, apart from a bill of 1899 which penalised workers who forced their fellow workers to join a union or go on strike, no action was taken. Instead, the *Kaiser* planned to win back the support of the middle class, which had been partly lost by the concessions to the workers. The new policy, 'the policy of concentration', emphasised the importance of military expansion and colonial achievements.

See pages 52–3

D *Bülow, Tirpitz and Holstein*

Although Hohenlohe remained Chancellor until 1900, the new policies were produced by a new group of ministers, who can truly be identified as Wilhelm's men:

● Count Bernhard von Bülow was Foreign Minister from 1897 and Chancellor from 1900–1909. Little complimentary has been written about von Bülow, chiefly because he succeeded in offending most of his colleagues as a part of his game of keeping the *Kaiser's* favour
● Alfred von Tirpitz became Secretary to the Navy in 1897. Tirpitz was an able organiser and a convincing speaker, who won over both the *Reichstag* and the German public to the cause of naval expansion
● Friedrich von Holstein, a survivor of the Bismarck era, became a senior adviser in the Foreign Office in 1878. Like the *Kaiser*, he disagreed with Bismarck's policy towards Russia, and from 1890 onwards was Wilhelm II's chief adviser on foreign affairs, even though he only once met him.

Bülow, Tirpitz and Holstein were the chief influences on Government policy in the crucial period at the turn of the century.

The passage of the Navy Laws was the dominant issue in German politics between 1896 and 1900. In 1896 Britain had 33 battleships and 130 cruisers. Germany had six and four, respectively. The *Kaiser* and his advisers were convinced that Germany could not attain the status of a world Power until it too had a navy. To try to equal Britain's fleet was out of the question. Consequently, Tirpitz propounded his 'risk theory' – the German fleet had to be large enough to damage any attacker sufficiently to make it not worth risking a battle.

See pages 109–10

The Navy Laws were intended to provide the additional ships, men and ports to bring this about. The first Navy Law (1897) proposed the building of seven battleships and nine cruisers before 1904. The *Reichstag*, often hostile to military expansion, was won over by Tirpitz. The newly formed Navy League quickly came under his influence and was used to spread the gospel of navalism to the general public. The *Kaiser* himself explained the need for a fleet at the time of the Boer War – 'I am not in a position to go beyond the strictest neutrality and I must first get for myself a fleet. In 20 years' time, when the fleet is ready, I can use another language.'

A second Navy Law, approved in 1900, proposed building three battleships each year over a 20-year period. The third Navy Law (1906) increased the tonnage of the ships and added six cruisers to the annual programme. It also allowed for the widening of the Kiel Canal to enable ships of Dreadnought size to pass through. By this time, German naval expansion was far beyond the bounds of domestic policy, and had become a key factor in Anglo-German relations.

During his period as Chancellor, Bülow concerned himself mainly with foreign affairs, leaving domestic matters to his Interior Minister, Count Arthur von Posadowsky. Caprivi's policy of making concessions to the workers was revived. In 1900, accident insurance was extended to more occupations and pensions for the elderly and the disabled were increased. In 1901 industrial courts for the settlement of disputes were made compulsory in all towns with more than 2000 inhabitants. From 1903 workers were entitled to receive sickness benefits for 26 weeks rather than 13, and in 1908 additional restrictions were imposed on the employment of children.

On the other hand, when the commercial treaties drawn up by Caprivi expired in 1902, they were not renewed. Instead, responding to the pressures of the Agrarian League, agricultural tariffs were restored to their former levels and food prices consequently rose.

Bülow's Government faced two internal crises:

- the first arose in 1906. There had been native risings against German rule in South West Africa, where Catholic missionaries reported that the colonial rulers had treated the natives harshly. The Catholic Centre Party joined the Social Democrats in criticising the Government and opposing a bill to provide money for the colonial government in South West Africa. Since the Centre Party held the balance in the *Reichstag*, this amounted to defeat for the Government's supporters. To some extent, Bülow welcomed the opportunity to end the Government's dependency on the Catholics. The *Reichstag* was dissolved and the 'Hottentot' election took place, so-called after the rebellious Africans. It was a lively affair, in which both sides actively criticised the other. The outcome was as Bülow hoped: a victory for the Conservatives despite the fact that the Catholics and the Left won three million more votes than the Right as there had been no change in constituency boundaries since 1871. The new coalition of Government supporters, known as the 'Blue-Black Bloc', passed some legislation of a conservative nature, such as the extension of the sedition laws. However, the support of the Progressives prevented the

KEY ISSUES

How significant were the German Navy Laws?

See pages 109–10

See Table 16 on page 37

Government from extremism, since they proved almost as moderate as the Centre Party, suggesting (but not winning) an end to the Prussian three-tier franchise system

● on 28 October 1908, an article appeared in the *Daily Telegraph* based on talks between Wilhelm and his English host at Highcliffe in Hampshire. In the article, Wilhelm expressed his great wish for close relations with Britain. He explained how he had supported and helped Britain during the Boer War. He said that the fleet was intended for the protection of Germany's colonies, especially in the Far East, where both China and Japan were a serious threat. It was not to be used against Britain. The article proved to be dynamite, not in England but in Germany. What right had the *Kaiser* to make such important policy statements? Were they not the prerogative of his ministers? Was it for him to decide that Germany wanted Britain's friendship? Bülow was held responsible for allowing the article to be published. He had been sent a proof copy of the article but had passed it on without reading it. He offered his resignation, but it was refused. There followed a period in which the *Kaiser* was sharply criticised, not only for his high-handedness, but also, not for the first time, for the kind of friends he kept, some of whom were suspected, if not proven, homosexuals. Talk of constitutional changes to reduce the *Kaiser*'s power was widespread, but nothing was done since the Conservative majority in the *Reichstag* could not agree on any acceptable alternative.

The Blue-Black *Bloc* collapsed in July 1909. Naval building had incurred enormous expenses. To raise the required money, an inheritance tax and an increase in contributions from the individual states to the federal budget were proposed. The Conservatives refused to support these. The Progressives refused to support anything else. Eventually a Finance Bill was passed with Conservative, Centre and Polish support, but Bülow took the opportunity to resign, on the grounds that he no longer had the confidence of the *Reichstag*. In fact, his relations with the *Kaiser* had become increasingly strained and only Wilhelm's difficulty in choosing a successor had kept him in office so long.

E *Bethmann-Hollweg*

Eventually, Wilhelm chose the Interior Minister (since 1907), Theobald Bethmann-Hollweg, of whom he had once said, 'He always knows the answer and tries to instruct me. I can't work with him.' On his own admission, Bethmann knew little of foreign affairs, thereby leaving Wilhelm greater freedom of action.

The Government's relations with the *Reichstag* continued to prove difficult, since defence and finance, on which Left and Right had such different views, were the dominant issues. The 1912 election changed the composition of the *Reichstag* and made the Social Democrats, with 110 seats, the largest single party. With the newly united Progressive People's Party and the Centre, they could command 243 of the 391 seats. Only the lack of co-operation between these parties gave the Government a chance to pass its own legislation.

Finance was the greatest problem. The Socialists would not countenance any increase in indirect taxation and the Conservatives opposed any increase in property taxes. In 1913 a bill to expand the army, at a cost of a billion marks, was introduced. It was supported by the Conservatives, since it was a strongly nationalist measure. However, to meet the enormous cost, a special national defence tax on property was proposed. Being a tax on wealth, it was supported by the Socialists, even though they opposed the army for which it was earmarked.

In 1913 there was a crisis over an incident in the Alsatian town of Zabern. A young lieutenant had not stopped his men treating the townspeople roughly and a lame cobbler was injured. The townspeople who subsequently demonstrated against the army's actions were rounded up by the soldiers and locked in the barracks. There were public and official protests, and the Governor-General appealed to the *Kaiser* to settle the matter. Only when the Governor threatened to resign did Wilhelm act. Rather than punish the soldiers concerned, he ordered them to be sent away on manoeuvres. In the *Reichstag*, all parties but the Conservatives joined the protests, but they achieved nothing – even the colonel who was responsible for the town was acquitted by a court martial. The incident forcefully underlined the superiority of the military, and the inability of civilian authorities to influence them.

Michael Balfour, in *The Kaiser and his Times*, concluded that 'the atmosphere in Imperial Germany during the years before the war cannot have been pleasant. The country was being run by an exclusive minority whose strength was waning and whose outlook was becoming increasingly repugnant to the general public.' Neither the public nor their elected representatives in the *Reichstag* had any influence on events of importance. Instead, the *Kaiser* and his entourage, through the hapless medium of the Chancellor, determined and dictated policy. At the same time, as Perry has written:

> Germany became a state of soldiers and war rather than one of citizens and law. The army not only remained independent of any control other than that of the monarch himself but also through prolonged and universal military service it was able to influence the thinking of the greater part of the German nation. German society was one in which the upper classes were soaked in the ethos of the barrack square, in which social distinction was measured almost entirely by military rank.

Few protested about this. There were strikes, but on purely economic grounds, and they were swiftly settled. The Social Democrats, the likely focus of opposition, were apparently satisfied by the prospect of parliamentary power, a power that was illusory. The vast majority of the people seemed content. Economic expansion had provided them with more material benefits than they had ever had before. Their Government had made Germany powerful and respected around the world. In any case, harsh punishments were given to those foolish enough to protest.

Change and continuity in the second German Empire

Historians studying twentieth century German history, particularly that of the Nazi period, have often displayed an interest in events before World War I, in order to determine whether there was any continuity in the German experience. Did the extremes of the Nazi era have their origin in this earlier period? Or was the *Kaiser*'s Germany a completely different phenomenon?

Were events after 1918 determined by the events of the war itself and its aftermath, with the pre-war German regime bearing no responsibility? Do historians put too much emphasis on the role of individuals like Wilhelm II in influencing the course of events, and give too little due to the importance of social and economic events outside of individuals' control?

The German historian Fritz Fischer caused a storm in the 1960s by rejecting the arguments of earlier historians who were reluctant to trace the roots of Nazism to the pre–1914 period, but preferred to concentrate on the disillusionment and problems present from 1918 onwards. Fischer detected a link between Hitler's extreme nationalism and the *Weltpolitik* of the *Kaiser*'s Germany. Historians who followed the Fischer line also began to study the impact of massive industrialisation on Germany and the social dislocation caused, for example, by the expansion of towns. The argument went something like this: Germany's inflexible political structure, created in 1871, could not cope with the pressures created by these developments, which spawned for example, the growth of Social Democracy. Therefore those with influence in Germany either consciously or subconsciously channelled these pressures into an aggressive foreign policy and even a desire for foreign domination, as a sort of safety valve. By implication this argument made Germany largely responsible for causing World War I.

This line of argument was further developed in the 1970s by the so-called 'Bielefelder' school of historians, in particular Hans-Ulrich Wehler. These historians emphasised the authoritarian, militaristic, anti-democratic nature of the politics of the Second Empire. They saw domestic politics as a struggle to deflect the threat of social revolution at home by a forward foreign policy. Critics of these arguments, such as Hillgruber and Hildebrand, countered with a more 'traditional' view that German foreign policy had its own dynamics and was not an extension of domestic politics to the extent that the Wehler school argued.

Historians in the 1980s and 1990s, including British historians such as Eley and Blackbourn in *The Peculiarities of German History* (Oxford, 1985), took what might be seen as the middle ground. Rather than emphasising one interpretation, they often highlighted the diversity of pre-1914 Germany: how, for example, the states were very different from each other and the fact that there were considerable divisions within ethnic, religious, class and gender groups. German society was developing in several directions at once, and generalisations are dangerous. In the words of G Layton 'Imperial Germany on the eve of the First World War was a land of contrasts – a complex mixture of forces for change and forces for conservatism. However, it was an essentially civilised nation. It enjoyed a highly sophisticated cultural tradition and an advanced education system ... in 1914 Germany could have evolved along any one of several different lines of historical development ... and in the long-term, genuine parliamentary democracy was just as feasible as authoritarian dictatorship.' Extract from *From Bismarck to Hitler: Germany 1890–1933* by G. Layton (1995). Reprinted by permission of Hodder & Stoughton Ltd.

4 ⤳ GERMANY DURING WORLD WAR I

Like the citizens of all the combatant nations, Germans entered the war on a wave of patriotic enthusiasm. All political parties declared a truce in the national interest, and although enthusiasm was muted after the failure to achieve a decisive victory, there was for a long time no open discontent. The major political development was that soon after the outbreak of war, the *Kaiser*'s influence declined, and the war was increasingly run by the generals and the War Ministry. In 1916 Generals Hindenburg and Ludendorff were effectively put in charge of Germany. Bethmann-Hollweg was forced out of office in 1917.

Germany's economy was put under unbearable strain by the War. Shortages at home caused social strains, culminating in revolution in 1918.

5 ⤳ ECONOMIC HISTORY

The German economy expanded widely and rapidly during this period. Great advances were made in the production of crucial basic materials which were needed for armament manufacture, the expansion of transport facilities, and the production of consumer goods.

Germany's coal production between 1890 and 1913 increased by 213 per cent while Britain's rose by 58.6 per cent. Productivity per miner

TABLE 17

Coal production (in thousands of metric tons) 1871–1913

	Germany		Great Britain
	Output	Number of miners	Output
1871	37 900	125 000	118 000
1880	59 100	179 000	149 000
1890	89 100	262 000	184 000
1900	149 800	414 000	228 800
1910	192 300	621 000	268 700
1913	279 000	689 000	292 000

	Germany	Great Britain
1870	1391	6060
1880	2729	7875
1890	4037	8033
1900	7549	9003
1910	14793	10380

TABLE 18

Pig iron production (in thousands of metric tons) 1870–1910

	Germany	Great Britain
1870	169	286
1880	660	1320
1890	2161	3637
1900	6645	5130
1910	13698	6374

TABLE 19

Steel production (in thousands of metric tons) 1870–1910

KEY ISSUE

What were the main features of Germany's economic expansion?

---

increased consistently throughout the period, with the exception of the decade 1900–10. Overall, in 1871 each miner produced about 300 tons per annum; in 1913 the figure was over 400 tons.

Pig iron production increased almost eleven-fold in Germany while it almost doubled in Britain. Steel production rose an incredible 80-fold in Germany and 22-fold in Britain. It was such remarkable increases in these primary industries that provided the basis for Germany's rapid economic expansion before the Great War. There were also considerable increases in applied and modern industries, most notably the electrical and chemical industries. Siemens had experimented with electric traction in 1879 and by the 1880s the German Edison Company (later AEG) was installing lighting systems. In census returns there had been no category for electrical workers in 1882. By 1895, 26 000 listed themselves in this new category, and by 1907 107 000, of whom more than 30 000 worked for AEG (*Allgemeine Elektrizitats-Gesellschaft*). The value of cable exports rose from £150 000 in 1891 to £2 500 000 in 1908.

Similar advances occurred in the chemical industry. In 1878 only a million tons of sulphuric acid were produced in the whole world. By 1907 Germany alone produced 1 402 000 tons. Ammonia production rose from 84 000 tons to 287 000 tons between 1897 and 1907. The production of crude potassium salts at Stassfurt rose from 906 000 tons in 1881 to 4 607 000 in 1911. Most of these chemicals were sold on the home market, primarily for use as fertilisers.

The increased availability of modern machinery and the use of fertilisers contributed to expansion in agricultural production. For example, the yield of sugar per ton of beet increased from one ton of sugar from 12 of beet to one of sugar from six of beet over a 40-year period. There were other agrarian advances. More than four million acres were brought under cultivation for the first time in the last 20 years of the century. Yields of crops and the number of livestock, except for sheep, also increased, although even in 1912 Germany was not self-sufficient in animal products.

TABLE 20

Sugar beet production in Germany 1866–1910

	Average yield of beet p.a. (tons)	Average yield of raw sugar p.a. (tons)
1866–70	2 500 000	211 000
1889–90	8 722 000	1 110 000
1906–10	13 423 000	2 116 000

The effects of this rapid advance were far-reaching. German workers were likely to be better off than ever before. Their jobs were secure and there were more consumer goods available. On the other hand, working conditions were often unpleasant and more and more Germans were crowded into the industrial centres. Significantly, the world's first slum clearance programme was undertaken in Hamburg in 1893, while at the same time many German cities were having trams, street lighting and similar amenities installed.

The new conditions stimulated the development of working-class movements. Workers could see both the wealth that they had created for others and the prospect of more material possessions for themselves, each of which encouraged them to demand higher pay. At the same time, their working hours and conditions led them to demand improvements from their employers. Yet the Party which represented them – the SPD in the *Reichstag* – was apparently stifled by the franchise system and the constitutional weaknesses of the *Reichstag*. In such conditions the development of extra-parliamentary forms of protest, and of revolutionary ideas, might have been expected. Therefore the *Kaiser* sought ways to distract his people's attention from this situation and to isolate potential enemies. Hence the concessions offered to the workers by the Caprivi and Bülow ministries.

PICTURE 6   *The choice facing the German worker*

It has also been argued that Germany's ambitious foreign policy was an attempt to capture public support for a Government that faced serious difficulties. In this way, opposition to the *Kaiser* and his ministers could be seen as unpatriotic and the opponents outlawed as extremists while the majority of the people supported the all-conquering Government. Historians following the lead of Fritz Fischer have taken the view that 'German foreign policy after 1897 must be understood as a response to the internal threat of Socialism and democracy'.

Similarly, the continued pre-eminence of the army not only gave the *Kaiser* a powerful force with which to quell rebellion but also helped to identify opponents as fringe extremists. For to oppose the army was not just unpatriotic but actually threatened the country's security. Taken to its logical conclusion, this argument sees the *Kaiser*'s efforts to distract his people from opposition as a critical factor in the events that led up to the outbreak of war in 1914.

6 ✑ FOREIGN POLICY

A *The end of Bismarck's policy*

For over 20 years Bismarck had worked to maintain a favourable position for Germany in Europe. Primarily, this necessitated the isolation of France so that it could not realistically hope to recapture the lost provinces of Alsace and Lorraine. An alliance of France and its ancient enemy, Britain, was unlikely. Austria-Hungary, by race and the treaty of 1879, was a guaranteed friend. Consequently, Russia was the key to Bismarck's policy. Despite the mutual rivalry of Austria-Hungary and Russia in the Balkans, Bismarck was able to keep both on his side during the 1880s. The Reinsurance Treaty of 1887 was crucial to this situation: Germany promised to support Russia's claims to the Straits and to remain neutral in the event of war unless Russia attacked Austria-Hungary, while Russia agreed to remain neutral unless Germany attacked France.

See page 87

KEY ISSUE

What were the main features of Bismarck's foreign policy?

Bismarck had broken with Wilhelm II over the renewal of this treaty which many felt was incompatible with Germany's promises to Austria-Hungary in 1879. In any case, the *Kaiser* and his advisers were convinced that the most likely wars in Europe would be between Germany and France or Austria-Hungary and Russia. In neither case could Russia and Germany be on the same side.

Consequently, the dismissal of Bismarck ended Russo-German friendship. Instead, friendly noises were made in Britain's direction, and agreement was reached with the British over Heligoland and East Africa in 1890. The following year the Triple Alliance of Germany, Austria-Hungary and Italy was renewed.

See page 88

The discussions and subsequent treaty between Russia and France convinced the German generals that they would have to fight a European war on two fronts. Their military plans were therefore tailored to this end. The most notorious of these was drawn up by the new Chief of General Staff, Count Alfred von Schlieffen, in 1891. This moved the anticipated attack on France from Lorraine to the Vosges and planned for an attack on France before Russia, since it was known that the Russian army would take longer to mobilise. The details of the attack through Belgium were not brought in at this stage. Significantly, the lines of military-diplomatic activity were thus drawn up as early as 1894. Of the five major Powers of Europe, only Britain was outside the existing agreements, so Germany's relations with Britain provided the only degree of manoeuvrability in European diplomacy.

B *The friendship of Britain*

Wilhelm II's attitude to Britain was critical to relations between the two countries and to international peace. His attitude was determined largely by his parentage. From his mother he inherited an admiration for English liberalism and the accepted view of English pre-eminence. From his father's family he inherited the strict Prussian military code of behaviour and views on the accepted order of society. In later life he both loved and loathed England. Even in 1911 he told Theodore Roosevelt how he 'adored' England. On the other hand he wrote of 'the same old arrogance, the same old overestimation' of the British. Above all, he was determined to be respected by the British and to win acclaim for what he regarded as his very real achievements.

KEY ISSUE

How close did Germany and Britain come to making an alliance before 1914?

These influences perhaps explain the *Kaiser*'s peculiar approach to Britain. In 1896 he sent a telegram to the Boer President, Kruger, congratulating him on defeating the Jameson Raid 'without appealing for the help of friendly powers'. Yet in the *Daily Telegraph* interview he was to explain how he had helped the British to defeat the Boers. Again in contrast, he had suggested to Tsar Nicholas in 1897 that they should join together to thwart British plans to expand. Since he seems to have wanted both to befriend Britain and to show its people his own country's strength, it has been suggested that he was trying to show the British that Germany's friendship was crucial to its survival – to 'frighten them into an alliance'.

Before 1900, it seemed possible that this tactic might succeed. In 1898 Joseph Chamberlain suggested an Anglo-German colonial agreement, but Wilhelm rejected it on the grounds that Britain was merely seeking an ally against Russian expansion in the Far East. After the turn of the century, the likelihood of an alliance diminished rapidly. Britain's unpopularity over the Boer War and German influence in Turkey were the major stumbling blocks. At the same time, though, the German Government believed there was little possibility of Britain reaching agreement with any other major Power, in view of their past conflicts, and therefore saw no need to woo Britain too enthusiastically.

German naval building was a last attempt to frighten Britain into friendship. However, it had the reverse effect of making the British determined to counter it. Britain's agreements with Japan, France and Russia during the 1900s placed it firmly in the camp of Germany's enemies, and such agreements as were subsequently made were restricted to specific, and relatively minor, issues.

Germany's failure to reach agreement with Britain had important effects on the whole of German foreign policy. Given Italy's ambivalence, Germany was wholly reliant on Austria-Hungary. This in turn brought Germany increasingly into the disputes over the Balkans. Moreover, the end of British isolation removed the final question mark from international diplomacy and for the first time gave Germany reason to believe that it, and not Britain, was the isolated country of Europe.

See pages 117–18

C *Weltpolitik*

Golo Mann has written that 'great states, that is states which under given conditions regard themselves as great, want to be influential beyond their own boundaries. History confirms this a hundred times.' Such was the ambition of Wilhelm II of Germany.

To achieve this, Germany had to win colonies, so that its influence could be directly brought to bear in different parts of the world. In addition, its power had to be sufficiently respected that it could influence events in Europe even when they did not directly concern Germany. To achieve either ambition, military power would be required, if not to be used then to exist as a threat – hence the naval and military expansion of the period. The German search for world power was to become the dominant issue of world politics and diplomacy after 1900.

This search was encouraged by the 'Leagues'. There were three main leagues devoted to the promotion of Germany's world power:

See pages 42–3

KEY ISSUE

How successful was Wilhelm II's Weltpolitik?

- the Pan-German League, established in 1890, included some 60 *Reichstag* members in 1914. It sought the acquisition of colonies and the establishment of German predominance in Europe. In particular, the League hoped that on the death of Franz Josef, the German areas of northern Austria-Hungary would be brought under German rule, so fulfilling their hopes for a *Grossedeutschland*, a Greater Germany
- the *Deutsche Kolonial Gesellschaft* – 'German Colonial League' – was founded in 1882; and was more directly concerned with the acquisition and exploitation of colonies, several of which it actually governed for a time
- the Navy League, with one million members, was directly sponsored by the Government to promote Germany's claims for a larger navy.

Admiral Müller explained Germany's need for world power in 1896:

World history is now dominated by the economic struggle. This struggle has raged over the whole globe but most strongly in Europe, where its nature is governed by the fact that central Europe is getting too small and that the free expansion of the peoples who live here is restricted as a result of the present distribution of the inhabitable parts of the earth and above all as a result of the world domination of England.

> The war which could – and many say must – result from this situation of conflict would ... have the aim of breaking England's world domination in order to lay free the necessary colonial possessions for the central European states who need to expand ...

D *Colonial policy*

Despite Bismarck's lack of enthusiasm, a number of German entrepreneurs had established interests in Africa and the Far East during the 1870s and 1880s. To protect the interests of their companies, and to protect others from the worst extremes of the companies, colonial armies and Government representatives were sent out. South West Africa became a German possession in 1883. After a dispute with Britain over its ownership in 1884, the German Government declared it to be a German protectorate ruled by the Colonial League. In 1892 it was brought under direct Government control. Similarly, the areas in East Africa claimed by Karl Peters came under the German East Africa Company in 1885. In the same year, the German Government announced that it had established a protectorate over the land between the Umba and Rovuma rivers in East Africa. For several years parts of this area were disputed with Britain, until in 1890 Germany surrendered its claim to Uganda in exchange for Heligoland. In the same year, the East Africa Company surrendered its sovereignty to the Government. Similar events took place on the West coast. In 1884 a protectorate was proclaimed over the coastal part of Togoland and in 1885 a protectorate was established over the Cameroons. Thus Germany's African colonies were established before 1890.

See Map 4 on page 27

KEY ISSUES

How successful was Germany's colonial policy?

Herein lies the paradox of German colonial policy. During and after the 1890s the colonial ambitions of Germany reached their peak, and there was much talk of the desirability and necessity of expanding Germanic ideas and people. In 1896 the *Kaiser* boasted that 'thousands of our countrymen live in far-flung corners of the earth' and that 'German goods, German knowledge, German industriousness, cross the ocean.' Yet the actual gains were minimal. In 1898 Germany was granted a 25-year lease on the port of Kiaochow but its ambitions in the Phillippines were thwarted by the USA. In 1899 the Samoan islands of Savaii and Upolu were taken together with the Mariana and Palau islands. Germany's other Far Eastern possessions had, like those in Africa, been taken in the 1880s – the North-east of New Guinea, the islands of the Bismarck Archipelago and the Solomon and Marshall islands.

Germany's relations with the Ottoman Empire proved more fruitful. The Berlin-Baghdad Railway was a grandiose and potentially profitable project to build a railroad from the heart of Europe to the heart of the Middle East. In 1888 Turkey gave its approval to the first stage of the construction. However, successive extensions caused friction amongst the Great Powers, mostly about which Power would control which section of line.

The reality of German achievements did not match the aspirations. Much was written in Germany about 'our railway' and the extension of German 'world power' in a new area. In fact, the railways in the Turkish Empire were built by British and French as well as Germans. The new railway never became the great trade route that it was intended to be, since it took so long to build and it remained cheaper to take the goods by sea. There was some German influence in Turkey – especially through the provision of German officers to train Turkish troops – but it was never paramount, especially after the Young Turk revolution of 1908.

E *Germany and Morocco*

German policy towards Morocco was an essential part of *Weltpolitik*. By 1900 businessmen from several European countries were keen to exploit the resources of Morocco. France already controlled neighbouring Algeria, and hoped for a pre-eminent share or a complete take-over of Morocco. In the *Entente Cordiale* of 1904 the British had recognised French interests in Morocco and agreed, in secret articles, to the likelihood that it would be partitioned between France and Spain. France obtained similar understandings from Italy and Spain.

Germany was not consulted about these negotiations, and was technically under the impression that the policy of the European Powers was one of 'open door'. The German Foreign Office was of course aware that discussions were taking place and the likely content of them. Bülow and Holstein, initially without the *Kaiser*'s approval, saw Morocco as a means of testing the loyalty of the British to their new friend, France. Would Britain support France when Germany challenged French rights to influence in Morocco? The Madrid Convention of 1880 had given all the powers equal rights in Morocco. And if France did not want Germans there, it would have to give them somewhere else in exchange. There was nothing to be lost and quite a lot to be gained from challenging France.

KEY ISSUES

What were the international repercussions of German's policy towards Morocco?

In March 1905 the *Kaiser* visited Morocco, riding through Tangier on a white charger, a gift from the Sultan of Morocco. He then visited France's minister there and told him that Germany expected rights in Morocco to which it was entitled. He next told the Sultan that Germany recognised his independence and reminded him not to introduce European reforms without good reason. He returned to his ship and left, in the process of which one of the escorting tugs rammed a British vessel.

The repercussions of the visit were not long in coming. Some members of the British and French Governments, most notably the French Foreign Minister, Delcassé, saw the situation as an opportunity for a showdown with Germany, and sought to escalate the crisis. The rest of the French Cabinet was less enthusiastic. Delcassé was forced to resign and Prime Minister Rouvier took over the Foreign Ministry. France then accepted the Moroccan (though German-inspired) invitation to attend an international conference, and Rouvier contemplated the possibility of offering Germany concessions elsewhere in exchange for a free hand in Morocco. By the failure of the Anglo-French side to take swift and firm action – a failure that was unavoidable – Germany had won the first round of the diplomatic game.

The conference was convened at Algeçiras in January 1906. Germany now found itself deserted by all but Austria-Hungary and Morocco. France and Britain were supported by Russia and the minor powers present. Germany had to be satisfied with a share of the international control of Moroccan finances, while France and Spain were to share the control of the customs and police forces. Far more importantly, Bülow and Holstein had failed to crack the new Anglo-French *Entente*. Rather, it had been strengthened by the experience of a common enemy. Round two was lost and Holstein resigned from the Foreign Office.

By October 1908 Wilhelm had apparently resigned himself to the fact that Morocco would remain French and there was little that Germany could gain there. Shortly afterwards, French troops entered the German embassy in Casablanca, removed three deserters from the Foreign Legion, and arrested the secretary for hiding them. German nationalists protested loudly and urged action, but the *Kaiser*, who thought little of deserters in any case (especially as they turned out to be a Swiss, a Pole and an Austrian), made little of the matter and even reprimanded the diplomat concerned.

In February 1909 an end to the arguments over Morocco seemed to have come when an agreement was signed by which Germany acknowledged France's 'special political interests' in exchange for a French promise to respect Germany's economic interests. Morocco's continued independence and territorial integrity were accepted by both sides.

F *The Agadir crisis*

It was the incompetence of the Moroccan 'independent' Government that provided the German Foreign Office with a new opportunity for action. In May 1911 the French sent troops to Fez to quell anti-foreign riots. The German Government was consulted before they were sent. The German Foreign Minister, Kiderlen-Wachter, was divided between the opportunity to make gains (by arguing that the French had broken the agreement reached in 1905) and his anxiety to improve relations with Britain and France. To advance German claims, the gunboat *Panther* was sent to the port of Agadir in South Morocco on 1 July, ostensibly to protect German citizens in the area, though in fact a petition requesting such protection was only forthcoming when requested by the German Foreign Office via the Hamburg-Morocco Company.

In the ensuing crisis, Germany demanded the whole of the French Congo as compensation for giving up all claims in Morocco. Lloyd George then claimed that Britain could not be ignored. Throughout the summer, negotiations continued between Kiderlen and Joseph Caillaux, the conciliatory French Prime Minister, while extremists in both countries, and in Britain, spoke of the likelihood of war. British army manoeuvres were ended and discussions held with the French on the shipment of troops to France. In Germany, von Moltke wrote, 'If we sources, along with analyses and exercises, will be found in *Imperial and Weimar Germany 1890–1933* by J Laver (Hodder and Stoughton, 1992), in *From Bismarck to Hitler: Germany 1890–1933* by G Layton (Hodder and Stoughton, 1995), and in *The Second Reich* by W Simpson (Cambridge University Press, 1995). For a slightly different perspective, which includes considerable personal detail about the Kaiser and his court, *The Kaiser and His Times* by M Balfour (Cresset Press, 1964), is recommended. A useful survey of different interpretations is *Germany in the Age of Kaiser Wilhelm II* by J Retallack (Macmillan, 1996). Important German contributions, although not easy, are *The German Empire, 1871–1918* by H-U Wehler (Berg Publishers, 1985) and *Germany Without Bismarck: the Crisis of Government in the Second Reich* by J Rohl (Batsford, 1967). Foreign policy is covered in detail in *Germany and the Approach of War* by R Berghahn (Macmillan,1993).

8 ⌐ STRUCTURED QUESTIONS AND ESSAYS

1.   (a) Briefly explain the role of the Chancellor in the constitution of the Second German Empire; (3 marks)
     (b) Explain the importance of Prussia in the German Constitution and the German state generally before World War I; (7 marks)
     (c) Explain how much influence Kaiser Wilhelm II had on German affairs in the period 1890–1914. (15 marks)
2.   (a) Briefly explain the difference between 'reformist' and 'revolutionary' ideas in Left-wing German politics in the late nineteenth century; (3 marks)
     (b) Explain the principal policies of the Social Democratic Party in pre-1914 Germany; (7 marks)
     (c) Explain the growth in influence of the SDP in the 20 years before 1914. (15 marks)
3.   (a) Outline the main developments in the German economy between 1890 and 1914; (10 marks)
     (b) Explain why the German economy grew at such a remarkable rate during this period. (15 marks)
4.   (a) Explain briefly the meaning of *Weltpolitik*; (3 marks)
     (b) Outline the main reasons for the Kaiser's determination to practise *Weltpolitik*; (7 marks)
     (c) How successfully did the Kaiser achieve his foreign policy objectives before 1914? (15 marks)
5.   'Economically advanced, but politically backward.' How accurate is this assessment of Germany between 1890 and 1914? (25 marks)
6.   To what extent was Germany responsible for World War I? (25 marks)

9 ⌐ SOURCE-BASED EXERCISE ON GERMAN FOREIGN POLICY

Study the following Sources A–D on Wilhelm II and German foreign policy and answer the questions which follow.

William played a smaller part in the formation of policy than was permitted by the constitution or supposed by the public. Bismarck's departure was undoubtedly his doing, but in the controversies leading to it there was much to be said on the side of the Kaiser, who was in any case only anticipating by a few years the action of natural causes. As regards the failure to renew the Reinsurance treaty, the Morocco crisis of 1905-6 and the Agadir episode, William was a somewhat unwilling accessory to the acts of other people ... The only major policy for which prime responsibility must be laid at the Kaiser's door is that regarding the fleet ... In building such a fleet, William was only carrying to their logical consequence the aspirations of his subjects.

SOURCE A
A modern historian's views from M Balfour The Kaiser and his Times *(1964)*

A state which has oceanic or world interests must be able to uphold them and make its power felt beyond its own territorial concerns. National world commerce, world industry, and to a certain extent fishing on the high seas, world intercourse and colonies are impossible without a fleet capable of taking the offensive. The conflicts of interests between nations, the lack of confidence felt by capital and the business world will either destroy these expressions of the vitality of a state or prevent them from taking form, if they are not supported by national power on the seas, and therefore beyond our own waters. Herein lies by far the most important purpose of the fleet.

SOURCE B
German naval expansion. Memorandum of the Oberkommando of the German Navy, June 1914

VISITING GRANDMAMMA.

Grandma' Victoria. "NOW, WILLIE DEAR, YOU'VE PLENTY OF *SOLDIERS* AT HOME; LOOK AT THESE PRETTY *SHIPS,*—I'M SURE YOU'LL BE PLEASED WITH *THEM!*"

SOURCE C (PICTURE 8)
A British cartoon about naval rivalry

Supreme Court of the Empire, thus giving it a judicial rather than a political function.

None of these three groups could challenge the Tsar's omnipotence, which was reinforced by his position as head of the Church.

To what extent was Russia an autocracy under the Tsars?

Alexander II undertook some reforms in the 1860s. *Zemstvos* or local parliaments were set up on a county and provincial basis. They were to be local parliaments, elected by an electoral college system that favoured the richest citizens. *Zemstvo*s were responsible for transport, health, education, the poor, famine relief, and the encouragement of agriculture and industry in their area. As *zemstvos* were set up throughout the country, there were, for the first time, bodies prepared to bring reforms and improvements – hospitals, roads, pavements, schools, sewers and the like – although they had no official administrative power.

The *mir*, or village commune, was also established in the 1860s. In 1861, Alexander II had ended the system by which peasants were owned by landlords and had no land of their own. They were freed from serfdom and given some land. This land was initially paid for by the State, and the peasants then had to repay the debt. The *mir* was responsible for collecting these redemption dues as well as taxes. To ensure that peasants would not escape their debts, the *mir* issued passports and until 1903 no peasant could leave his village without a passport and the consent of the *mir*. The *mir* also handled court cases that involved only peasants. In essence, the *mir* was one method of coping with local issues and controlling Russia's enormous population with minimal expenditure.

2 ⏎ POLITICAL BACKGROUND: THE TSARS

reactionary policies which are repressive or a reversal of previous reforms. A reactionary politician is one to the right of conservatism

Alexander II (1855–81) was at first a reforming Tsar, ending serfdom, reducing censorship, creating *zemstvos*, introducing a new legal system which had juries and trained judges, introducing a less arbitrary system of conscription and reducing the length of military service. However, by modern standards he was **reactionary** beyond all measure, banning trade unions in 1874 and maintaining an enormous army and police force. The 'Tsar Liberator' was killed by a bomb thrown by a member of the 'People's Will' in March 1881 – the seventh attempt on his life.

He was succeeded by his son, Alexander III (1881–94). It has been said of him that he set out to undo all that his father had done, carrying out a series of measures to reassert the authority of the aristocracy:

● the discussions between *zemstvo* officials and the Imperial Council that had been initiated by the Minister of the Interior, Loris-Melikov, were ended

● in 1889 the proportion of peasant votes for *zemstvo* deputies was reduced; instead the peasants were to be presented with a list of candidates from whom they could choose. Also in 1889, 'land captains' were appointed in each area. These were virtually governors, since they headed the legal and administrative systems and could overrule the decisions of the *zemstvos*

● Alexander III was advised by Constantine Pobiedonostev, tutor to the Tsar and his son, Nicholas, and Procurator of the Holy Synod. He advised the Tsar to control the education system more closely, to dismiss disloyal judges, to enforce the use of Russian in schools where it was not the local language, such as Poland and the Baltic states, and to force conversions to Orthodoxy, the 'official' religion of the Russian Empire

● the Jews suffered particularly. A vicious campaign forbade them to settle in certain areas and limited their numbers in universities. Pobiedonostev pronounced that a third of the Jews in Russia must die, a third emigrate and a third assimilate. In 1891–2 thousands were cleared out of Moscow and forced into ghettos.

Alexander's son, Nicholas, was born in 1868. During the 1890s he led an easy life as a young army officer. However, in 1894 Alexander III died suddenly. A week later, Nicholas married Princess Alix of Hesse-Darmstadt, his own choice and originally opposed by his family because she was German. On hearing of his father's death, Nicholas said to his brother-in-law, 'What am I to do? I am not prepared to be Tsar. I know nothing of the business of ruling.'

Liberal elements, especially among the *zemstvo* leaders, had high hopes of their new Tsar. However, in his first formal speech, acknowledging the congratulations of the *zemstvo* leaders, Nicholas said, 'It is

PICTURE 9 *Tsar Nicholas II and his family, photographed around 1905*

KEY ISSUE

What obstacles to reform were there in tsarist Russia?

known to me that voices have been heard in some assemblies of persons carried away by senseless dreams of the participation of *zemstvo* representatives in the affairs of the internal government. Let all know that ... I shall preserve the principle of autocracy as firmly and undeviatingly as did my father.'

In other ways too the omens were not good. In May 1895 Nicholas was crowned in Moscow, wearing a 9lb crown that slipped over his nose. That evening, 7000 guests attended a ball in the Kremlin. The next day 1300 poor people were killed and hundreds more injured, as they were crushed in a rush to get presents at an open-air celebration of the coronation. That night, although he wanted to mourn his people, Nicholas was persuaded to attend a ball at the French Embassy.

3 ∽ ECONOMIC HISTORY

A *Economic background*

Two factors dominated the economy of nineteenth-century Russia. The population was increasing rapidly and the overwhelming majority of that population was engaged in farming. Table 21 illustrates these points.

The emancipation of the serfs in 1861 did little to improve the agricultural efficiency of the countryside. Since landlords could not, or would not, pay labourers and since the peasants could not afford land themselves, almost a quarter of the previously cultivated area fell into disuse. Peasants received very small land holdings, usually of less than 10 acres and rarely more than 20. Inheritance systems reinforced this trend. In some areas, land was inherited in the normal way by the eldest son. In others, a man's land was redivided on his death on the basis of family size. If his family did not require as much land as they had, then some would be taken by the *mir* and given to another, larger, family. Given small farms and, except in Black Earth areas, poor soil, crop yields were sometimes as low as half as much grain per acre as the richest agricultural countries, Britain, Germany and the Low Countries.

The rapidly increasing population put great pressure on existing resources of food, especially in times of bad harvest. Famines, in which hundreds of thousands, even millions, died, such as that of the winter of 1891–2, were common.

Industry remained backward. Most natural resources lay in the east and were not exploited. Russian coal production was less than 5 per cent of that of Britain in the late nineteenth century. Even in the 1890s more than a quarter of Russia's coal was imported. The iron industry also lagged behind the rest of Europe, relying mainly on old-fashioned charcoal forges and importing half of the pig iron that was needed. By all the usual indices – miles of railway track, mechanisation in the textile industry, size of the national debt – Russia in 1890 was economically backward.

Date	Total population (millions)	Percentage of population living in towns of over 5000 people
1730	14	3
1751	7.8	
1796	36	
1817	46	
1870	77	
1890	95	
1896	12.4	
1900	103	
1913	122	14.6

TABLE 21
Russian population growth

KEY ISSUE

How backward was the Russian economy?

On the other hand, there had been some progress. Between 1860 and 1876 coal production had risen 16-fold and steel production 10-fold. Foreign manufacturers had helped to achieve this. The Swedish Nobel brothers had financed oil production in Baku while the Welshman John Hughes had established a coal, iron and rail works in the Krivoi Rog Basin. Railways expanded particularly quickly. In 1861 there had been only 1000 miles of railway track – by 1880, there were 14 000. So although the general picture was of backwardness and stagnation, there was advance and expansion in some fields.

B *Witte's reforms in the 1890s*

Such advances as there were resulted from the initiative of the ministers of finance. They were instrumental in deciding the extent of taxation and the priorities of government expenditure. Reutern, Minister from 1862 until 1878, had encouraged the first foreign entrepreneurs such as the Nobels, Hughes, and the textile manufacturer Knoop. Bunge, Minister from 1878 until 1886, adopted a *laissez-faire* attitude to the economy, reducing taxes in the hope of establishing a prosperous peasantry that would provide the demand necessary to stimulate industrial progress. In 1881 he reduced the salt tax, and in 1886 the poll tax. Taxation fell to only one-third of its 1860s levels.

However, Bunge's policy ran into difficulties because of the military expenditure. His successor, Vyshnagradsky (1886–91), adopted an entirely different policy – relentless austerity to build up reserves of capital. Taxation was increased. In years of good harvest, like 1887–8, this policy was successful. But in a time of shortage, such as 1891–2, it was quite impossible for the peasantry to surrender a third of its crops for taxation.

Vyshnagradsky was replaced by Sergei Witte (1891–1900), a mathematics graduate who had risen through the administrative service of the railways. He had a clear plan for the economy to establish heavy industry and an extensive railway system, financed by foreign capital. The basis for long-term growth would thus be established. Two subsidiary aims were also necessary – the promotion of technical education and the avoidance of wars, which were expensive and disruptive to planned economic growth.

Railway building advanced rapidly. The basic pattern already existed, so Witte's scheme was to extend existing routes to more outlying areas in the south and east, and to improve existing tracks by making them double, by providing more stations, engines and rolling stock. The eastwards expansion through the construction of the Trans-Siberian Railway was the major project, linked to Witte's idea of developing whole new areas in the east by forced resettlement and the development of shipping in the Far East. Construction on the railway was started in 1891 and lasted almost 15 years. The railway proved so expensive that in places only a single track could be built, and in the end only six trains a day could be run. The expansion of the railway system in European Russia was far more successful, where the amount of track was

KEY ISSUE

How significant were Witte's policies for Russian development?

1893	2 500 000 roubles
1897	80 000 000 roubles
1898	130 000 000 roubles
1913	2 200 000 000 roubles

TABLE 22

Foreign investment in Russia

See page 9

tripled and the total mileage covered by some railroads increased by 46 per cent.

Witte also succeeded in attracting foreign capital into Russia. He stabilised the currency by forbidding speculation and amassing gold by high exports of agricultural goods – healthy for the economy, less so for the peasants, all of whose surpluses were removed by taxation. By 1897 Witte was able to put Russia on the gold standard. Table 22 indicates the extent to which foreign capital was attracted into the country.

Although this resulted in large parts of Russian industry being owned abroad, especially in Paris – pig-iron and steel in particular – it did provide much of the required capital. In 1890 only 60 million roubles had been invested in new industries. In 1900 430 million roubles were. By then, 40 per cent of all industrial enterprises in Russia had been established in the single decade 1890–1900.

Education too was encouraged. In 1894 there had been only eight technical schools in Russia. Ten years later there were 100, in addition to new polytechnics in Kiev, Warsaw and St Petersburg. The literacy rate rose from 20 per cent in 1890 to 38 per cent in 1914. In many ways, these efforts were inadequate in that only 150 million roubles were spent on education in the decade 1890–1900, compared with 120 millions *each year* on railways. However, investment in education was not a popular policy with the traditional autocrats, who preferred an ignorant and subservient populace.

Above all war was avoided until 1904. Witte persuaded his master and his colleagues to play down Russia's role in Central Asia and the Balkans, potential areas of conflict. The agreement with Austria-Hungary of 1897 was one result of Witte's influence. In the same year, the Hague Conference on disarmament was held on Russia's initiative. For once, power considerations were made to serve economic objectives rather than vice versa.

Overall, Witte's initial objectives seem to have been achieved. Coal production was doubled. In the Donets basin, it was tripled. Iron production increased five- or six-fold, depending on the area concerned, mainly as a result of the new industrial centres in the south. Russia displaced France as the fourth greatest iron producer in the world and advanced to fifth place in steel production. In the oil industry, production increased ten-fold over the period 1883–1900. In the cotton industry, the labour force doubled and over 200 000 spindles were added each year. The overall growth rate achieved in the 1890s was more than 8 per cent per annum – the highest for any decade in Russia in the nineteenth century. The income from industrial production rose from 42 million roubles per annum in the period 1888–92 to 161 millions for 1893–97. Russian growth rates in industry were the fastest of any European country, but this was mainly because Russia was starting from a weak economic base, and Russia actually slipped down the 'league table' amongst Great Power economies.

Witte was criticised for the facts that:

● some 30 per cent of capital invested in Russia came from abroad. This dependence on foreign capital left Russia in constant debt to other countries so that any crisis in Europe threatened Russian financial stability

● high indirect taxes and the heavy exactions of crops were also necessary to raise capital. Witte took 15 per cent of the crop each year, compared with Reutern's 5 per cent. The result of this was that consumption levels fell by about 25 per cent, the demands of the Government being worsened by the requirements of a higher population. Since industrial production was so low, there was no alternative to exporting crops. Usually, grain made up half the total of Russian exports – even in the famine year of 1899 it constituted 42 per cent of the value of exports

● as well as ignoring the urgent needs of agriculture, Witte paid little attention to more advanced and sophisticated forms of industry. Modern equipment such as machine tools and electrical goods was imported from the West, making servicing difficult and costs high. Steel works, for instance, often had plenty of modern furnaces, rollers and the like, but only wheelbarrows with which to move the finished steel around the plant

● Witte concentrated on showpieces and industries that could demonstrate Russia's might, rather than on essentials. The Trans-Siberian Railway is one such example. Equally, the metallurgical resources of the Ukraine in western Russia were exploited, but not those of the Urals, where a single mountain could have flooded the iron ore markets of Europe.

Ultimately, it is possible to trace the events of 1905 and 1917 to Witte's reforms, since they produced the disaffected peasantry and the urban proletariat who were to be the activists in those years.

The period 1900–6 was a period of depression, in which some of the achievements of the Witte era were undone. In 1902, over 2000 businesses closed, including a third of the great iron mines at Krivoi Rog. However, from the high growth rates resumed after 1906 it may be argued that the momentum gained in the 1890s was not lost.

4 ⌐ POLITICAL HISTORY UNDER NICHOLAS II

A *The opposition to the autocracy*

The economic spurt of the 1890s imposed strains on the political and social structure of Russia. The industrial growth rate at that time was higher even than rates in Germany and the USA. In the last decade of the nineteenth century, the number of industrial workers in Russia increased by almost a million. This led to crises in urban accommodation, new consumer demands and forced a complete upheaval of the transport system. The shock waves of industrialisation spread from the towns to the overburdened peasantry. Moreover, the process of industrialisation was artificial, being imposed by Government policy rather than resulting from natural increases in demand.

The relationship between the economic changes and the development of the opposition was evident:

- there was direct protest from those who suffered the most – factory workers in terrible slums, starving peasants in the countryside
- the economic boom brought increased contact with Western ideas about government and society.

The most moderate of the Tsar's opponents were the 'Westernisers', also known as modernisers and as liberals. These often came from the educated, professional classes and were concerned that Russia should keep up, militarily and economically, with the other Great Powers. Rapid industrialisation was seen as the key to this. The liberals also admired Western democratic processes and hoped to see them emulated in Russia, if only to give their own supporters some influence in government. There was no named group of liberals making such demands but the *zemstvos* had liberal views, as did those employed by them – the new 'experts', like doctors, engineers, teachers and lawyers.

As their experience of local administration increased, the *zemstvos* from neighbouring areas met to discuss their common problems and complaints. In 1896 the first Annual Congress of *Zemstvo* Presidents was held. A proposal for universal elementary education was discussed and plans for a national assembly put forward. After the second Congress the following year, it was banned by the tsarist authorities as being **seditious**. In 1902 some of its members joined the 'League of Liberation', an organisation intended to unite the moderate opposition. Nicholas's rejection of their ideas was to prove fatal.

The liberals themselves foresaw this. This is an extract from their open letter to Nicholas after he rejected hopes for allowing their participation in government as 'senseless dreams' in 1895:

'We do not know whether you clearly understand the situation created by your 'firm' utterance. But people who do not stand so above and so far off from actuality can easily comprehend what is their own and your position concerning what is now the state of things in Russia ... No *zemstvoist* has put the question as you put it, and no voice was raised in any *Zemstvo* assembly against autocracy ... The question was only to remove the wall of bureaucracy and court influences which separate the Tsar from Russia; and these were tendencies which you in your inexperience and lack of knowledge ventured to stamp as 'senseless dreams' ... If autocracy in word and deed proclaims itself identical with the omnipotence of bureaucracy, if it can exist only so long as society is voiceless, it is lost. It digs its own grave, and soon or late, at any rate, in a future not very remote it will fall beneath the pressure of living social forces.

You challenged the *Zemstva* and with them Russian society, and nothing remains for them now but to choose between progress and faithfulness to autocracy. Your speech has provoked a feeling of offence and depression; but the living social forces will soon recover from that feeling. Some of them will pass to a peaceful but systematic struggle for such scope of action as is necessary for them. Some others will be made

---

KEY ISSUE

Why was there growing opposition to the autocracy in the decades before 1914, and what forms did this opposition take?

seditious material or action deemed to be a serious threat to the stability of the Government or State

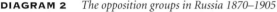

DIAGRAM 2   *The opposition groups in Russia 1870–1905*

more determined to fight the detestable regime by any means. You first began the struggle; and the struggle will come.'

The more extreme opposition was fractured into endless groups. Many historians have interpreted the history of these groups in different ways, making it difficult to provide a simple account of their development. The great variety of interpretations is hardly surprising, since the Tsar's 100 000 police and 50 000 'security gendarmerie' encouraged secrecy. The following account is intended to simplify the history of these groups.

During the reign of Alexander II, the more extreme opposition can be broadly described as 'populist'. Its members believed that the emancipation of the serfs should lead to the extensive redistribution of the land and increased wealth among the peasantry. Moderate populists believed that this would in turn lead to industrial progress as the result of increased demand and political changes would follow naturally. Extreme populists believed that these processes could be hastened by terrorist activities which would encourage reform and end the hated autocracy.

The populists were much influenced by the writings of Peter Lavrov, who hoped for a peaceful social revolution. In *Historical Letters* (1868–9) he wrote that the people must be shown the poverty of their conditions and led to a new society in which they were not exploited. He appealed to the young and educated to educate the masses. Some of them took him more literally than others. In 1874, following a famine in the Volga region, thousands of them went out into the villages to preach the populist message to the peasants. They met with little success, since the peasants understood nothing of their message and in many villages treated them as they had treated other wayside preachers – to mockery, a beating, even a lynching. The Government did understand and locked up more than 1500 young populists.

In the following years, the populists split into more identifiable groups with differing views on the means, rather than the ends, of social and political revolution. In 1876 the 'Land and Liberty' (or 'Land and Freedom') movement was founded. It was a small but well-organised group, whose chief demand was for the land to be handed over to

1891	Beginning of construction of Trans-Siberian Railway Beginning of severe famine in Russia
1892	Witte appointed Minister of Finance and Commerce
1894	*Secret alliance signed between France and Russia* Accession of Nicholas II
1896	*Railway concessions granted by China to Russia in Manchuria*
1898	Formation of Social Democratic Labour Party
1901	Formation of Socialist (or Social) Revolutionary Party
1903	Split of SDP into Bolshevik and Menshevik wings
1904	*Outbreak of Russo-Japanese War*
1905	Bloody Sunday in St Petersburg Potemkin mutiny *Treaty of Portsmouth ended war* October Manifesto issued by Tsar Risings crushed
1906	Fundamental Law issued by Tsar First Duma met Stolypin appointed Prime Minister Agrarian reforms began
1907	Second and Third Dumas elected
1908	*Bosnian crisis*
1911	Assassination of Stolypin
1913	Election of Fourth Duma
1914	*Outbreak of World War I*

TABLE 23

Date chart of main events in Russia 1890–1914. (Foreign affairs in italics)

the peasants. It organised demonstrations, and some of its members engaged in terrorist activities. Among their victims were the Governor of St Petersburg, General Trepov, the Crimean War hero General Mezentsov and Prince Kropotkin, Governor of Kharkov. In 1879 one of its members even attempted to kill the Tsar.

In the same year, the moderates, led by George Plekhanov, formed a new group, the 'Black Partition' (or 'Black Earth Populists'). They were opposed to violence and believed in the gradual education of the peasants into realising the need for change.

Their more extreme colleagues formed the 'People's Will' (or 'People's Freedom') movement, dedicated to hastening the course of events through terrorism. One of their first decisions was to condemn the Tsar to death. After seven attempts and nearly two years they succeeded.

The separate populist groups remained apart until 1900 when they were reunited as the Socialist Revolutionary Party, an umbrella group for all those with left-wing views. The new party followed the traditional populist policy of the redistribution of the land as the first priority. It advocated both a mass movement and closely-organised terrorism. Among the victims of the 'Combat Organisation', the heirs to the 'People's Will', were two Ministers of the Interior, Sipyagin (1902) and Plehve (1904) and the Tsar's uncle and brother-in-law, the Grand Duke Sergei (1905).

The foundation of the 'Emancipation of Labour' group in 1883 was to prove of far greater significance than the populist movements, although at the time it went unnoticed. It was founded in Switzerland by a group of ex-populists led by Plekhanov, Vera Zasulich and Paul Axelrod. Plekhanov was the leading theorist of the group, which for the first time applied Marxist theory to the Russian situation.

Marx's works had been translated into Russian in the 1860s, but few saw the relevance of books that wrote of the exploitation of the working class in industrial society to agrarian Russia. It was believed that capitalism would make slow progress in Russia, because of the lack of finance, entrepreneurs and markets, and therefore a theory of revolution based on the reactions of the masses to capitalism was inapplicable. Plekhanov dismissed this view and argued that capitalism *would* develop in Russia and that therefore 'the revolutionary movement in Russia can only triumph as the revolutionary movement of the workers'.

ANALYSIS

The Marxist view of economic and social development

Marx believed in a pattern of historical development that had in essence gone through three stages and was destined to progress through two more.

THE FIRST STAGE: PRIMITIVE COMMUNISM

In early times Marx identified a primitive economic system in which there was no organised government or class structure. People scratched a living mainly from the land.

THE SECOND STAGE: FEUDALISM

Following the development of a class structure, societies were dominated by aristocracies and absolute monarchies. The mass of the people were peasants. As trade and commerce expanded, the rising middle class would assume at least a share of power in order to further its own economic interests – what Marx believed had happened in the more advanced economies of Western Europe.

THE THIRD STAGE: CAPITALISM

In developing industrial societies, the middle classes, represented in particular by industrialists and financial interests, would exercise power, often through parliaments. The majority of the population would now be the *proletariat* or industrial working class. Workers would not receive the rightful rewards of their labour, which instead boosted the profits of the bosses. Eventually the workers would develop revolutionary ambitions and overwhelm the rich but numerically much smaller ruling class.

THE FOURTH STAGE: SOCIALISM

Having taken over the State, the workers would run it in the interests of their own class – 'the dictatorship of the proletariat'. Goods and services would be distributed fairly in a more equal society, and gradually the organs of state, with their repressive functions redundant, would begin to 'wither away.'

THE FIFTH STAGE: COMMUNISM

All would be equal in a community without an organised State power. Everyone would contribute willingly: 'From each according to his ability, to each according to his needs.'

For Marx, writing in the late nineteenth century, Russia was still a peasant society without a developed industrial base, and therefore had scarcely begun to emerge from the feudal into the capitalist stage. Lenin believed that revolutionary Socialists like himself need not wait for the natural course of development, but work to instil a revolutionary consciousness in the small proletariat, with leadership provided by a disciplined, *élite* Party. Such a Party would seize power in the name of the workers and institute 'state socialism', rather than wait for capitalist development to take its 'natural' Marxist course. Lenin's concentration on the organised Party, not something to which Marx had given much thought, was probably his most significant contribution to 'Marxist' thinking.

At that stage, the divisions were not final. In 1904 the Mensheviks won control of the Central Committee and Lenin founded his own rival paper, *Vperyod* ('Forward'). In 1905 the split became permanent when the two groups held separate congresses, in London and Geneva. Weak and divided, Russian social democracy in 1905 was hardly a force with which to be reckoned.

One further source of opposition to the Tsars must not be discounted. Less than half the population of the Russian Empire was Russian by nationality. Many of the minority nationalities were strongly opposed to the rule of the Tsar. The Poles, for example, hoped to re-establish their own kingdom. The Armenians, too, disliked Russian rule and in 1890 founded the Armenian Revolutionary Federation. The 'Russification' policy of the central Government under Alexander III further encouraged hostility among the minorities. All teaching had to be carried out in Russian, not only in Poland, always a centre of opposition, but also in the German Baltic areas, Finland and Central Asia.

The Jews were especially persecuted because of their association with the assassination of Alexander II, and the first of over 200 *pogroms* – attacks on Jews and their property – took place in May 1881. Legal restrictions were also placed on them, so that they were forced to live in towns and were barred from practising law and trading in alcohol. They were even, in 1890, forbidden to vote in *zemstvo* elections, and their numbers in further education were fixed. In 1897, they formed the *Bund* to co-ordinate their opposition. Members of the *Bund* attended the Minsk Conference that attempted to found the Social Democratic Party in 1898.

B *The 1905 Revolution*

The revolutionary events of 1905 were preceded by a series of decisions and accidents. There were signs of discontent among both the urban and rural poor. An increasing number of strikes were organised in the cities, especially St Petersburg, as part of a campaign to win reduced hours and better wages. The famines of 1897, 1898 and 1901 worsened the plight of the already desperate peasantry, and in 1902 there were uprisings in the provinces of Poltava and Kharkov.

Thousands of miles away, tension with Japan had reached a new peak. In 1895, Russia had persuaded Japan to give up Port Arthur and the Liao-tung Peninsula to her. Subsequent agreements with China had increased Russian influence and Russians had substantial investments in northern China. This expansion was opposed by Japan and there were negotiations about the influence each was to have on the Chinese mainland.

A peaceful solution was almost certainly possible, but without the restraining influence of Witte, who had been dismissed in 1900, the Russian ministers advised the Tsar to ignore it. Plehve, Minister of the Interior, actually welcomed 'a short, victorious war that would stem the tide of revolution'. Japanese requests for negotiations were ignored. On 8 February 1904 the Japanese fleet torpedoed the Russian fleet stationed in Port Arthur while the Japanese army cleared the Korean peninsula of Russian troops.

See page 85

KEY ISSUE

What were the causes and consequences of the Russo-Japanese War?

The war proved disastrous for Russia's military pride. A second Japanese army was landed on the Liaotung peninsula and cut off Port Arthur. The Russian armies fought bravely in spite of inept orders, short supplies and inadequate reinforcements. In March 1905 they were defeated at Mukden. In the meantime, Port Arthur had fallen to Japanese troops in January 1905 and in the course of ten months 100 000 Russian troops had been lost.

Desperate for victory, Nicholas ordered his Baltic fleet to leave Kronstadt in October 1904. Barred from the Suez Canal, the fleet rounded the Cape. On 27 May 1905, it was sailing through the straits of Tsushima when it was attacked by the Japanese. More than 30 battleships – almost the entire fleet – were destroyed in an afternoon. So much for a 'short victorious war'.

The war had a major impact on Russia. Plehve was blown up by Socialist Revolutionaries in July 1904, prompting Nicholas to remark: 'I have a secret conviction that I am destined for a terrible trial.' Two days later his son and heir, Alexis, was born. A week later the remains of the Far East fleet ventured out of Port Arthur. Its commander was killed in his flagship, the *Tsarevich* ('Tsar's son'). Shortly afterwards it was learnt that Alexis had haemophilia. The winter of 1904–5 had already brought discontent and news of the fall of Port Arthur coincided with a strike at the Putilov engineering works in St Petersburg. Spontaneous strikes were called in other cities. By 22 January 1905, 105 000 workers were on strike.

This prompted action from more moderate quarters. Father Gapon, an ex-prison chaplain and head of the Association of Russian Factory and Mill Workers, one of the unions set up by the Government to channel workers' demands, met with *zemstvo* leaders and Socialist Revolutionaries. They drew up a petition to present to the Tsar. 'We are not considered human beings ... we are treated like slaves' it began. It requested 'the ending of the war, full civil liberties, a political amnesty and a constituent assembly'. It had 135 000 signatories.

On Sunday 22 January, the petitioners, led by Gapon, proceeded to the Winter Palace, the Tsar's residence in St Petersburg. As they marched, they sang hymns and carried pictures of the tsar. When they reached Palace Square, they were met not by the Tsar, who was not in residence, but by Cossacks and dragoons who fired on them. Officially, 96 protesters died and 333 were wounded. Probably 1000 died and thousands more were wounded. The Tsar himself recorded that it was a 'painful day' but others were less charitable – Ramsay Macdonald called him a 'blood-stained creature' and 'a common murderer'.

A wave of protests followed. Almost half a million workers came out on strike. There was more terrorism. The Tsar's uncle, Grand Duke Sergei, the Governor of Moscow, was assassinated in February. In March, the Tsar promised a 'consultative' assembly, religious toleration, language rights for the Polish minority and cancellation of a part of the redemption dues for the peasants.

These concessions proved inadequate, and instead unions were set up among groups that had never before been so organised – engineers,

> **KEY ISSUE**
>
> *What was the significance of Bloody Sunday?*

- the members of the *Duma* theoretically had the power to veto legislation, but as they had little control over government finance and none over the Council of Ministers, which remained responsible only to the Tsar, this power was limited.

These arrangements were announced by the Tsar in the Fundamental Law of 6 May 1906, less than a week before the *Duma* was due to sit. Nicholas also proclaimed himself an autocrat with control over the army and foreign policy and stated that no alterations could be made to the new arrangements without his approval. Four days earlier, he had sacked Witte, secure in the knowledge that the $400 million loan he had obtained from France would keep him financially independent of the *Duma*. Witte's replacement was the conservative Ivan Goremykin. The Tsar had seemingly scotched any chance of democratic government before it got off the ground.

Nevertheless, on 10 May 1906, the newly elected members of the *Duma* met for the first time. There were no 'parties' by modern standards, but there were a number of identifiable groups:

- the *Octobrists*, who had about 40 representatives, took their name from the October Manifesto, which they accepted as providing the right degree of democracy. They were, however, keen to build up Russia's economic strength and establish a wealthy peasantry
- the *Cadets* (Constitutional Democrats), of whom there were nearly 200, had been formed by Milyukov in October 1905. They were the political party of the *zemstvo* liberals and sought direct and universal suffrage and further redistribution of land in the peasants' favour
- the Social Democrats were technically absent, since they had boycotted the elections on the grounds that they were sham democracy. In fact, about 20 of them, chiefly Mensheviks, had ignored the boycott and had been elected
- the other members were not affiliated to any particular group. Sixty or so represented particular national groups – Ukrainians and Poles especially – and stood for the independence of their group from the Russian Empire. The other members, about 200 of them, were poorer people with no agreed policy, although some can be identified as a labour group. The lack of party organisation and the few votes that were called makes it difficult to be definite about the numbers and constitution of the different groups.

The first session of the *Duma* lasted only 10 weeks. The deputies attempted to win more power for themselves, demanding, for instance, that ministers should be responsible to them, not the Tsar, and that the Imperial Council should be abolished. They also made a series of demands for nation-wide reforms, such as the breaking up of the great estates and the abolition of the death penalty.

The experiment in constitutionalism had backfired on the Tsar. He could control the electoral system but not the people who were elected. Rather than give way again, he decided to reimpose his authority. In July he declared the *Duma* dissolved on the grounds that it was unable to function. Troops were sent to the Tauride Palace to prevent any meeting continuing. Contrary to his own Fundamental Law, Nicholas set no date for new elections but announced that the next *Duma* would meet the following February. In protest at this, about 200 *Duma* members, mainly Cadets, crossed the border into Finland and from the town of Viborg called upon the people to refuse to pay their taxes or to serve in the army. Their manifesto was generally ignored.

The Second *Duma* differed from the First in two respects:

- the Social Democrats put up candidates, and some 50 of them were elected
- the Cadets decided to attempt to co-operate with the Government. However, they could not prevent other members repeating the radical demands of the First *Duma* or refusing to co-operate with the Government's plans for agrarian reform and the repression of terrorism. Consequently, after three months, the *Duma* was dissolved on the (false) grounds that a Social Democrat member was plotting to assassinate the Tsar.

In an attempt to ensure more compliance, the Tsar altered the electoral quotas. In so doing, he again broke the Fundamental Law of 1906 which stated that it could not be changed without the *Duma's* approval. The number of electoral college votes for workers was reduced, as was that for the national minorities, while that for estate owners was increased, giving them more than half the seats.

Not surprisingly, the subsequent *Dumas*, which sat from 1907–12 and 1912–17, respectively, were more obedient. Seton-Watson gives the following membership figures for these two *Dumas*:

1907: Octobrists 154; other right-wing 127; Cadets 54; left-wing 33
1912: Octobrists 121; other right-wing 145; Cadets 100; left-wing 23

The Third *Duma* contained a majority of Octobrists and right-wingers, who gave their approval to Stolypin's repressive measures. The Fourth *Duma* was also conservative and thus, by 1914, the Tsar had achieved the rubber-stamp democracy that he had wanted.

Yet even the conservatives of the Fourth *Duma* were roused to action by the inefficiency of the Government during the Great War and formed a 'Progressive Bloc' in 1915 to recommend reform. The Tsar's failure to respond to this symbolised the last chance for democracy. Oberlander summarised the significance of the failure of the *Dumas* as follows: 'The tsarist regime was not overthrown, it succumbed to its own inertia. The Russian parliamentary system was completely undermined by the lack of trust between the tsarist regime and the First and Second *Dumas*, which were more or less representative of the people.'

> **KEY ISSUE**
>
> *How successful were the Dumas?*

D *Stolypin's economic reforms*

Peter Stolypin became Prime Minister in June 1906, having made his name as Governor of Saratov province during 1905, when he had put down revolutionaries with great harshness. He remained a believer in repression. The extra powers granted to provincial governors on his initiative in 1906 – during which the First *Duma* had been dissolved – resulted in over 100 executions.

Nevertheless, Stolypin saw the need to establish Russia as a strong, capitalist state, preferably with the Tsar as its head. To achieve this, he wanted to create a class of wealthy peasants who would provide enough grain for exports while earning enough money to be a consumer class for industrial goods. Those peasants who could not survive would provide the industrial workforce. Reforms in this direction should also win new support for the Tsar from the wealthy peasants.

PROFILE

PETER STOLYPIN (1862–1911)

Stolypin was by far one of the Tsar's most able ministers, coming from a noble family that had served the regime for centuries. He had a better perception than most of the bureaucratic class of the problems of the countryside, since he was appointed Prime Minister directly from a provincial area, one in the West of Russia which had not experienced the communal system of farming. This moulded his belief that the best guarantee of stability was a prosperous landowning class and not a communal system of subsistence farming. He was a brave and ruthless servant of the Tsar. He told the British historian Bernard Pares in 1906, 'I am fighting on two fronts. I am fighting against revolution, but for reform.' He had no truck with the ambitions of the *dumas* for more power, and lacked the diplomatic skills which might have brought compromise. Although in some ways far-sighted, Stolypin's high-handedness alienated many at all levels of society.

Stolypin was assassinated after five years of power, when he himself had declared that he needed 20 years to change Russia. Extract from *A People's Tragedy. The Russian Revolution 1891–1924* by Orlando Figes, published by Jonathan Cape. Used by permission of The Random House Group Limited.

> He adhered so rigidly to his own aims and principles that he lost sight of the need to negotiate and compromise with his opponents. He antagonised the old political elites by riding roughshod over their traditional privileges and lost the support of the liberals by suppressing the Duma whenever it stood in his way. This political inflexibility stemmed from his narrow bureaucratic outlook. He acted as if everything had to be subordinated to the interests of the state, as if these were defined by his reforms, and believed that this placed him above the need to involve himself in the dirty business of party manoeuvring. He thought he could get his reforms by administrative fiat, and never moved outside the bureaucracy to mobilise a broader base of support. Although he acknowledged that the key to his programme was the creation of a conservative peasant landowning class, he never considered the idea of sponsoring a smallholders' party. There was a Stolypin but no Stolypinites. And so when Stolypin died his reforms died with him.

To these ends he introduced the Agrarian Reform Act of 1906 and a series of complex subsidiary legislation between 1906 and 1911:

● the land captains were abolished and the peasant passport system ended so that peasants became as free to move around as any other Russian

● the peasants were also released from their obligations to the *mir* and could choose to own their land as individuals rather than as part of the *mir*. If a majority of members of the *mir* favoured individual land holding, then the *mir* was disbanded. When a peasant received his individual land holding, it was in the form of a single farm, rather than parts of land scattered throughout the *mir*'s holding. By 1916, 1.2 million peasants (about 24 per cent) owned their own land, and a further 750 000 applications were waiting a decision

● Stolypin also encouraged resettlement, as a result of which about half a million people went to the east with Government assistance. The Peasants' Land Bank was extended to make it easier for peasants to set up their own farms. In 1907, redemption payments were ended, by which time 670.3 million roubles had been repaid out of a total due of 2012 millions.

KEY ISSUE

How successful were Stolypin's agricultural reforms?

These measures should have combined to provide a rural revolution. In fact, they had failed to do so by the time of the political revolutions of 1917. When Stolypin was assassinated in a Kiev theatre in 1911, the Tsar and Rasputin were in the audience. As the assassin had been both a revolutionary and a police agent, it is not certain on whose orders he had acted. Stolypin's scheme for closing the *mirs* was ended in 1916, since it was impossible for peasants serving in the Great War to reorganise their land.

ANALYSIS

The condition of Russia in 1914

Historians have debated the extent to which tsarist Russia was a stable society in 1914, and how successfully Russia was developing as an economic power in the light of developments since the 1890s. Could the regime have gone on to develop peacefully, perhaps on the lines of Western European constitutional states? Or was the regime too inflexible? Could the regime have survived but for the disasters of World War I?

The revolutionaries themselves were not confident that Russia was ripe for revolution. A group of Bolsheviks wrote in their Party newspaper *Forward* in 1910 that

Our party is in a very serious condition ... Our organisations have grown much smaller ... many local groups have disintegrated altogether ... because of countless arrests and banishments, and also because of the desertion of the intelligentsia, there is an enormous shortage of forces for leadership and propaganda ... Work in the armed forces and among the peasantry has died down altogether.'

The following statistics show Russia's ranking in some economic areas:

Comparative production of major industries in million tons, 1914

	Russia	France	Germany	USA	Britain	Russian ranking
coal	36	40	190	517	292	5
oil	9.1	0	0	33.1	0	2
iron	4.6	5.2	6.8	31	10.4	5
steel	4.8	4.6	8.3	31.8	7.8	4

Contribution of industry to Gross National Product in 1910
Russia 30%   Austria-Hungary 47%   Germany 70%   Britain 73%

Value of foreign trade in 1913, in million £

Britain	1223
Germany	1030
France	424
Austria-Hungary	199
Russia	190
Turkey	67

In February 1914 Peter Durnovo, a member of the State Council, wrote a pessimistic memorandum to the Tsar. He forecast a war between Britain and Germany and speculated on Russia's position. He realised that Russia would be on Britain's side. However, 'The main burden of the war will fall on Russia, since England is hardly capable of large-scale participation in a continental war, while France will probably confine itself to strictly defensive tactics.' He declared that Russia itself was not prepared for a 'stubborn' struggle, particularly since it was so dependent on foreign industry. He told the Tsar that German interests, which lay 'on the sea', did not conflict with Russian interests, whilst Russia could only benefit from the continued development of German economic strength. A war would cripple Russia financially, and would also 'undoubtedly lead to a weakening of the conservative monarchical principle of which they [Germany and Russia] are the only two reliable bulwarks.' There would inevitably be a 'social revolution' in the defeated country, and it would spread to the victorious country. Russia would be 'flung into anarchy as she suffered in 1905–6 ... the defeated army will prove too demoralised to serve as a bulwark of law and order ... the legislative institutions, lacking real authority, will be powerless to stem the rising popular tide, which they themselves had aroused.'

Given the popular enthusiasm for war in 1914, this much more pessimistic assessment was in several respects very accurate in its portrayal of what was to happen in 1917. The unanswerable question is this: if Russia had avoided war in 1914, would revolution also have been averted, or as Marxists anticipated in their more optimistic moods, would radical change eventually occur anyway because it 'lay in the logic of history'?

Stolypin's reforms had left untouched the 140 million acres held by the nobility and had taken no account of the increasing rural population. Like Stalin after him, Stolypin concentrated on reforming the system of landholding as the key to agrarian reform. In other countries, which had undergone a natural rather than an imposed agricultural revolution, innovations – such as machinery and fertilisers – had preceded rather than followed changes in the landholding system. Certainly, Stolypin encouraged new techniques: over 1500 model farms and agricultural schools were set up between 1907 and 1913. However, these were intended to bring changes to the newly created farms rather than bring changes that would *require* new farms. Not surprisingly, crop yields remained at their old levels, about half those of Western Europe.

Stolypin's measures had come too little, too late.

5 ⌐ FOREIGN POLICY

A *Imperial policy*

CENTRAL ASIA

During the nineteenth century Russia extended its trading influence and governing control over parts of Central Asia. Several Russians had undertaken conquests on their own initiative. General Chernayev, acting against official orders, had captured Tashkent in 1865. Next, the three Khanates, previously ruled by the Uzbeks, were captured. The first, Bukhara, was captured as a result of the battle of Dzhizak. Khiva became a Russian dependency in 1873 and Kokand was taken in 1876. Prince Gorchakov, the Russian Foreign Minister, justified these conquests on grounds of security, since each new boundary brought contact with another hostile people. The conquests were also economically valuable, providing minerals and cotton-growing areas. The building of railways after 1880 increased this value and gave them strategic importance. In 1879 the Transcaucasian Railway was started, reaching Samarkand in 1888. In 1898 a line from Merv to Kushk on the Afghan border was started.

There was no further expansion after 1890. However, Russian activity in Central Asia remained of diplomatic importance. The British Government was concerned that Russia planned to continue its expansion and

See Map 6 on page 84

the port of Port Arthur. In addition, the Russians bribed the Chinese negotiators to get permission to build a railway from Harbin to Darien.

The next years saw significant developments in Russian Far Eastern policy:

- negotiations with Japan over Japanese influence in Korea. Since 1895 Japan had won such power there that Russia realised it had little chance of challenging it. The Nissi-Rosen Convention of 1898 agreed that each Power would respect Korean sovereignty and not interfere in the internal affairs of Korea. As far as Japan was concerned, Russia was promising to keep out. Japan offered Russia a free hand in Manchuria in exchange for Japan having a free hand in Korea, but Russia had rejected this
- other European Powers acquired railway rights in China. The Boxer Rebellion of 1900 had led to a joint West European force going to China but Russia, keen to maintain its pre-eminence, took the opportunity to occupy all the major cities of northern Manchuria and increase the number of troops in the railway zone. The other Western Powers became concerned by Russia's influence. The Anglo-Japanese Treaty of 1902 promised neutrality in the event of a Far Eastern war while Germany supported Russia by declaring that 'the fate of Manchuria was a matter of absolute indifference to Germany'
- the Tsar became increasingly keen to exploit the resources of Manchuria, and, if possible, Northern Korea. An ex-cavalry officer, Bezobrazov, persuaded Nicholas to let him have two million roubles to investigate the natural resources of the Yalu River, especially timber. Bezobrazov recruited a number of Chinese thugs to act as guards during the investigations. Their excesses did little to endear the Russians to the Chinese and Japanese in the area.

KEY ISSUE

What were the causes of the Russo-Japanese War?

Japan became more and more concerned by Russia's action. In 1903, the Japanese Government offered negotiations and repeated its offer of 1898 – a free hand for Russia in Manchuria in exchange for a free hand for Japan in Korea. The Russian Government made no reply. Then the Tsar appointed Admiral Alexeev, a friend of Bezobrazov, as Regent of the Far East. In October 1903 Russia replied to the Japanese offer by saying that Korean independence should be acknowledged by both sides and that the area to the north of the 39th parallel should be neutral. Manchuria was not mentioned. The Japanese rejected the Russian proposals and again asked for the same rights in Korea as the Russians had in Manchuria. Subsequent negotiations during the winter of 1903–4 made no progress, and on 8 February 1904, the Japanese attacked Port Arthur, launching the war that led to Russia's humiliation.

See page 74

After the war, Russia attempted to maintain its influence in northern China. In 1907, a treaty with Japan settled each nation's fishing rights and the use of the South Manchurian Railway. A secret protocol acknowledged Japan's rights in Korea and southern Manchuria and Russia's influence in northern Manchuria and Mongolia. In 1910 Korea was formally annexed to the Japanese Empire and renamed Chosen.

After 1911 Russia won from China special interests in Mongolia, setting up a bank and sending military and financial advisers.

B *European policies*

RUSSIA'S POSITION IN 1890

In 1872, Russia had joined Germany and Austria-Hungary in the *Dreikaiserbund* (Three Emperors League). This was an informal agreement by which each agreed to benevolent neutrality if any of them were involved in war with an outside Power. In 1881 this arrangement was formalised into a treaty, renewable every three years. It was also agreed that Austria-Hungary should ultimately annex Bosnia and Herzegovina.

By 1887 there was considerable opposition in Russia to the renewal of the treaty. This was led by MN Katkov in *Moskovskiye vedomisti*: he argued that an alliance with Austria-Hungary restricted Russia's hopes of territorial gains in the Balkans. The German Government was also concerned by the treaty's incompatibility with its promises to Austria-Hungary in 1879, that Germany would go to Austria-Hungary's aid in the event of war with Russia.

As a result of their mutual concerns, Russia and Germany signed the Reinsurance Treaty of 1887. By this, each promised benevolent neutrality in the event of the other being involved in war, unless Russia attacked Austria-Hungary, in which case Germany claimed the right to support its ally. Germany also promised to support Russian influence in the Balkans. However, the treaty was not renewed in 1890, for the new German Government was still concerned that it conflicted with German promises to Austria-Hungary. Only Bismarck had been able to maintain alliances with both the Great Powers which threatened each other in the Balkans. So Russia entered the 1890s without allies.

The Tsar and his Government still hoped to maintain and extend Russian influence in the Balkans. Bulgaria had accepted Russian friendship until 1885. In that year, Prince Alexander had supported the union of Eastern Rumelia with Bulgaria, thereby annoying the Russian Government, which forced his abdication. The new ruler, Ferdinand of Coburg, once again accepted Russia's influence. In addition, Serbia, officially Austria-Hungary's client, looked increasingly to Russia as an ally against Austria-Hungary. Consequently, Russia, which in any case regarded itself as the natural leader of the Slav peoples, had the friendship and support of both the new Balkan Powers in the 1890s.

Russia was equally keen to see the decline of the Ottoman Empire, by force if necessary. This would not only bring the prospect of territorial gain, but might also resolve the issue of the Straits of Constantinople in Russia's favour. In 1841, Britain, Russia, France, Austria and Prussia had agreed that the Straits should be closed to all warships as long as Turkey was at peace. In 1871 this had been revised so that the Sultan could allow warships through if he considered his independence threatened. These arrangements were reasonably satisfactory to Russia as they gave its southern flank a measure of protection, but they also made it difficult for the Russian Black Sea fleet to be used. In 1904–5, this fleet

KEY ISSUE

What were Russia's ambitions in the Balkans?

had been barred from the Straits during the war with Japan, so thereafter the Russian Government was keen to have the 'Straits Convention' revised so that the Straits were permanently open to its warships.

THE ALLIANCE WITH FRANCE

See pages 107–8

Russo-French friendship began in the late 1880s. The Russian ambassador in Paris, Baron Mohrenheim, was influential in allaying French fears about the autocracy and in 1889 and 1890 France began to lend money to Russia.

In 1891 the Triple Alliance of Germany, Austria-Hungary and Italy was renewed. Four years earlier Britain had signed the Mediterranean Agreements with Austria-Hungary and Italy, and seemed friendly to the Triple Alliance. France and Russia were both isolated. In July 1891 a French naval squadron visited Kronstadt. In August an agreement was signed promising mutual consultation in the event of possible war. If either were in danger each would agree to 'measures which this eventuality would require the two Governments to adopt immediately and simultaneously'. Discussions were initiated on what these measures should be.

In August 1892 France and Russia agreed on a military convention which was finally ratified by both sides in January 1894:

- if France were attacked by Germany (or by Italy and Germany), Russia would provide between 700 000 and 800 000 men against Germany
- if Russia were attacked by Germany or by Austria-Hungary and Germany, all available French forces (1 300 000 men) would be used against Germany.

KEY ISSUES

Why, and with what consequences, did Russia sign an alliance with France?

These terms were never made public, but the commitment of the two countries to each other was widely known. In 1896, and again in 1901, Nicholas II visited Paris, and in 1897 President Faure visited Russia. French loans continued to support and develop the Russian economy.

RELATIONS WITH GERMANY, AUSTRIA-HUNGARY AND GREAT BRITAIN

In 1904–5 the possibility of a Russo-German alliance arose. Germany had failed to come to agreement with Britain and Russian friendship might be valuable not only against Britain but also as a means of securing France's agreement to the permanent accession of Alsace-Lorraine. For Russia, Germany's friendship might provide both security against Austria-Hungary and support for Russian claims in the Balkans and the Straits of Constantinople.

In October 1904 the *Kaiser* suggested a Franco-Russo-German alliance against Britain to the Tsar. Nicholas' immediate reaction was enthusiastic, but he insisted on discussing it with France before signing anything, while the *Kaiser* wanted a Russo-German alliance signed before France was brought into the negotiations. The idea was therefore shelved. In July 1905 the *Kaiser* persuaded the Tsar to sign the Treaty of Björko, but it was never ratified and Russo-German relations thereafter worsened.

See page 57

For a short time, agreement with Austria-Hungary seemed a possibility. After Russia's defeat in the Far East, there seemed little chance of making gains in the Balkans by military action. Consequently, there was some discussion in the Third *Duma* in 1907 of the possibility of agreement with Austria-Hungary. However, the Bosnian crisis of 1908 and Austria-Hungary's closeness to Germany ended all hopes in this direction.

See pages 113–14

Before the turn of the century, Russia and Britain seemed likely enemies because of their rival ambitions in Central Asia. However, after 1904 they were both friendly to France and Anglo-Russian discussions began in 1906. A Convention was agreed in August 1907:

- Persia was divided into three zones of influence (one British, one Russian, one neutral)
- the position of both Powers in Afghanistan was agreed (Russia was to leave and maintain relations with the Afghan Government only through Britain)
- Tibet was to be under Chinese sovereignty.

See Map 6 on page 84

This convention was the basis of the Russo-British *Entente*.

Germany was given assurances that the agreement was not intended to damage it, and in fact, apart from the Bosnian crisis, Russo-German relations improved considerably. In 1908 an agreement on the Aaland islands was signed and in 1910 there was a settlement on the Baghdad Railway. In February 1914 PN Durnovo, the Russian ex-minister of the Interior, wrote in a memorandum: 'The vital interests of Russia and Germany are nowhere in conflict ... The future of Germany is on the seas where for Russia, essentially the most Continental of the powers, there are no interests at all.'

KEY ISSUE

What was the significance of the Anglo-Russian Entente?

RUSSIA AND THE BALKANS

The Balkans were relatively quiet during the 1890s. Both the chief protagonists were involved elsewhere – the Russians in the Far East, the Austro-Hungarians with internal problems. Serbia became increasingly Russophile, and the Austro-Serbian treaty was not renewed in 1895. Draga Mashin, the wife of King Alexander (1889–1903), was keen to improve relations with Russia. After her assassination with her husband in 1903, the new King, Peter I, of the Karadjordjevic dynasty, was equally pro-Russian. At the same time, Russian influence in Bulgaria remained assured. In 1895 the anti-Russian Prime Minister, Stambolov, was assassinated. The heir to the throne, Prince Boris, was converted from Catholicism to Orthodoxy. In 1902 a military agreement was signed. Russia seemed pre-eminent.

However, the next 10 years saw a reversal of Russia's fortunes. In the Bosnian crisis of 1908 Russia was unable to back Serbia for fear of German involvement and thus lost some of Serbia's confidence. In the following years, the Russian Foreign Ministry tried hard to create a barrier against further Austrian expansion, particularly encouraging the alliance of Serbia and Bulgaria that was signed in 1912. Unfortunately, while Russia saw this alliance as a way of blocking Austrian expansion,

See page 114

The rioting and agitation in the capitals and in many localities of Our Empire fills Our hearts with great and deep grief. The welfare of the Russian Emperor is bound up with the welfare of the people, and its sorrows are His sorrows. The turbulence which has broken out may confound the people and threaten the integrity and unity of Our Empire.

The great vow of service by the Tsar obligates Us to endeavour, with all Our strength, wisdom, and power, to put an end as quickly as possible to the disturbances so dangerous to the Empire. In commanding the responsible authorities to take measures to stop disorders, lawlessness and violence, and to protect peaceful citizens in the quiet performances of their duties, We have found it necessary to unite the activities of the Supreme Government, so as to ensure the successful carrying out of the general measures laid down by Us for the peaceful life of the State.

We lay upon the Government the execution of Our unchangeable will:

1   To grant to the population the inviolable right of free citizenship, based on the principles of freedom of person, conscience, speech, assembly, and union . . .
3   To establish as an unbreakable rule that no law shall go into force without its confirmation by the State Duma and that the persons elected by the people shall have the opportunity for actual participation in supervising the legality of the acts of authorities appointed to Us . . .

SOURCE B
The October Manifesto,
17 October 1905

. . . The troubles that have broken out in villages . . . fill Our heart with deep sorrow . . . Violence and crime do not, however, help the peasant and may bring much sorrow and misery to the country. The only way to better permanently the welfare of the peasant is by peaceful and legal means; and to improve his condition has always been one of our first cares . . . We have decided:

1   To reduce by half, from 1 January 1906, and to discontinue altogether after 1 January 1907, payments due from peasants for land which before emancipation belonged to large landowners, State and Crown.
2   To make it easier for the Peasant Land Bank, by increasing its resources and by offering better terms for loans, to help the peasant with little land to buy more . . .

SOURCE C
Manifesto to better the
conditions . . . of the peasant
population, 3 November 1905:

The Government continues to stride over corpses. It puts on trial before a court-martial the brave Kronstadt soldiers of the army and navy who rose to the defence of their rights and of national freedom. It put the noose of martial law on the neck of oppressed Poland.

The Council of Workmen's Delegates calls on the revolutionary proletariat of Petersburg to manifest their solidarity with the revolutionary soldiers of Kronstadt and with the revolutionary proletarians of Poland through a general political strike, which has proved to be a formidable power, and through general meetings of protest.

SOURCE D
The St Petersburg Soviet, 13 October–3 December 1905 – proclamation calling the second general strike, 1 November 1905, in support of the rebellion of the Kronstadt sailors

...
4. The supreme autocratic power is vested in the Tsar of All the Russias. It is God's command that his authority should be obeyed not only through fear but for conscience' sake ...
7. The Tsar exercises the legislative power in conjunction with the Council of the Empire and the Imperial Duma ...
9. The Tsar approves of the laws, and without his approval no law can come into existence.
10. All governmental powers in their widest extent throughout the whole Russian Empire are vested in the Tsar ...
17. The Tsar appoints and dismisses the President of the Council, the ministers themselves, and the heads of the chief departments of administration, as well as all other officials where the law does not provide for another method of appointment and dismissal ...

SOURCE E
The Fundamental Laws of the Russian Empire, 23 April 1906

We summoned the representatives of the nation by Our will to the work of productive legislation. Confiding firmly in our divine clemency and believing in the great and brilliant future of Our people, We confidently anticipated benefits for the country from their labours. We proposed great reforms in all departments in the national life. We have always devoted Our greatest care to the removal of the ignorance of the people by the light of instruction, and to the removal of their burdens by improving the conditions of agricultural work.

A cruel disappointment has befallen Our expectations. The representatives of the nation, instead of applying themselves to the work of productive legislation, have strayed into spheres beyond their competence, and have been making enquiries into the acts of local authorities established by Ourselves, and have been making comments upon the imperfections of the Fundamental Laws, which can only be modified by Our imperial will. In short, the representatives of the nation have undertaken really illegal acts, such as the appeal by the Duma to the nation.

The peasants, disturbed by such anomalies, and seeing no hope of the amelioration of their lot, have resorted in a number of districts to open pillage and the destruction of other people's property, and to disobedience of the law and of the legal authorities. But Our subjects ought to remember that an improvement in the lot of the people is only possible under conditions of perfect order and tranquillity. We shall not permit arbitrary or illegal acts, and We shall impose Our imperial will on the disobedient by all the power of the State . . .

SOURCE F

Dissolution of the First Duma, 21 July 1906

SOURCE G

Pictures 11–13 show Russian posters about the aftermath of the 1905 revolution

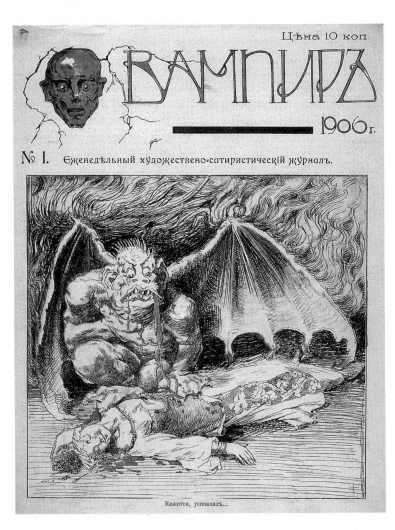

PICTURE 11

'He seems to have pacified her'

PICTURE 12 *'In this world there is a Tsar. He is without pity. HUNGER is his name.'*

PICTURE 13 *'The voter'*

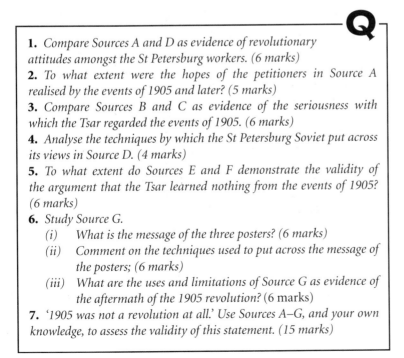

1. Compare Sources A and D as evidence of revolutionary attitudes amongst the St Petersburg workers. *(6 marks)*

2. To what extent were the hopes of the petitioners in Source A realised by the events of 1905 and later? *(5 marks)*

3. Compare Sources B and C as evidence of the seriousness with which the Tsar regarded the events of 1905. *(6 marks)*

4. Analyse the techniques by which the St Petersburg Soviet put across its views in Source D. *(4 marks)*

5. To what extent do Sources E and F demonstrate the validity of the argument that the Tsar learned nothing from the events of 1905? *(6 marks)*

6. Study Source G.

   (i)   What is the message of the three posters? *(6 marks)*

   (ii) Comment on the techniques used to put across the message of the posters; *(6 marks)*

   (iii) What are the uses and limitations of Source G as evidence of the aftermath of the 1905 revolution? *(6 marks)*

7. '1905 was not a revolution at all.' Use Sources A–G, and your own knowledge, to assess the validity of this statement. *(15 marks)*

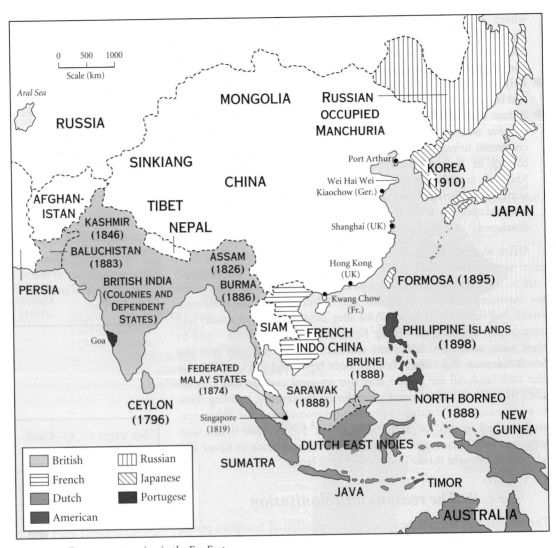

MAP 9   *European expansion in the Far East*

the natives, while almost all those who went genuinely believed that they would improve the peoples they met

● economic gain was, implicitly or explicitly, an important motive. The new colonies were seen as 'undeveloped estates', in a famous phrase of Joseph Chamberlain, whose cultivation would bring reward for both owners and occupiers. In some cases, such as Egypt, the colonies began as an independent area of European investment in which it became necessary to intervene in order to protect the interests of the investors. Often, the colonies were seen as sources of otherwise expensive raw materials and as enormous new markets for European manufactures

● Marxist historians considered that imperial expansion was the logical extension of the development of monopoly capitalism, as

KEY ISSUES

What were the motives for empire building?

capitalist states sought new markets. Such expansionism would lead to war and eventually to international revolution, after Powers armed their working masses. One drawback of this theory is that it fails to explain why, for example, Britain went to war against Germany rather than, for example, France or Russia, from whom far more potential overseas territory might be won

- European expansion can also be seen as the result of **geopolitics**. By 1885, almost all the boundaries of Europe were settled and agreed upon. Only the Balkans remained open to question. Expansion by any Power in that area was likely to be extremely hazardous, as it was liable to upset the delicate balance between the Powers. In contrast, Africa was a huge continent, where gains could more easily be made without risking conflict with another European Power and, it hardly needs to be said, without great risk to the Europeans involved

- there was an important element of national prestige and 'keeping up with the Jones's' in the scramble for Africa. Prestige at home and abroad was unlikely to be easily won by military victory in Europe, but it could be achieved by victory and expansion overseas. Once one European Power won the admiration and respect of its people and rivals in this way, it was hard for the others to resist.

> **geopolitics** the study of the effect of a nation's geographical position on its politics

These many and mixed motives were rarely clear to the participants in the colonial stampede, whose actions were more often reactions to particular circumstances than clearly rationalised policies.

C *Colonial conflicts in the 1890s*

Inevitably, there were disputes over the borders between the separate acquisitions of the Powers. This was especially true of West Africa, where a number of countries had taken possession of coastal areas and then expanded inland. In most cases, the disputed areas were settled by agreement. For example, in 1886 France and Portugal defined the frontier between French and Portuguese Guinea, while in the same year Britain and Germany agreed on the borders of Togoland and the Gold Coast.

However, there were cases where no agreement was possible. In 1897–8 both Britain and France sought to win control of Western Nigeria. In 1890 an agreement had been signed on the northern limits of British Nigeria. However, the French were eager to link their possessions to the north of this with their colony of Dahomey. French troops were sent to the area and took two towns, Busa and Nikki, in 1897. Britain protested strongly at this action but nothing was done during 1898 when both sides threatened to send more troops to the area. Eventually, a new agreement was reached in June 1898, when a boundary from northern Nigeria to the coast was drawn, by which France kept Nikki but gave Busa to Britain.

Also in 1898, British and French interests clashed on the other side of the continent. The Sudan was of considerable importance to both countries, since it lay between the British areas of East Africa and Egypt, and

In 1899 the agreement was extended to provide that the balance of power should be maintained as well as the maintenance of peace. The agreement was also made indefinite. In 1912 a naval agreement was added to the previous arrangements, so that the navies as well as the armies of the two countries should work together.

1904: The *Entente Cordiale* between Britain and France. The agreement's main provisions settled the colonial differences between the two. France accepted Britain's occupation of Egypt, provided that the Suez Canal was free for navigation, while Britain recognised France's interests in Morocco and promised diplomatic support in winning France's demands there. France gave up her claims to Newfoundland in return for some territory near French Gambia.

The agreement cannot be regarded as an alliance, as there were no reciprocal arrangements for support. However, it cleared the ground for subsequent negotiations, and in January 1906 military and naval discussions between the two began. Britain refused to promise support in the event of a German attack, but nonetheless agreed to discussions about military co-operation should such co-operation be decided on. This in effect created a 'moral obligation' of Britain to France, although the nearest they came to any formal agreement was in November 1912 when an exchange of letters between the foreign ministers, Grey and Cambon, led to agreements to consult if either country were threatened by attack.

KEY ISSUE

How significant was the Triple Entente?

PICTURE 15 *'Let Germany be careful now'*

See page 84

1907: Agreement between Britain and Russia, thus creating the so-called *Triple Entente* between these two countries and France. This agreement also settled colonial disputes but made no firm commitments on either side. Persia was divided into three separate spheres of influence and Russia accepted that Afghanistan was outside its sphere of interest, while Britain promised not to interfere with Afghanistan's domestic affairs. Both accepted China's dominant position in Tibet. In a separate agreement, Britain expressed its support for a revision of the Straits Agreements in Russia's favour, while in a third agreement Russia acknowledged Britain's pre-eminence in the Persian Gulf.

In this summary, only those treaties and alliances that were to have direct bearing on the Great War have been included. Thus the Russo-German agreements of the 1880s have been omitted, as has the Anglo-Japanese Agreement of 1902 and the agreements between the Triple Alliance and Romania (1882) by which Romania was protected from Russian attacks.

See page 50

Although the reasons for the agreements, and even the terms of them, were often innocuous, the end result was clear. After 1907, Europe was clearly divided by two alliance systems. In one respect, this provided the balance of power that many statesmen regarded as essential for the maintenance of peace. On the other hand both blocs had extensive military plans for defending themselves against the other. Inevitably, these defensive plans also included attacks that would lead to widespread declarations of war. For this to come about, the leaders did, however, have to want war. As Italy was to prove in 1914 it was possible to avoid war within the terms of the treaties. Consequently, the role of the alliance system in the outbreak of the war is complex and it did not even 'make the war a large one', since almost any of the Powers could have avoided their commitments if they had so desired.

See page 159

KEY ISSUE

To what extent was the 'alliance system' a cause of World War I?

Similarly, the existence of enormous and well-equipped armies and navies did not necessarily make war any more or less likely. It is difficult to monitor precisely the build-up of these forces, since no Power wanted to reveal the extent of its forces to likely enemies. Consequently, the account below is gathered from a variety of sources (hence the different currencies) in an effort to bring together a coherent account of the build-up of forces.

The most publicised and potentially dangerous acceleration came in the field of naval expansion. Since Britain held its navy to be vital, any attempt to rival it by another Power, particularly Germany, would meet a spirited response. Yet many German statesmen saw naval expansion as the only way to assure Germany of world-power status, since Germany's central position in Europe made the acquisition of overseas colonies essential. In addition, only Britain's acceptance of a large and powerful German navy would give Germany the prestige it so desired. The Navy Laws were intended to provide for this expansion.

See page 52

Rumours about the naval plans and activities of each side so alarmed the other that attempts at reconciliation between the two were permanently soured. The Haldane mission of 1912 offered Germany support for an extension to its African empire in return for a halt to naval building, but it came to nothing, as Germany would not stop its naval expansion without concrete compensation. On both sides, the building and plans became almost an obsession that dominated relations between them. In

KEY ISSUES

Why, and with what consequences, was there a 'naval race' between Britain and Germany?

See page 41

See Tables 25 and 26

fact, Britain's fleet remained considerably larger throughout the period: by the outbreak of war in 1914, Germany had 33 battleships with seven under construction, whilst Britain had 55 with 11 under construction.

It is less easy to monitor the increases in army size, since this was related to the number of people of the right age for military service and the different regulations regarding length and type of service. Some broad trends can, however, be identified. The German conscription system underwent two major changes:

● in 1893 the period of service was reduced to two years, but the total size of the standing army was increased
● in 1913 the army was increased by a total of 170 000 men and plans were made to have a wartime army of some 5 million men.

In response to this, both France and Russia increased the length of service – in France, it went up from two years to three and in Russia from three to three and a half. Defence expenditures also increased. DF Fleming, in *The Origins and Legacies of World War I* (1968) estimated that British expenditure rose from $295 million in 1908 to $375 in 1913, French expenditure from $220 million to $410 million and Russian expenditure from $300 to $460 million.

TABLE 25

Proportion of population in the armed forces 1880–1914 (from The Kaiser and His Times by M Balfour)

Date	Size of army	Size of navy	Total	% of population
Germany				
1880	401 650	7 350	409 000	0.90
1891	511 650	17 000	528 650	1.07
1901	604 100	31 200	635 300	1.16
1911	622 500	33 500	656 000	1.01
1914	791 000	73 000	864 000	1.30
Great Britain				
1880	198 200	59 000	257 200	0.73
1891	209 000	97 600	306 600	0.80
1901	773 500	114 900	888 400	2.10
1911	247 000	128 000	375 000	0.83
1914	247 000	146 000	393 000	0.85

	Germany		Great Britain	
Date	Total defence expenditure (million marks)	% of yearly average national income	Total defence expenditure (million marks)	% of yearly average national income
1886–90	510	2.35	626	2.35
1891–5	586	2.59	664	2.29
1896–1900	637	2.4	820	2.3
1901–5	848	2.69	1966	5.33
1906–10	1294	3.23	1220	2.93
1911–13	1468	3.1	1071	2.12

TABLE 26   *Percentage of National Income devoted to defence 1880–1914 (from The Kaiser and His Times by M Balfour)*

By a range of indices, therefore, it is possible to detect an 'arms race' between the Great Powers. However, it is harder to identify the role that this trend played in the outbreak of the war. Did not this wealth of arms in fact act as a deterrent to war, since so many men would inevitably die? This was the argument to be used to support nuclear deterrence in a later age. Or was it rather an inducement to war, so that the Powers could find out what their men and machines could do? Or did it merely provide generals and statesmen with the confidence, or even over-confidence, to press their demands on their enemies, in the knowledge and belief that their forces were so strong they would not be attacked?

3 ✐ THE BALKANS

A *The Bosnian crisis*

The Treaty of Berlin (1878) allowed Austria-Hungary to occupy and administer the Turkish provinces of Bosnia and Herzegovina that lay on its southern border. Since they bordered Serbia, whose Government hoped to win for itself those areas of Austria-Hungary where there was a majority of Serbs, the two Turkish provinces were of great strategic importance to the Habsburgs. In 1881 they won the secret agreement of Germany and Russia to their plan to keep the provinces permanently. However, in 1903, by the Mürzsteg Agreement, Austria-Hungary agreed with Russia to maintain the *status quo* in the Balkans for a five-year period.

During those five years, several pressures made Habsburg action more likely. Events within the Empire led the Government to believe that it was increasingly urgent to end the opposition of the southern Slav peoples – the Croats, Slovenes and Serbs – to the Emperor's rule. The Young Turk Revolution of 1908 forced the Turkish Emperor, Abdul Hamid, to accept constitutional government. This made a revival of the Turkish Empire more likely, which in turn threatened Austria-Hungary's occupation of the provinces. Moreover, representatives of Bosnia and Herzegovina were invited to attend the new Turkish parliament, indicating that the Turkish Government had by no means abandoned them. The Austrian Foreign Minister, Aehrenthal, decided that some action was urgently needed. However, the possibility of Russian opposition to Austria-Hungary's annexation of the provinces had first to be removed.

Aehrenthal met his Russian counterpart, Izvolsky, in September 1908. They agreed in principle that if Russia accepted Austria-Hungary's annexation of the provinces, Austria-Hungary would support Russia's claim for a revision of the Straits Convention so that Russian warships could have access to the Mediterranean through the Dardanelles. No one else was present at the meeting, and only Aehrenthal kept a written record.

Subsequently, two details of the agreement were to be questioned by the Russians. At what stage was the annexation actually to be announced – before or after the Russians had seen the other Powers? And was it or was it not agreed to hold an international conference to ratify the changed circumstances in the Balkans?

See Map 10 on page 112

Background information on the Balkans situation in the period can be found on pages 9–11

See pages 9–10

See pages 87

KEY ISSUE

What was the significance of the Bosnian crisis in international relations?

Izvolsky's delight in winning Austria-Hungary's approval for his plans for the Straits was enough to send him rushing off to the other European capitals to win their approval. After all, Austria-Hungary had most to lose by a revision of the Straits Convention, and once its approval

MAP 10 *The Balkans 1878–1914*

was won the other Powers should not be hostile. On 26 September the German Foreign Minister, von Schön, agreed in principle to the plan, but on condition that Germany received some compensation, probably in the form of Russian support for Germany's plans for the Berlin-Baghdad Railway. On 28 September, the Italian Government agreed to Russia's plans in exchange for Russian support for Italian claims to Tripoli and parts of the Balkans, notably Albania. By 4 October Izvolsky had reached Paris, where he had to win over the French.

Aehrenthal too had been busy. On 23 September he promised Prince Ferdinand Austria-Hungary's support for Bulgaria's independence from Turkey, thus removing another likely source of hostility. Bulgaria, like Bosnia and Herzegovina, had been asked to send representatives to the Turkish parliament, so the question of its relationship to Turkey was made more urgent. On 4 October Aehrenthal informed Izvolsky in Paris that he planned to go ahead with the annexation. The next day Bulgaria's independence was declared and on 6 October the annexation of Bosnia and Herzegovina by Austria-Hungary was announced by Aehrenthal.

The announcement had immediate and widespread repercussions. The outraged Turkish Government immediately imposed a boycott on all trade with Austria-Hungary and made military preparations as did Serbia. Greece and Montenegro opened negotiations with Turkey and Serbia. In Paris, Izvolsky was powerless. His own Government in St Petersburg, denying any knowledge of his secret agreement with Aehrenthal, instructed him to oppose Austria-Hungary and support Serbia. Consequently, he was forced to claim that he had been tricked by Aehrenthal and oppose the annexation. However, his opposition was only half-hearted since he still hoped for Austrian support for revision of the Straits Convention as a form of compensation for the annexation at an international conference.

On 9 October the British Foreign Secretary Lord Grey told Izvolsky, now in London, that Britain would only support Russia's plans if Turkey agreed to them. Turkey refused to do so. Grey did, however, agree to Izvolsky's plans for an international conference, which Izvolsky now pressed hard for as the only way of saving face.

By this time, the lines were clearly drawn on both sides. Serbia's troops were mobilised and Serbia and Russia demanded a conference to discuss the annexation and possible compensation for the other Powers, especially Serbia and Montenegro. But Austria-Hungary refused – it would accept an international conference only to approve the annexation. Germany supported Austria-Hungary but accepted Russia's claims to the Straits provided that Germany received compensation.

On 12 January 1909 Austria-Hungary reached agreement with Turkey, by which Turkey accepted the annexation in exchange for two million pounds compensation. Since Turkey was the chief loser by the annexation, this agreement considerably strengthened Austria-Hungary's position. Nonetheless, Serbia's troops remained mobilised. However, Serbia could not act without Russian support, in which case Austria-Hungary would depend on German support. Germany's Chief of Staff, Moltke, assured his Austrian counterpart, Conrad von Hötzendorff, that such support would be forthcoming – the first time Germany had made such a firm promise to its ally.

This state of affairs remained until 21 March when Germany took the initiative. A note was sent to Russia demanding that it accept the annexation and end its support for Serbia. If Russia did not agree, 'events would run their course' according to the German note. Izvolsky, presented with an opportunity to escape a war that Russia could not fight, gave way and accepted the note, muttering about the iniquity of the German '**ultimatum**'.

ultimatum a final warning or demand for terms, prior to a declaration of war

Ten days later, on 31 March, Serbia sent Austria formal recognition of the annexation and accepted that it did not affect its interests. Significantly, Serbia also promised to stop anti-Austrian propaganda and to be a good neighbour.

The annexation was a major triumph for Austria-Hungary and Germany, at least in the short term. The Russian Government was furious at the outcome and was left more determined than ever not to be forced to give way again. Instead Russia sought to consolidate its position in the Balkans. It began by helping Bulgaria to pay Turkey the compensation required as a result of the declaration of independence.

More significantly, Serbs were outraged by Austria-Hungary's success. More and more extreme groups were formed and were not outlawed by the Government. Leading among these was the 'Union or Death' movement, founded in 1911 by 'Apis' (Captain Dragutin Dimitrjevic´). The movement was known as the 'Black Hand'. It was committed to the liberation of all Serbs living under foreign rule by secret and terrorist means.

B *The Balkan Wars*

In the aftermath of the Bosnian crisis, Russia tried to construct a Balkan *bloc* of Serbia, Bulgaria and Turkey as a bulwark against further Austrian expansion. However, Russia accepted that the differences between the two emerging Powers and Turkey were too great and therefore encouraged, in the first place, negotiations between Bulgaria and Serbia. For an alliance of these two could be used as well against Turkey as against Austria-Hungary. After initial disagreement over Macedonia, a Serbo-Bulgarian treaty was signed in March 1912. By it, three zones of Macedonia were defined – one each for Serbia and Bulgaria and a third neutral zone. It also included a mutual guarantee of existing boundaries and promised support in the event of a Great Power trying to take land from Turkey.

When, on 29 May 1912, Greece and Bulgaria signed a treaty of alliance, there was born a Balkan League of the four Balkan Powers (Serbia, Bulgaria, Greece and Montenegro), each of which opposed both Turkey and the Great Powers. The Great Powers realised the likelihood that this League would declare war on Turkey and, in a note of 14 August, urged the four to act cautiously.

However, the Balkan Powers were not to be denied. Using the frequent outbreaks of rioting in Macedonia as a pretext for action, they mobilised their troops on 30 September 1912 and, on 18 October, declared war. Turkey, already weakened by war against Italy, was in no state to fight back. The Bulgarian army advanced rapidly southwards and reached the Chatalja lines outside Constantinople by the end of October, where its attack was held. Russia warned Bulgaria against entering Constantinople. In the West, the Serbian army took northern Albania and reached the coast by mid-November. In the south, the Greek army took Salonika. Apart from three forts and an area of about 30 kilometres outside Constantinople, all European Turkey was in the hands of the Balkan League. On 3 December an **armistice** was signed between Turkey and Serbia and Bulgaria. Greece remained technically at war.

The Great Powers, especially Austria-Hungary, had good reason to be horrified by the success of the Balkan League. Austria-Hungary was totally opposed to Serbia having an Adriatic coastline, and advocated instead the establishment of an independent Albania. In contrast, Russia and France supported the idea of an enlarged Serbia. In late November both Austria and Russia began to mobilise their troops to oppose and support Serbia respectively, while Germany and Britain endeavoured to moderate their allies' demands. Again, Russia was forced to back down rather than risk war, but until March 1913 400 000 extra Russian troops and 220 000 Austrians were mobilised.

On 17 December the peace conference opened in London. Little progress was made as the Turks refused to give up Adrianople and Crete. In fact, they declared war again on 3 February under their new nationalist ruler, Enver Bey. The Turkish army was again defeated swiftly and on 16 April a new armistice was signed following the capture of Adrianople by the Bulgarian army.

By the end of May, negotiations were ended and the Treaty of London was signed on 30 May. Greece gained Crete, Salonika and much of southern Macedonia, although it was largely inhabited by Bulgars. Bulgaria received Thrace and Serbia won central and northern Macedonia. Albania became independent from Turkey. These terms were not decided by negotiation between the countries involved but by the Great Powers, who agreed the terms in advance and then imposed them on the Balkan Powers.

Consequently there was considerable dissatisfaction at the terms. Serbia resented being kept from the Adriatic coastline, and felt that its share of Macedonia was inadequate. Bulgaria refused to acknowledge that Serbia was entitled to more of Macedonia than had been agreed by the 1912 treaty, and claimed that, under the terms of that treaty, the division of Macedonia should be left to arbitration by the Tsar. On 1 June 1913 the Serbians formed an alliance with Greece, their obvious intention being to win on the battlefield what had been denied them in the treaty. Bulgaria had similar intentions.

On 29 June the second Balkan War broke out. The Bulgarian commander ordered an attack without receiving Government authorisation. Even though the Bulgarian Government disowned his actions, it was enough for Serbia and Greece to declare war on Bulgaria. Romania and

armistice a truce or suspension of hostilities

KEY ISSUE

What were the causes and consequences of the two Balkan Wars?

See Map 10 on
page 112.

Turkey joined the war on Serbia's side and the encircled Bulgars were rapidly humiliated.

On 10 August the Treaty of Bucharest was signed. Bulgaria was forced to give the Dobrudja from Turtukia on the Danube to Ekrene on the Black Sea to Romania. Serbia and Greece kept possession of those parts of Macedonia that they had captured, leaving Bulgaria a small part of the Aegean coastline around the port of Dedeagach. By a separate treaty, Adrianople was returned to Turkey.

Flushed with success, the Serbs invaded Albania on 23 September, claiming that Albania had raided parts of Western Serbia. Only when Austria-Hungary intervened and demanded a Serbian withdrawal was the invasion ended. Even then, Greek troops remained in Albania until April 1914 when Greece was awarded some Aegean islands in exchange for evacuating Albania.

Each of the new Balkan Powers had made significant gains of both territory and prestige. These gains challenged the plans of Russia and Austria-Hungary for the domination, if not annexation, of the Balkans. In addition, the new strength of Serbia threatened Austria-Hungary's southern borders. Since neither the Great Powers nor the combatants saw the Balkan Wars as bringing a final settlement, all sought ways of improving their position in the area.

In November 1913 the German General, Liman von Sanders, was sent to reorganise the Turkish army and was made commander of the First Army Corps, based in Constantinople. Russia and France protested loudly at the presence of a German general in such a sensitive area, and a crisis was only averted when the Turks and Germans agreed to reduce his powers.

In June 1914 the Tsar, accompanied by his Foreign Minister, Sazonov, visited Bucharest in an effort to win Romanian support for Serbia in the event of it being attacked by Austria-Hungary. The Romanians refused this, but did agree to support and help Russia in the event of the Straits being closed by a Greek-Turkish war. In June 1914 Germany and Austria-Hungary held discussions on future Balkan policy. Austria-Hungary favoured friendship with Bulgaria and Turkey while Germany favoured rapport with Serbia, Greece and Romania. No decision was reached, and none was needed since events overtook the discussions.

4 ⤳ THE OUTBREAK OF WAR

In late June 1914, Archduke Franz Ferdinand visited the provinces of Bosnia and Herzegovina. The trip was ill-planned. It coincided with Austrian army manoeuvres in the area and with the anniversary of the medieval battle of Kosovo when the Serbs had fought valiantly to ward off their Turkish conquerors. The Serbian 'Union or Death' society (or 'Black Hand'), which had been founded in 1911 with the purpose of campaigning, by terrorist means, for Serbia's rights over the provinces, was tempted to take the opportunity for a violent protest. In the event, though, it was not the Black Hand that fired the fatal shots.

See page 114

A group of six young Bosnians, who were not members of the group, planned their own attack on the heir to the throne when he visited Sarajevo on 28 June. One of them, Gavrilo Princip, was able to reach the Archduke's car and shoot both the Archduke and his wife.

The assassination provided the Austrian Government with an excuse for military action against Serbia. The Serbian Government could be held culpable in that its officials allowed the assassins through the frontier and knew of the existence and aims of the Black Hand. However, before any action was taken, Franz Josef had to be sure of German support. On 5 July an Austrian diplomat, Count Hoyos, took a letter from the Emperor to Berlin. The letter explained that:

> ... the Sarajevo affair was not merely the bloody deed of a single individual, but was the result of a well-organised conspiracy, the threads of which can be traced to Belgrade; and even though it will probably prove impossible to get evidence of the complicity of the Serbian Government, there can be no doubt that its policy, directed towards the unification of all the Southern-Slav countries under the Serbian flag, is responsible for such crimes, and that the continuation of such a state of affairs constitutes an enduring peril for my house and my possessions.

He also wrote of the necessity to 'eliminate Serbia as a factor of political power in the Balkans'. The implication was clearly that Austria, with German support, would crush Serbia militarily.

The *Kaiser*, through his Chancellor, replied the following day that Franz Josef could 'rest assured that His Majesty will faithfully stand by Austria-Hungary, as is required by the obligations of his alliance and of

KEY ISSUE

Was Sarajevo the cause of war or an excuse for it?

his ancient friendship'. This note has become known as Germany's 'blank cheque' to Austria, since it virtually promised German support for whatever action Austria chose to take. It is unlikely that the *Kaiser* and his advisers realised the full implications of this. Their reading of the situation was that Russia, as before, would not intervene on Serbia's behalf and therefore a local Balkan issue between a Great Power and a small neighbour would be swiftly and simply resolved.

At the time observers did not see the ensuing events as inevitable. David Lloyd George, writing in his *War Memoirs* in 1938, recalled:

> When I first heard the news of the assassination of the Grand Duke Ferdinand, I felt that it was a grave matter, and that it might provoke serious consequences which only the firmest and most skilful handling could prevent from developing into an emergency that would involve nations. But my fears were soon assuaged by the complete calm with which the rulers and diplomats of the world seemed to regard the event. The Kaiser departed for his usual yachting holiday in the Norwegian fjords. His Chief Minister left for his usual shooting party on his estate in Silesia. The Acting Head of the German Foreign Office went off on a honeymoon trip. A still more reassuring fact – the military head of the German Army, von Moltke, left for his cure in a foreign spa. The President of the French Republic and his Prime Minister were on a ceremonial visit to Russia and only arrived back in Paris on July 29th. Our Foreign Office preserved its ordinary tranquillity of demeanour and thought it unnecessary to sound an alarm even in the Cabinet Chamber. I remember that some time in July, an influential Hungarian lady, whose name I have forgotten, called upon me at 11, Downing Street, and told me that we were taking the assassination of the Grand Duke much too quietly; that it had provoked such a storm throughout the Austrian Empire as she had never witnessed, and that unless something were done immediately to satisfy and appease resentment, it would certainly result in war with Serbia, with the incalculable consequences which such an operation might precipitate in Europe. However, such official reports as came to hand did not seem to justify the alarmist view she took of the situation.

During the first two weeks of July, the Austrian cabinet debated its policy, and by 14 July had decided on war, even though its envoy to Belgrade reported that there was no conclusive evidence of the Serbian Government's complicity in the assassination. By 20 July an ultimatum to Serbia had been prepared, but was not sent until 23 July, to allow the French President, Poincaré, to leave St Petersburg after a state visit.

The ultimatum demanded that the Serbian Government should publish its intentions to be a good neighbour in its press, that all anti-Austrian organisations should be disbanded, that any anti-Austrian official employees should be dismissed from their posts, that all anti-Austrian propaganda in schools should be ended, that two Serbian officials known to have been involved in the plot be arrested and tried, and that Austrian officials be allowed to join the Serbs in the inquiry into the plot.

On hearing of Austria's demands, the Russian Government announced that it would not allow Serbia to become a part of the Austro-Hungarian Empire. Austria announced that it did not intend to take over Serbia, but on 25 July the Russian Government decided to mobilise against Austria and to declare war if Serbia were attacked.

Initially, the Serbian Government decided to accept all the demands in the Austrian ultimatum, but then decided to buy time and tempt the Austrian Government into negotiation by rejecting just one of them. So, on 25 July, the Serbians replied in conciliatory terms, but refused to accept the demand that Austrian officials be allowed to play a part in the inquiry. The critical part of the reply read: 'As far as the co-operation in this investigation of specially delegated officials of the Imperial and Royal Government is concerned, this cannot be accepted, as this is a violation of the constitution and of criminal procedure'. Even before sending the reply, the Serbian Government realised that this one point could mean war, and Serbian troops were mobilised.

When the reply was received in Vienna, Austria-Hungary mobilised against Serbia. The only remaining question was which countries would feel obliged or tempted to intervene. On 26 July the British Foreign Minister, Grey, suggested that a conference be held to discuss the crisis. Only France supported the idea fully, while both Austria and Germany rejected it. On 28 July war was officially declared, and Austrian forces bombarded Belgrade, thereby ending negotiations between Russia and Austria, although Bethmann Hollweg made a vain effort to renew these the next day. At the same time, he contacted the British Government, and promised that Germany would not take territory from either France or Belgium provided Britain remained neutral. Grey replied that his Government could not accept such an offer.

The actions of the Russian Government were critical. On 29 July the Tsar agreed to his Government's demands for general mobilisation – against both Germany and Austria-Hungary. Then, however, he changed this order to partial mobilisation, against Austria-Hungary alone, when he heard from Berlin that Germany was trying to force Austria-Hungary to lessen its demands. However, this change of plan proved technically impossible, since mobilisation plans against both had already been put into effect and men were on the move. On 31 July the German Government sent an ultimatum to Russia demanding the withdrawal of forces aimed at Germany within 12 hours.

The Germans also sent enquiries to Paris as to the attitude of France in the case of a Russo-German war, and refused a British request that the neutrality of Belgium be accepted. During the evening of the same day, Austria-Hungary declared a general mobilisation. On 1 August the French replied to Germany's enquiry that 'she would be guided by her own interests' and at 3.55 pm French troops were mobilised. Five minutes later Germany's forces were mobilised and at seven o'clock that evening Germany declared war on Russia on the grounds that its ultimatum had expired.

KEY ISSUE

Why did a crisis in the Balkans become a European war rather than a localised conflict?

On 2 August the British Government agreed to help France protect its coast against German attack, while German troops entered Luxembourg and a demand was sent to Belgium that if German troops were allowed through Belgium its neutrality would be respected. The Belgian Government refused to accept this. On 3 August Germany declared war on France on the grounds that France had violated the German frontier.

German troops entered Belgium, and on 4 August Britain declared war on Germany on the grounds that Belgian neutrality, guaranteed in 1839, had been violated. (By the terms of this treaty, Britain, and the other Great Powers, had the right to intervene if Belgium's neutrality were violated, but were not obliged to do so.) When Austria-Hungary declared war on Russia on 6 August, all the Great Powers of Europe, save Italy, were at war with one another.

5 ↝ BIBLIOGRAPHY

A useful treatment of these complex issues will be found in *Rivalry And Accord: International Relations 1870–1914* by John Lowe (Hodder and Stoughton, 1988). A detailed study is *The Origins of the First World War* by J Joll (Longman, 1984). Also useful are *The Origins of the First World War* by G Martel and *The Scramble For Africa* by M Chamberlain (both in the Longmans Seminar Studies series). Another standard text is *July 1914* by I Geiss (Batsford, 1967). The detailed, but most important, *German Aims in the First World War* by F Fischer (Chatto & Windus, 1967) is a critical book for more advanced study.

6 ↝ STRUCTURED QUESTIONS AND ESSAYS

1. (a) What was meant by the term 'balance of power' in the context of international affairs in the late nineteenth century? (3 marks)
    (b) Explain why the Triple Alliance was formed between Germany, Austria-Hungary and Italy; (7 marks)
    (c) To what extent was Germany responsible for upsetting the balance of power in Europe by 1900? (15 marks)
2. (a) Briefly explain the meaning of the term '*Entente Cordiale*'; (3 marks)
    (b) Why did Britain and France make an agreement in 1904? (7 marks)
    (c) How significant were the changes in Anglo-French relations between 1890 and 1914? (15 marks)
3. (a) Explain the causes and consequences of the 1908 Bosnian crisis; (10 marks)
    (b) How important were the issues at stake in the Balkans between 1908 and 1913? (15 marks)
4. To what extent was *either* the arms race *or* the alliance system responsible for the outbreak of war in 1914? (25 marks)

5. 'German responsibility for World War I was no greater than that of any of the Great Powers of Europe.' Assess the validity of this statement as an explanation of the short-term and long-term causes of World War I. (25 marks)

7 ⌁ SOURCE-BASED EXERCISE ON THE ORIGINS OF THE GREAT WAR

The following are some interpretations of events leading to the outbreak of World War I.

The disaster had its roots since 1870 in the grand expansion and uncontrolled ambition of the new Germany. Bismarck had sown the seeds through his memorable triumphs for militarism and unscrupulous efficiency ... After his fall, it grew apace, unchecked by the statesmen and encouraged by the Emperor. In the many-sided quick changing displays of the brilliant William II two features alone never failed – arrogant megalomania and an instinctive preference for methods of violence. These, it is not unfair to say, became the national vices of pre-war Germany; and they made her an object of alarm to every leading nation save her Austrian ally.

SOURCE A
Sir Robert Ensor, England
1870–1914 *(1936)*

Millions of men had to be recalled to the colours, organised into fighting units, equipped with a vast apparatus of arms and services and sent by railway to their points of concentration, all within a few days. The lesson of 1870 was burnt into the mind of every staff officer in Europe: the nation which loses the mobilisation race is likely to lose the war ... In no country could the elaborate plans of the military be substantially modified to meet political requirements. For the Austrian government a declaration of war was a political manoeuvre, for the Russian government a mobilisation was a counter-manoeuvre; but such orders set in motion administrative processes which could be neither halted nor reversed without causing a chaos which would place the nation at the mercy of its adversaries ...

SOURCE B
Extract from Studies in War
and Peace *by Michael Howard.*
Reprinted by kind permission of
David Higham Associates Ltd.

'War guilt' is still an open question. Its solution, obscured by national or other bias, really depends on how it is posed. The role of 'evil genius' behind the explosion no doubt goes to the German leaders, who must be submitted to 'the Judgement of History' – they tipped the balance towards radical solution of the Serbian question, carefully stage-managed its course so as to have a kind of 'perfect crime', deliberately rejected attempts at mediation when the conflict threatened to go further, and deliberately risked this when Russia threatened to intervene. On the other hand, England was 'the apostle of peace' – trying not to aggravate the Austro-Serbian conflict and to ensure that it did not lead to war. Just the same, her policy of conciliation did as much to produce war as the Germans' 'calculated risks' – the Germans, sure that whatever happened England would stay neutral, went further in their adventurous way than they would have done had they known they were wrong.

In comparison with these two contrary attitudes – the effects of which were much the same despite differing intentions – other Powers' roles seem, as time passes, increasingly passive. After Sarajevo the Austrians' singularly artificial rage had more noise than bite – Conrad did want to settle accounts with Serbia, but could be restrained by Germany. In the final analysis Vienna only did what Berlin said – to a degree described, by Fritz Fischer, as 'grotesque' ... Sazonov and the Tsar were conciliatory; several times they declared Serbia guilty, and deserving 'punishment'. But the Central Powers rejected these offers. Paléologue (French ambassador to Russia), acting in France's name without a mandate, approved what they did – but in any case the Central Powers had clearly shown that they meant to disrupt the Balkan balance, blackmailing France and Russia into hesitation by threat of continental war ...

SOURCE C

Extract from The Great War 1914–1918 *by M. Ferro (1986). Reproduced by kind permission of Routledge (Taylor & Francis).*

The war of 1914 was due to the unbearable national tensions within Austria-Hungary and the attempt of that power to escape from them by action dangerous to peace. The continued existence of the Habsburg monarchy as a great power was the thing at stake in the war, at least to start with. To this extent the war was a European rather than a world conflict, and it was 'imperialist' only in the sense that Austria-Hungary had always been a multi-racial state and the subject races were now rebelling against it. But the Austrian crisis could not have grown into a general war among the powers had there not been tensions among them which prevented effective co-operation in the preservation of peace. These tensions were the result of imperial rivalries, and often concerned regions far beyond Europe and hardly touched by the ensuing war.

SOURCE D

JR Western, The End of European Primacy *(1965)*

SOURCE E

Extract from Germany's Aim in the First World War *by Fritz Fischer. Copyright © 1961 by Droste Verlag und Druckerei GmbH, Dusseldorf. English translation copyright © 1967 by W.W. Norton & Company, Inc.*

Economic expansion was the basis of Germany's political world diplomacy, which vacillated in its methods between rapprochement and conciliation at one moment, aggressive insistence on Germany's claims the next, but never wavered in its ultimate objective, the expansion of Germany's power.

As for the widespread view that war was inevitable, that it was due also to the past blunders and to the easy assumption that those blunders could not be rectified or their dangerous consequences postponed. Yet the handling of the Balkan Wars had proved the opposite less than twelve months before August 1914. The whole conception of inevitability in human affairs is often no more than a confession of political incompetence. It implies that tendencies, themselves created by human beings, cannot be checked, diverted or even reversed by human beings. The history of the nineteenth century contains many examples of how 'inevitable' developments can be successfully resisted for a very long time. The break-up of the Habsburg Empire and the triumph of the Revolution had both been regarded as inevitable by Metternich; but neither inevitability had occurred by 1900. In 1900 a war between England and the French and Russians had seemed inevitable; but by 1914 they were allies together.

SOURCE F
LCB Seaman, From Vienna to Versailles *(1955)*

After 1911 Europe's doom advanced with what now seem to be inexorable strides. The Bosnian crisis of 1909 had ended with the diplomatic defeat of Russia. The Agadir crisis ended with the diplomatic defeat of Germany. Would either of these great powers, or the blocs to which they belonged, accept defeat again without trying the further test of war? If not, there could only be one result: a continental civil war, continental suicide. It would take a miracle to prevent it.

There was no miracle. National ambition and greed for empire continued to work their mischief ... . Italy picked a quarrel with Turkey, in order to seize the great Turkish province of Tripoli (now called Libya) ... in 1911 they managed to defeat the Turks, and so enlarged their Empire, but in so doing they triggered off a more serious train of events.

The weakening of Turkish power was a signal to all her enemies, above all the Balkan states with their deep-seated hatred of the Turks. Now Serbia, Bulgaria and Greece combined to attack Turkey. The result staggered Europe. In seven weeks the Turkish grip on the Balkans which had lasted for five centuries was utterly smashed. And out of the ruin of the once-dreaded Ottoman Empire Serbia emerged as the strongest of the Balkan states, her territory practically doubled. This result was intolerable to the anti-Serb elements in the Austro-Hungarian Empire. The military party urged immediate war against Serbia. And now the perils of the power blocs, and the system of interlocking alliances by which Europe sought security, were clearly seen.

SOURCE G
Extract from The Mighty Continent *by John Terraine (Copyright © John Terraine 1974) by permission of PFD on behalf of John Terraine.*

Q

1. *From your reading of these extracts, you should have identified two broad approaches to examining the outbreak of the war. The first looks particularly at the attitudes and actions of individual countries, and statesmen, and examines their part in the events leading up to the war. The second concentrates rather on trends, such as imperialism and nationalism, and identifies their role in the causes of the war. Obviously, the two approaches are closely linked and often overlap. Nevertheless, to draw out the distinction in approaches, re-examine each of the passages and explain which of the two approaches it adopts. You may also wish to discuss the merits and defects of each approach to the examination of the causes of the war.*

2. *Re-examine the views of Fischer, Ensor and Ferro. Put yourself in the position of a German commentator and tackle the accusation that the 'disaster had its roots in the new Germany', and demonstrate instead how it was the Entente that provoked the war.*

3. *What role did the military chiefs play in the outbreak of war – were they a cause of conflict in the first place, an influence on the size of the war or the determinants of the timing and sequence of events?*

4. *Compare and contrast the views of Ferro and Western on the role of Austria-Hungary in the outbreak of war.*

5. *How inevitable was war in Europe in the early twentieth century?*

6. *What difficulties face the historian today in assessing the responsibility for World War I?*

The readings and exercises you have completed should have given you some fairly clear ideas about why there was a war in Europe.

Below are tabulated what have generally been regarded as the chief causes of the war; where necessary, some additional explanatory notes have been added.

(i)   Germany's desire for world-power. Evidence: its pursuit of colonies; its expansion of trade; naval development; claims that it was being 'encircled' and deprived of its rightful place in world affairs.

(ii) Germany's support for Austria-Hungary. Evidence: Germany's encouragement of a firm line against Serbia and promises to support Austria-Hungary in the event of war.

(iii) The alliance system that had developed in the years before 1914. Although the original treaties had been defensive and primarily concerned with colonial affairs, subsequent military negotiations and international crises had welded them into firm commitments that were brought into effect and made a Balkan conflict into, first a European war, and then a world war.

(iv) Widespread ignorance of what war would be like, or how politicians and military men might react in a crisis. There had been no major European war since 1871. Authors generally wrote of brightly coloured uniforms, massed ranks of infantry and victorious charges by the cavalry bringing a swift and glorious end to war. In all nations, this encouraged bellicosity. At the other extreme there were some thinkers who foresaw such horrific military and economic consequences should a war break out, that they assumed no civilised power could allow it to happen.

(v) The arms race. The development of new and powerful weapons in large numbers undertaken for the purpose of using such weapons, which were not seen as deterrents.

(vi) The nationalism of the Great Powers. Evidence: Organisations like the Pan-German League and Navy League pressing for power; the popular press and its enthusiasm for national prestige in all countries.

(vii) Affronted Great Power nationalism. Russia had been 'done' by the Bosnian affair, Germany by the Agadir crisis, leaving a conviction that it should not be allowed to happen again, and that a show-down was inevitable.

(viii) Nationalism of the different nationalities within Austria-Hungary, leading to threats to the stability of the Habsburg Empire. This in turn encouraged Austro-Hungarian leaders to quash firmly any attempt to threaten their power and to seek a swift and easy victory that would reunite the nationalities against a common enemy and, in victory, confer prestige on the Empire.

(ix) The imperial conflicts of the Great Powers, leading to frustration and encouraging the view that a show-down was necessary.

(x) The mobilisation plans of the generals which were seen as immovable and essential to success in the war when it came.

Consider each of points (i)–(x) carefully and then judge the importance of each of them.

6

World War I 1914–18

INTRODUCTION

This chapter does not aim to provide a detailed history of the war itself. There will be an outline of the main events in the main theatres of war on the Western and Eastern Fronts, and an outline of the impact of the war generally. Brief accounts of the developments within individual Great Powers are given in the chapters on those particular countries. In this chapter we have tried to provide a straightforward account of the chief events of the war to show broadly why events happened, when and where they took place and to provide a brief analysis of some of the standard problems of interpretation – the role of the navies, the ideas and actions of the generals, and the reasons for Germany's ultimate defeat.

It is difficult to write a meaningful chronological account of the war. For purposes of clarity we have broken the chapter down into years, itself an artificial division, since ideas and campaigns frequently ran on from year to year. Secondly, it is not possible to follow a strictly chronological pattern when the war was fought on so many fronts. For example, the campaigns on the Eastern Front in 1914–15 form a single topic, and have therefore been handled together before examining the Western Front in 1915.

To keep the order of events in mind, and therefore their interactions with each other, you might find it helpful to draw out a date chart before reading the chapter to fill in as you read. This could be divided not only into years, but also separate areas, for example:

	Western Front	Eastern Front	Balkans Front	Southern	Sea	Others
1914 Aug.						
Sept.						
etc.						

One final note of clarification: we have referred to the Anglo-French-Russian alliance, and its allies, as the '*Entente*' throughout. To call them the 'Allies' can be confusing since it was the Central Powers, Germany and Austria-Hungary, which strictly speaking formed the Triple Alliance.

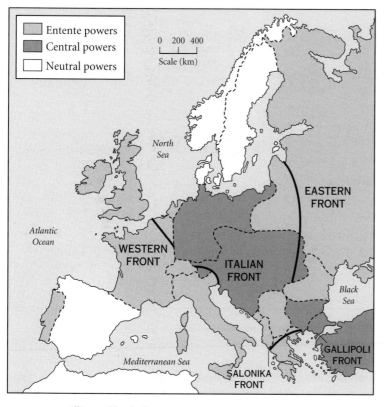

MAP 11   *Allies and battle fronts*

1 ⤙ THE WESTERN FRONT IN 1914

On 4 August the Schlieffen Plan was put into operation. The German armies would attack northern France through Belgium in a sweeping movement that would ultimately trap the French armies, whilst Paris would be encircled.

The Germans first repulsed French attacks in Lorraine and Luxembourg and then advanced. Paris seemed an easy target. The German Commander-in-Chief, Moltke, said 'in six weeks all this will be over'. However, the plan had to be adapted to take account of the Russian attack in the East which had come far sooner than expected.

The German advance was eventually halted at the battle of the Marne in September. This setback made any prospect of implementing the final stages of the Schlieffen Plan impossible for the time being. Both sides sought to find a way behind the others' armies and moved northwards towards the Channel. The ports there were also crucial strategic points, as through them would come additional British forces.

The German attack at Messines and Ypres in October was bloody but neither side made significant gains. Both sides resorted to a more defensive strategy: interlinking trenches were constructed, protected by

KEY ISSUE

Why did the Schlieffen Plan fail?

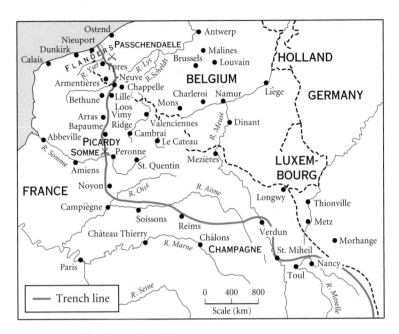

MAP 12   *The Western Front 1914–18*

The tactics of trench warfare are discussed further on page 138

See Map 12 above

barbed wire and strategically-positioned machine guns. From these, the enemy could be seen and fired upon at some distance, though no attack could be made, given the weapons available. By the end of November 1914 trenches were dug from the Belgian coast to the Vosges mountains.

2 ⤳ THE SOUTHERN AND EASTERN FRONTS IN 1914–15

The Russian army mobilised more quickly than expected and invaded Eastern Prussia. General Hindenburg moved against the Russians at Tannenburg and crushed them. Further north, the Germans also defeated the Russians at the Masurian Lakes. Further south, the Russians forced the Austrians out of Eastern Galicia. Pressure on Austria was relieved by Hindenburg. The Russian armies had certainly done all that was expected of them – they had held the German attacks, albeit at the cost of more than a million men, and taken pressure off France and Britain in the West. However, by mid-September the Russians had lost all of Poland, Lithuania and Courland (Latvia).

3 ⤳ 1915: WEAK POINT STRATEGY

Marc Ferro has called 1915 the 'year of weak point strategy'. Although commanders on both sides still believed the decisive battles would be

MAP 13 *The Eastern Front*

fought on the Western Front, they also realised that such battles would be costly, and that they were not prepared for them. Consequently, all sought alternative ways of striking at their enemy. The focus of the war therefore shifted to other areas and other combatants, most notably in Italy and the Balkans.

Nevertheless, there were still attacks on the Western Front. The French launched new offensives in January and February but failed to gain much territory. For their part, the Germans made a new attack on

Ypres in late April, using poison gas for the first time, but the defence held out. After further *Entente* attacks in the early summer and autumn the front lines in the West were barely altered; so it was not surprising that generals and politicians sought alternative areas for action.

Both sides courted the uncommitted powers. Turkey had joined the Central Powers in the autumn of 1914 and had attacked Russia across the Black Sea. Russia was keen to win over Romania and thus open up a second front against Austria-Hungary but Romania did not join the war until 1916. In September 1915 the Bulgarians joined the Central Powers and attacked Serbia.

In Britain Churchill, Lloyd George and Lord Kitchener favoured action in the Balkans, leaving the stalemate in the West to the French army, while Britain's fresher troops should be used to open up a new front, probably against Turkey. Britain hoped to draw German troops away from other fronts to help their ally and, given the prospect of territorial gains from Turkey, draw the Balkan states more conclusively into the conflict.

Those in favour of such schemes were known as 'easterners' while those who favoured continued major attacks in the west were called 'westerners'. In January 1915 the *Entente* decided on an operation against the Dardanelles with the aim of taking Constantinople. The Dardanelles – or Gallipoli – campaign began in February 1915. The initial operation was abandoned after several ships were sunk on entering the Dardanelles. But the first British troops were landed in April. The preparations had been poor, unlike those of the Turks. The invading troops found themselves trapped. When a second landing at Suvla behind the Turkish defences failed in August the operation was abandoned, and the remaining troops were evacuated in December and January.

Chronologically, the second weak point to be exploited was the Italian Front. Italy joined the war on the *Entente's* side in April 1915 following the secret Treaty of London. However, Italy was poorly prepared and the first few months of their war, the Italian army lost 250 000 men fighting against the Austrians.

The Central Powers had greater success in their weak point strategy by defeating Serbia. A further weak point attack came in the Middle East. British and Indian troops were landed at the mouth of the Persian Gulf, at Basra, to protect oil supplies in December 1914. This force captured Kut-el-Amara. There the force was besieged by the Turkish army from December 1915 until April 1916 and eventually surrendered.

'Weak point strategy' had not proved successful. With the exception of the defeat of Serbia and the entry of Italy, the situation at the end of 1915 was little different to the beginning of the year. Neither side had been prepared to commit any real strength to the weak points they attacked, being still convinced that the Western Front was of paramount importance.

4 ⌐ 1916: THE GREAT ATTACKS

The strategy of 1915 was almost completely reversed in 1916. Instead, both sides undertook carefully planned gigantic attacks – Verdun and

KEY ISSUES

How and why did the war become more extensive in 1916?

See page 159

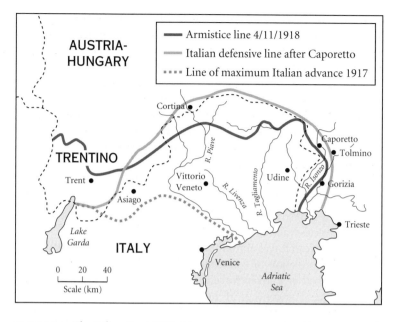

MAP 14 *The Italian Front 1914–18*

the Somme on the Western Front, the Brusilov offensive on the Eastern Front.

However, the first great attack was on the Italian Front. The Austrians attacked in the Trentino in May, although initial gains were lost. The Germans sought to attack in the West with sufficient force to draw *Entente* troops from other parts of the line to defend a single area. This would have a double effect of preventing them from attacking anywhere else and killing more and more troops, weakening both morale and fighting potential. The attack was launched on Verdun in February 1916.

French forces held on in desperate conditions, until later in the year the attack ended as German forces were more urgently needed to deal with the double *Entente* attack – from the British and French on the Somme and the Russians in Galicia. By August, more Germans were dying at Verdun than French, and the captured forts were once again in French hands. In all, some 380 000 French and almost 340 000 Germans were killed or wounded at Verdun.

The *Entente* had almost a two-to-one superiority on the Somme in terms of both men and guns. Following a ten-day artillery bombardment the main assault was launched in July. On the first day 57 000 British were killed or wounded. In all, over a million men died on the Somme that summer – some 400 000 Germans and British, 200 000 French, for almost no territorial gains. Meanwhile most Italian attacks on Austria ended in costly failures.

As in 1914, the most significant events of 1916 took place on the Eastern Front. A Russian advance in June achieved great initial success, but could not be sustained. Romania joined the *Entente* in August but was swiftly defeated.

'Great attacks' strategy had had little more success than weak point strategy. Despite the millions who died during 1916 the battle lines had changed little, the tactics hardly at all. Generals were convinced that the war would be won and lost in the West.

5 ⌐ 1917: THE ENTRY OF THE UNITED STATES AND THE DEFEAT OF RUSSIA

See page 135

KEY ISSUE

What impact did the involvement of the USA have on the war?

The entry of the United States on the *Entente's* side in April 1917 was, in fact, of little immediate significance. It came after Germany's announcement of the unrestricted use of submarine warfare, which threatened to harm America's trade considerably.

The American forces amounted to less than 150 000 in all. Nevertheless, the introduction of conscription in the USA at the end of April and the arrival of a token force in July in Paris gave promise of what was to come. The concept of 'holding on until the Americans arrive' was to have a great effect on the thinking and morale of both sides.

On the Western Front the Germans retreated to the new defensive positions of the Hindenburg Line. In April a joint Franco-British attack resulted in heavy losses and led to mutinies in the French army.

In June the British pushed the Germans back from the salient at Ypres in the battle of Messines, and in July a new attack was launched there. In this, the battle of Passchendaele (or the third battle of Ypres), nearly 500 000 British and Canadian troops died, in a three-month attack that was made wholly impossible by the rain and mud of autumn. French attacks further south intended to relieve pressure on the British were actually more successful. A final assault in the Cambrai region, in which a massed tank attack was used for the first time, made a considerable breakthrough in late November, but the infantry were unable to follow up the attack and were forced back by a German counter-attack. Yet again offensive tactics on the Western Front had proved fruitless.

In October an Austro-German attack against the Italians broke through at Caporetto. British and French troops were sent to help the Italians, and eventually the line was held.

See pages 235–7

The Central Powers were equally successful on the Eastern Front. Following the revolution in March, the Provisional Government of Russia could not agree on whether or not the war should be continued. Eventually in July it launched a new offensive, under Brusilov, in Galicia. However the attack was driven back. The Bolshevik revolution of November led to peace negotiations and an armistice on 15 December. While details of the peace settlement were discussed, German troops and materials could start to move westwards and reinforce the front line there for a fresh attack.

6 ⌐ 1918

From the German point of view, the prospects for both victory and defeat were delicately balanced at the start of 1918. On the one hand, one of Germany's main enemies, Russia, had surrendered, releasing men for use on the Western Front. The Balkans, with the exception of Greece, had been conquered and Italy all but defeated. On the Western Front, *Entente* attacks had been repulsed and German troops were almost without exception positioned on enemy soil.

On the other hand, Germany's allies, particularly Bulgaria and Turkey, hardly inspired confidence. Above all, the prospect of American forces arriving in Europe and American industry providing materials for the *Entente* augured ill. The longer the war lasted, the worse the situation would become. Everything pointed to the need for a knock-out blow on the Western Front, supported by a blockade of the British Isles.

German forces attacked in March and advanced some 40 miles. The *Entente*, faced by a critical situation, for the first time appointed a single overall commander, the French general, Foch. By 30 May German troops were back at the river Marne and less than 40 miles from Paris, having created an enormous bulge in the *Entente*'s line.

In July an *Entente* counter-attack finally forced the Germans back over the Marne. For both sides, the critical question was what to do next. The German troops were exhausted. Foch was keen to follow up his success, but Haig was more cautious. Eventually on 8 August, a day that Ludendorff called 'the black day of the German army', the British opened the attack. They advanced eight miles on the first day. Ludendorff ordered a general retreat to the Hindenburg Line.

By the end of September, the entire line was moving for the first time in the war. Although the advance was slower than Foch had hoped, it was enough to push Ludendorff into offering his resignation, though the *Kaiser* refused it.

With the breakthrough on the Western Front, attacks elsewhere made headway. British forces defeated the Turks in Palestine and moved northwards to Damascus and Beirut in early October. The Sultan signed an armistice on 30 October. Bulgaria asked for an armistice on 26 September. In the south, the Italians attacked the Austrians on a front from Trentino to the Adriatic, and on 30 October won the battle of Vittorio Veneto.

German generals and politicians were convinced of the need for an armistice before their armies were wholly destroyed and incapable of fighting. On 4 October the German and Austrian Governments asked Wilson for an armistice on the basis of the Fourteen Points.

The Germans had failed to achieve any of their war aims. These had been very ambitious: they included annexing large areas of Eastern Europe and establishing German dominance there, and bore some comparison with Hitler's later policies of a 'Greater Germany'. The German historian Fritz Fischer caused some controversy when he investigated these aims, and several historians seized on this to emphasise the expansionist aims of many German politicians and generals, and

> **KEY ISSUE**
>
> *Why were the Central Powers ultimately defeated?*

> See pages 142–3

KEY ISSUE

Why has there been a controversy over German war aims?

See page 195

abdication the surrendering of power by a monarch or emperor

claimed either that Germany had entered the war with these specified aims, or that they proved a continuous expansionist trend in German history. However, not all historians accepted these claims. After all, the fact that 'war aims' are developed and published during a war, does not automatically mean that they were on the agenda beforehand, and that a country went to war with the explicit intention of implementing them. The *Entente* had equally stated war aims during World War I which had never been articulated in 1914, when the priority had been simply to support friendly countries and prevent German military domination of Europe.

After the German request for an armistice there followed several weeks of negotiation over the terms. Wilson demanded that all occupied areas should be evacuated and that a democratic Government be formed in Germany. In the meantime *Entente* forces continued to advance on the Western Front. On 28 October sailors in Kiel refused to go to sea on a series of raids. When revolution broke out in Munich on 7 November, Prince Max of Baden, Chancellor since early October, announced the *Kaiser*'s **abdication** and sent an armistice commission to meet Foch. In exchange for peace, the Germans were to leave all occupied territory, including that gained by the treaties of Brest-Litovsk and Bucharest, and surrender large amounts of military and semi-military equipment (such as trains). The terms were accepted and at 11 am on 11 November the armistice came into force.

7 ⌐ THE UNEXPECTED WAR: BATTLE TACTICS OF WORLD WAR I

Most experts had expected a short war in which one decisive encounter would settle the issue. However, technological advances were such that the weapons available demanded entirely different tactics to earlier wars. In addition, the war became an economic one, in which battles were won and lost as much by the availability of supplies as by victories in battle.

A *Naval warfare*

Britain and Germany had spent millions of pounds developing powerful navies, particularly by building the mighty 'Dreadnoughts'. By 1914, Germany had 13 of these, Britain 20. However, the great fleets met once, and then but briefly. Quite simply, it was too risky to attempt the great showdown, in which a defeat might mean losing control of the sea and possibly the war itself. By mining the entrance to the English Channel and by keeping the Grand Fleet off northern Scotland, the Royal Navy was able to prevent the German High Seas Fleet leaving the Baltic and North Seas. If it risked escape, it risked disaster. The only major naval encounter of the war was the Battle of Jutland in 1916. The British lost 14 ships, the Germans 11. The German admirals decided that another major naval engagement could not be risked, so it was the

British who gained, since the German fleet remained unused in port. The only other naval engagements came early in the war and far from Europe, as when in November 1914 the German East Asia Squadron sank two British warships at Coronel off the Chilean coast.

The submarine proved a much more threatening weapon. At the start of the war, the Germans had only 30 such boats (U-boats), and even at the end only 130. Even so, they were able to cause sufficient damage genuinely to threaten Britain with defeat. This was possible because the war had, by virtue of its length, become an economic war, in which the continuing ability to maintain supplies was critical. In February 1915 the German Government announced that it was to begin a submarine **blockade** of Britain and would sink any ships approaching Britain with contraband supplies. The Germans caused great controversy by sinking the Cunard liner *Lusitania*, with the loss of 1198 lives, of whom 139 were American. It was carrying some arms and munitions and had been warned not to sail.

The British were able to stop and search ships before they entered or while they were in the unmined portion of the North Sea, and thereby effectively blockaded Germany. It was more difficult for the Germans to blockade Britain, since to do so ships had to reach the Atlantic, and therefore avoid the mines in the Channel and the northern North Sea. Only U-boats could do this, but sinking liners and merchantmen, the only means by which submarines could enforce a blockade, provoked widespread hostility, especially from the United States.

In February 1917, the Germans announced unrestricted submarine warfare, gambling that they could starve Britain into surrender. British losses were serious, but the introduction of escorted convoys soon reduced them. The German gamble failed, particularly since the USA entered the war.

KEY ISSUE

Why has there been a controversy over German war aims?

blockade the use of a navy to close the enemy's ports and prevent trade with the outside world

The impact of World War I

ANALYSIS

The war was in several respects remarkable, not just for the scale of the fighting and the numbers of men involved, but for the impact inside the countries which bore the brunt of the war. There is no space to analyse the domestic impact of the war in depth, but Britain will be taken as an example of how modern war involved the whole nation, combatant and non-combatant alike. Britain is a particularly good example, since before 1914 the impact of wars in which Britain had been involved had often been almost peripheral, with a small army in action and with everyday life going on much as before. But World War I was very different: for example it led to mass conscription for the first time in modern British history; it gave new opportunities to women because of the need for more labour; ordinary people were affected by rationing and direct enemy action for the first time in the form of air raids. These and other factors, combined with the trauma of such a long-drawn out costly war and its effects on people's attitudes, made the war experience a dramatic one for most people.

POLITICAL IMPACT

A national crisis called for drastic measures. When criticism of the Government's conduct of the war grew, in 1916 a coalition Government replaced the existing Liberal Government, in order to reflect the 'national' nature of the crisis. 'Successful' politicians, like the Prime Minister Lloyd George, were those who understood the need for new attitudes and new measures if the nation were to be geared to total war: hence innovations such as the War Cabinet and the convoy system, which went against traditional thinking.

WARTIME COLLECTIVISM AND CONTROLS

The initial mood in 1914 of 'Business as Usual' soon gave way to a recognition that large-scale state intervention in society and the economy was necessary to mobilise the population for victory. Whilst words like 'Socialism' were carefully avoided, some of the measures adopted would have not seemed out of place in a modern Socialist State in which the Government intervenes much more in everyday life than would have been thought conceivable by most people a generation before. DORA (the Defence of the Realm Act), passed in 1914, gave the Government widespread powers of intervention, used for example to nationalise the railways. New ministries were created, notably the Ministry of Munitions. The State took control of shipping and the mines. Conscription into the armed forces was adopted in 1916. Trade unions reluctantly agreed to a 'dilution of labour' by which semi-skilled and female workers were allowed into jobs hitherto reserved for skilled craftsmen. Taxation was increased and rationing of food introduced, towards the end of the war.

THE COSTS OF THE WAR

The costs of the war were enormous. Over 600 000 British nationals were killed and over one and a half million wounded. Economists calculated that the war cost two to four years of normal growth of capital resources, the using up of a quarter of overseas investments, a loss of overseas markets, and a massive rise in the National Debt from £650 million to £7000 million. There was a significant depreciation of assets. The costs of the war must have contributed significantly to Britain's economic problems in the decades after the war.

THE WAR AND SOCIAL CHANGE

Not always quantifiable, but nevertheless significant, were changes which the war brought about in attitudes and society. The loss of almost 10 per cent of the younger male population altered the population balance so that younger females significantly out-numbered males, and the trend of a declining birth rate, already evident before 1914, was significantly accelerated. Not all of the effects were negative: the working class saw an improvement in its income and standard of living; the war provided the first significant steps towards the emancipation of women, in recognition of the part they played on the home front, although there was still a long way to go; the war was a stimulus to scientific and technological progress. On the other hand, the horrors of war led many to question existing orthodoxies – for example the trend towards declining religious observance was accelerated. The war accelerated developments in the arts. Britain was still a class-conscious society, but some of the barriers between classes were weakened, as evident for example in the decline of the servant class.

The pre-war confidence in stability and progress was severely shaken, as the country mourned a 'lost generation'. Horror of the war had a significant impact on attitudes towards Germany in the period of appeasement in the 1930s when many people were desperately keen to avoid the trauma of another destructive war.

However, historians emphasise that many of the developments outlined above were not completely new: in some respects the war simply accelerated trends which were undoubtedly present but sometimes not appreciated before 1914: for example Britain's position of economic dominance was already being seriously undermined before 1914, and the war only accelerated the process.

Nevertheless World War I had a dramatic impact on all the combatant nations. The defeated nations were affected in the most dramatic ways: failure in war directly contributed to the Russian Revolution, and the German experience of the war and the peace settlement had an important impact on the rise of Nazism. However, victorious nations also lost their pre-war confidence. France suffered greater losses than Britain and its confidence as a Great Power had never really recovered by 1939. Dissatisfaction in Italy with the fruits of victory contributed to the rise of Fascism. Only the United States, which joined the war late and did not suffer the same traumas as the European Great Powers, emerged from the war richer and more confident, although determined not to be dragged into further European quarrels which had gone a long way towards destroying Europe's claim to be the dominant force in world affairs.

B *The generals and trench warfare*

The most vivid feature of the Great War was the horror of trench warfare. Enormous bombardments preceded infantry charges in which thousands of men ran, or walked, across open ground towards the enemy defences, and armed usually with rifles and grenades. As they reached the enemy, they were held up by the barbed wire; and shot to pieces in their thousands by machine guns. Why did the generals persist with such tactics?:

- at the simplest level, technology had again overtaken tactics. The machine gun combined with barbed wire, was a lethal method of defence. No similarly effective attacking weapon was developed in the early years of the war. Ultimately, the tank would prove to be this weapon, but it was barely used effectively until 1918. Heavy artillery was destructive but difficult to use for mobile offensive purposes. Communications were also difficult during trench warfare
- the generals were trained to believe that battles could only be won by attacking. Most disregarded the power of defences that were rarely a single line to be broken – they were complex arrangements involving not just lines of trenches but also machine gun posts in strategic places, large dug-outs, artillery and, often, buildings as well
- the generals were completely thrown by the scale of the war – in terms of time, geography, and the number of troops. This scale posed supply problems that had never before been contemplated: how was it possible to keep this number of men fully equipped, move them to the right place at the right time, feed them, clothe them?
- with the introduction of conscription, the generals believed that their conscripts were capable of only the simplest manoeuvres, even though many of them were obviously intelligent and able to do far more. However, the generals believed that they were the same 'bone-heads' that had joined before the war and treated them accordingly
- even more damaging was the failure of the allies to co-operate effectively. This was equally true of both sides. Both British and French were keen to make the decisive breakthrough in the west while Falkenhayn refused to help the Austrians in the Balkans and Italy. Paradoxically, they were more ready to help their more distant allies – the Russians to help the Italians, the British and French the Russians. Had the co-operation that eventually came in the summer of 1918 come a year earlier, better results might have been achieved.

KEY ISSUE

Why was trench warfare so predominant on the Western Front?

C *Germany's defeat*

In November 1918 the Germans undoubtedly had had the better of the four years of fighting. In the East the Russians had been beaten and surrendered enormous amounts of territory. In the West, the German front line was still on enemy territory when the German leaders asked for peace. Germany's losses were less than those of its enemies. Germany surrendered not because it had been defeated, but because it knew that it would be. The future was hopeless for Germany.

The entry of the United States had not made a great impact but the potential of America's contribution was enormous. Militarily, American troops were arriving at the rate of 300 000 a month by August of 1918. The Germans estimated that they might face an American army of five million men. They were also providing military equipment and assisting in escorting merchant convoys.

Even more importantly, the potential American economic contribution was enormous. In the first years of the war, production of coal, steel and iron was almost equal between the *Entente* and the Central Powers – each produced about 350 million tons of coal and 20 million each of iron and steel. After America's intervention, the *Entente* production was 841 million tons of coal, 58 million of steel and 50 of iron, while that of the Central Powers was slightly less than in 1914. From slight economic inferiority the *Entente* suddenly had a three-fold advantage.

As important as the entry of the United States were the effects of economic decline in Germany itself. This was in part the result of the British blockade on Germany. Obviously, many goods still reached Germany through neutral countries, especially Holland, Denmark and Sweden. Even so, the slow but steady effects of the blockade were increasingly felt. For example, animal fats were almost unattainable, as what there were were used for making glycerine for explosives. It has been estimated that the Germans were receiving only about 1000 calories a day by the end of the war. German statistics attributed an ever increasing number of deaths to the effects of the blockade – 88 000 in 1915, 120 000 in 1916, 260 000 in 1917 and 294 000 in 1918 – a total of three-quarters of a million people, as many as the British lost on the Western Front.

German agriculture was hit disastrously by the war. The conscription of agricultural workers hit Germany harder than the other combatant countries, with the result that production fell by up to 70 per cent in some sectors, compared with 50 per cent in Russia and 30–50 per cent in France. Rationing was first organised in Germany, and price controls were brought in in 1916. The production of *ersatz* (substitute) products increased as the war went on – 'K' bread made with potatoes, cloth made out of paper and nettles, shoes with wooden soles. Simultaneously, workers demanded shorter hours because they found it so difficult to work on such small rations. Most importantly, the harvests of 1917 and 1918 both failed, so that production was about half what it had been before the war, as Table 27 shows.

Rations were reduced accordingly – seven pounds of potatoes, 250 grammes of meat, less than 100 grammes of fats per week. Again, the economic decline affected Germany's future even more than its present. How could its people keep up their morale and enthusiasm for the war through another winter? Could they even survive it?

In such circumstances, the collapse of Germany's allies and the ultimate failure of the spring offensive were but nails in the coffin. Germany's fate was all but sealed before March 1918. The last days of September settled matters, when the *Entente* launched major attacks on the Western Front.

> ### KEY ISSUE
>
> *How significant was the blockade of Germany to its eventual defeat?*

	1912–13 (pre-war average)	1918
Potatoes	52	26.4
Rye	11.9	7.2
Oats	9.1	4.3
Wheat	4.9	2.5
Barley	3.6	2.1

TABLE 27
German agricultural production (in million tons)

8 ⌐ BIBLIOGRAPHY

Most of the numerous books on the Great War have detailed bibliographies that will lead the student to more specialised works, so this selection consists chiefly of introductory works. M Ferro's *The Great War* (Routledge & Kegan Paul, 1973) and A Marwick's *World War I* (Units 15–17 of the Open University *War and Society* course) adopt a rather different approach to the standard textbooks. AJP Taylor's *The First World War* (Penguin, 1966) is still a good readable account, as is John Terraine's *The Western Front 1914–1918* (Hutchinson).

More detailed, and highly readable, accounts of the battles on the Western Front are provided in the books of Lyn Macdonald, who supplements her accounts of the battles with many first-hand accounts from participants. Also of interest, as they cover areas largely ignored by this chapter, are *Gallipoli* by A Moorehead (Hamish Hamilton, 1956), *The War behind the War 1914–18: The History of the Political and Civilian Fronts* by FP Chambers (Faber, 1939) and *The Deluge* by A Marwick (Macmillan, 1965).

9 ⌐ STRUCTURED QUESTIONS AND ESSAYS

1. (a) What do you understand by the phrase 'Western Front' in the context of World War I? (3 marks)
    (b) Explain briefly why trench warfare developed early on the Western Front; (7 marks)
    (c) What finally determined the outcome of the war on the Western Front? (15 marks)
2. (a) What do you understand by the phrase 'Central Powers' in the context of World War I? (3 marks)
    (b) Explain briefly why the Germans failed in their plan to achieve a quick victory over the *Entente* Powers in 1914; (7 marks)
    (c) Why did the Central Powers eventually lose World War I? (15 marks)
3. 'In 1914 the war was expected to be over by Christmas, yet by 1918 it was expected to last another two years.' Why were both of these expectations proved false? (25 marks)
4. Why were the fortunes of the Germans ultimately different on the Western and Eastern Fronts? (25 marks)

The Peace Treaties and the Successor States

1 ⌐ THE TREATY OF VERSAILLES

A *The peacemakers and their aims*

When the Armistice was signed, the victorious Powers had no detailed plans of what should be done next, mainly because they had not formulated clear war aims in 1914 and had since concentrated on actually winning the war. Where aims were formulated, they were usually kept secret.

The German historian Fritz Fischer argued that Germany's aims were extensive and ambitious. Bethmann-Hollweg's memorandum of September 1914 spoke of the need to weaken France to a state of dependence on Germany and of the construction of a *Mitteleuropa* of Germany, France, Austria-Hungary, Poland and Scandinavia, with the Low Countries as vassal states. There were also plans to push back Russia and

See page 122 and
Chapter 5

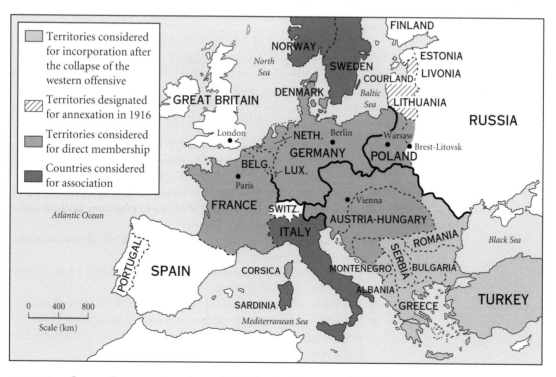

MAP 15   *German Government secret map of 1914 showing German territorial aims*

take over a new eastern Empire, part of which would form a defence against the new Russia (*Vorland*) and the rest of which, to the South, would be colonised and developed economically by Germany (*Kulturland*). Overseas, an enormous African Empire including the Congo, French Equatorial Africa and parts of West Africa would be created, so satisfying Germany's need for world power.

See page 52

The aims of the *Entente* powers were less ambitious:

- France sought the return of Alsace-Lorraine and the reduction of German power by the creation of a protective Rhineland Republic and a new political structure in Germany. In return for its agreement, Russia would be allowed the Straits of Constantinople and Poland
- Britain's aims were mainly colonial, and included many of Germany's and Turkey's colonies, although these would be shared with France and Russia. In January 1918, Lloyd George spoke of the need for Germany and its allies to return all the areas they had occupied – Belgium, Serbia, Montenegro, and parts of France, Italy and Romania, of the creation of a Polish state, of self-government for the nationalities of Austria-Hungary, and of 'reconsideration' of France's losses of 1871, Alsace and Lorraine.

KEY ISSUE

How different were the war aims of Germany and the Entente Powers?

See pages 244–5

Shortly afterwards, Germany signed the Treaty of Brest-Litovsk with Russia in March 1918 and the Treaty of Bucharest with Romania in April 1918. Germany and its allies took possession of large areas of Eastern Europe. *Entente* politicians could now demonstrate the greed of the Central Powers, and the consequent need to make sure of their defeat.

However, the ideas of America's President Woodrow Wilson formed the basis of the peace. Although America had been the least involved of the Great Powers in the War, Wilson's 'Fourteen Points' were the only coherent blueprint for peace. His ideas were outlined to the American Congress on 8 January 1918. Wilson hoped that by eliminating the causes of war, such a conflict would be avoided in the future:

- the alliance system had drawn the Powers into a local conflict by virtue of the secret obligations the Powers had made to each other, so Point 1 specified 'open covenants openly arrived at'
- naval rivalry between Britain and Germany had contributed to the arms race, so Point 2 demanded 'absolute freedom of navigation alike in peace and war'
- Point 3 called for the removal, as far as possible, of all economic barriers between nations
- Point 4 stated that 'armaments would be reduced to the lowest point consistent with domestic safety'
- Point 5 called for 'an impartial adjustment of all colonial claims'
- Point 14 was particularly ambitious: 'A general association of nations to be formed to afford mutual guarantees of political independence and territorial integrity to great and small states alike.'

This last would also ensure that the territorial adjustments Wilson planned for in Points 6–13 would be secured. These were:

(6) evacuation of Russian territory and the free determination of Russia's own future

(7) evacuation and restoration of Belgium

(8) evacuation and restoration of French territory and the return of Alsace-Lorraine to France

(9) readjustment of Italy's boundaries 'along clearly recognisable lines of nationality'

(10) autonomy for the peoples of Austria-Hungary

(11) evacuation and restoration of Romanian, Serbian and Montenegrin territory, including access to the sea for Serbia

(12) the Ottoman Empire to be broken up – areas of Turkish population were to form an independent Turkey but other areas and peoples 'to be given the opportunity for autonomous development'. The Straits of Constantinople were to be permanently open to all ships

(13) the creation of an independent Poland in all those areas 'indisputably Polish' and this state to have secure access to the sea.

Many of these aims could only be achieved at the expense of existing Powers – Germany, Austria-Hungary and Russia – and even then little seemed to have been done for French security. France and Britain broadly endorsed the plans, but would not accept the clause about freedom of the seas and also demanded compensation from Germany. Both Germany and Austria-Hungary agreed in October 1918 that the Points could form the basis of the peace.

PICTURE 17 *The 'Big Three' at Versailles: David Lloyd George, Georges Clemenceau and Woodrow Wilson*

See page 4

KEY ISSUE

What were the strengths and weaknesses of the Fourteen Points?

See pages 159–60

KEY ISSUE

How similar to each other were the peace aims of the 'Big Three'?

Yet there were some glaring faults in the Fourteen Points:

● it would not be possible simply to divide the Habsburg Empire into separate national states. There were more than a dozen such nationalities, not neatly segregated into separate areas
● the war was sure to be followed by economic hardship in the countries that had fought, and they were therefore unlikely to favour plans to abandon tariffs. In addition, they were likely to want to keep large armies at the ready in the period immediately after the war
● the Fourteen Points hinged on Wilson's interpretation of the causes of the war and the consequent remedies. Were the arms race and commercial and colonial rivalry actually the causes of the war, or were they merely symptoms of an underlying malaise, a nationalism that would have found its expression in war in any case?

The bulk of the peacemaking was to be done by the 'Council of Four': Britain, France, Italy and the United States. The attitudes of the other three leaders differed considerably from Wilson's idealism:

● Orlando, Italy's Prime Minister, was under great pressure to win considerable areas for Italy and so justify the suffering and losses of the Italian people. Moreover, Italy had the Treaty of London to support its claims to areas of Austria-Hungary
● Clemenceau, France's Prime Minister, had endorsed the Fourteen Points, but in secret scorned what he called the 'Fourteen Commandments'. He wanted to ensure that France could never again be threatened by Germany. He sought to secure France's eastern frontier
● Lloyd George, Britain's Prime Minister, was agreed on the need for redrawing Europe's frontiers but was flexible in his attitude to Germany and its future. He did not want to see Germany destroyed, an outcome which would harm British trade and create a dangerous power vacuum in central Europe. However, his flexibility was hampered by the British press, which demanded the *Kaiser* be hanged and that Germany be 'squeezed till the pips squeak'. During the peace negotiations Lloyd George also received a telegram signed by 370 MPs demanding that Germany be forced to pay full compensation.

B *The history of the peace conference*

The signature of the Armistice was followed by a seven-month 'limbo' until the Treaty was signed. Germany and its allies were barred from the conference, so leading to subsequent accusations that it was a *Diktat*: a dictated peace. At the same time, Germans continued to starve and the *Entente* Powers spent more than five million pounds providing food for the German people.

There were 32 states represented at the Peace Conference in Paris. The bulk of the detailed work was done by the 58 commissions and committees set up to deal with specific matters.

There were many disagreements at the Conference but by 7 May the bulk of the terms were agreed on and were presented to the German delegation, which objected vigorously that they were not in keeping with the Fourteen Points to which *it* had agreed. But the only German resistance was to **scuttle** the entire fleet, which had been taken to Scapa Flow, rather than let the victors take possession of it. A week later the Treaty was formally signed in the Hall of Mirrors at the Palace of Versailles, where Wilhelm I had been crowned *Kaiser* in 1871.

> **scuttle** to deliberately sink one's own fleet to prevent its capture

C *The terms of the Treaty of Versailles*

The final version of the Treaty ran to over 200 pages and 440 clauses, including the constitution of the League of Nations. Only the most significant clauses are dealt with here:

- the West bank of the River Rhine and an area 50 kilometres wide on the East bank were **demilitarised**. The *Entente* powers would man the Western bank and the bridgeheads until 1930. In addition, Britain and America guaranteed aid to France if it were attacked by Germany. In the event, the American Senate refused to accept this agreement, and Britain's promise, which had been dependent on America, lapsed too. Consequently, France's search for security was to continue into the 1920s

> **demilitarised** the removal of weapons, fortifications or troops from a particular area

- the Saar Basin was to be held by an inter-Allied force for 15 years, for the first five of which France was to receive the coal mined there
- Germany's armed forces were limited – the army to 100 000 men. Limitations were also placed on the size and number of guns. The navy was to be limited to six battleships of over 10 000 tons. No submarines or military aircraft were allowed. The victorious Powers explained that these restrictions were imposed 'in order to render possible the initiation of a general limitation of the armaments of all nations', a general limitation that was never to take place
- France received Alsace and Lorraine, and with them two million people and three-quarters of Germany's iron resources. Germany also gave up Eupen, Moresnet and Malmedy to Belgium and northern Schleswig to Denmark

> **mandate** a former colony delegated to the temporary control of another Power

- Germany's colonies were confiscated and put in the care of the victorious Powers until such time as they were ready to become independent. This was known as the '**mandate**' system, and by it the League of Nations oversaw the controlling Powers
- Germany had to give up land to the newly independent Poland, created in part also from Russia and Austria-Hungary. Poland had also, by Point 13, been promised access to the sea. This made it extremely difficult to draw a boundary, since the population of that area, from Danzig in the north to Silesia in the south, was mixed. Consequently, West Prussia and Posen, both of which contained many Prussians, were given to Poland, thus repudiating for Germans the right to **self-determination** that was so assiduously applied to other peoples. In

> **self-determination** the right of a people to determine their own form of government or the nation to which they belong

plebiscite a vote by a people on one particular issue, normally to determine the boundary of their country

other areas it was agreed to hold **plebiscites** to decide whether they should go to Poland or Germany. As a result, Allenstein and Marienwerder were left in East Prussia, and thus remained part of Germany, while the future of Silesia was not decided until 1921

● Danzig presented the greatest problem as it was a largely German town, whereas most of the surrounding area was Polish. As a compromise it was put under League of Nations' control. A similar arrangement was made for Memel. As a result of the construction of Poland, Germany lost some two million subjects and a wealth of minerals, as well as having one part of the state – East Prussia – separated from the rest by a part of Poland known as the Polish Corridor

---

KEY ISSUE

To what extent did the peace settlement fulfil the Fourteen Points?

● the 'War Guilt Clause' stated that 'Germany accepts the responsibilities of Germany and her allies for causing all the loss and damage to which the Allied and Associated Governments and their allies have been subjected as a consequence of the war imposed upon them by the aggression of Germany and her allies'. Reparations were to be paid. although the final sum was unfixed. There was disagreement over Germany's capacity to pay. A Reparations Commission was to

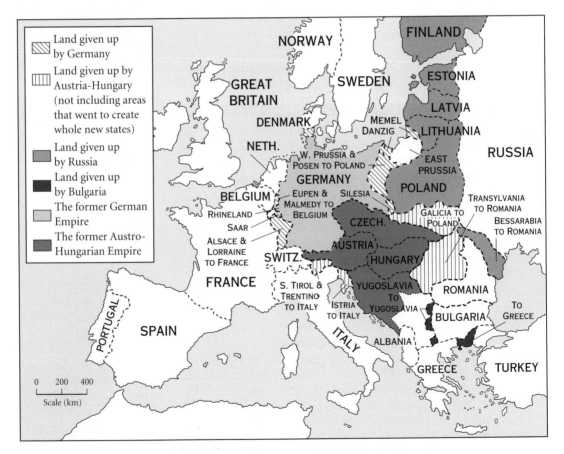

MAP 16 *Territorial changes after World War I*

decide the figure. Under the final bill, the Germans were to pay five billion dollars before May 1921. All merchant ships of more than 1600 tons, half of those between 800 and 1600 tons and a quarter of the fishing fleet were to be handed over immediately, and an additional 200 000 tons of shipping was to be built for the Allies each year for the next five years. Other goods, such as coal and timber, were to be delivered to France, Belgium and Italy. Germany was to pay the cost of the Allied occupation force.

See pages 283–4 and 290

Article 231 was to be the source of enormous discontent in later years. To the Allied leaders in 1919, the War Guilt Clause was a technical device to justify their charging such an enormous amount. So far as the German people were concerned, and their leaders were keen to tell them, the clause fixed the guilt for the war on Germany in a moral way, and few Germans could stomach being told it was their fault. This interpretation was repeated so often and seemed so obvious that in the inter-war period most Europeans accepted it.

Finally, the 'war criminals' were to be punished. The *Kaiser*, who had fled to Holland, was to be **extradited** and tried by special tribunal 'for a supreme offence against international morality and the sanctity of treaties'. In fact, the Dutch Government refused to hand him over, as to do so would contravene international law.

KEY ISSUE

Why was the 'War Guilt' clause controversial?

extradited removing a person from one country to that of another in which he or she is alleged to have committed a crime

2 ～ THE CENTRAL AND EAST EUROPEAN SETTLEMENTS

The settlement of Central and Eastern Europe was bound to be complicated. The abdication of the last Habsburg Emperor, Karl, on 11 November 1918, led to the separation of Austria and Hungary. Both the new states claimed that they were not the successor to the Habsburg Empire and should not be treated as an aggressor nation as Germany had been, but ultimately both were held to be so and both were charged reparations. In the confused last months of the war, several of the nationalities of the Empire had declared their independence and, in early 1919, arrived in Paris to press their claims. The *Entente* leaders were all agreed on the need for such 'self-determination', but it was difficult to put it into practice.

See Map 16 on page 146

A *The Treaty of St Germain*

The Treaty of St Germain held the new Austrian Republic to be the successor of the Empire and was therefore, like Germany, charged reparations and forced to limit its army to 30 000 men. The Austrian Government was forced to cede Bohemia and Moravia to Czechoslovakia, Dalmatia and Bosnia-Herzegovina to Yugoslavia, and Galicia to Poland. Bukovina was handed over to Romania and Trentino, the South Tyrol and Istria, including the port of Trieste, to Italy.

PEACE AND FUTURE CANNON FODDER

SOURCE H (PICTURE 20)
*Will Dyson's cartoon about the
Peace Conference*

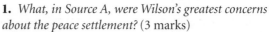

The Tiger: "Curious! I seem to hear a child weeping!"

Q

1. *What, in Source A, were Wilson's greatest concerns
about the peace settlement?* (3 marks)
2. *Compare the attitudes expressed in Sources A, B, D and E towards
the peace settlement.* (6 marks)
3. *To what extent do Sources F, G and H support the attitudes in
Sources A, B, D and E?* (8 marks)
4. *Use the Sources and your own knowledge to explain why reparations were such a controversial issue after World War I.* (6 marks)
5. *What is the attitude towards the peace settlement of the speaker in
Source C? Comment on the speaker's tone and arguments. How much
fact, and how much propaganda, is there in his speech?* (8 marks)
6. *Using your own knowledge, explain which of these Sources was the
most accurate, and which the least accurate, in their analysis of the
peace settlement and its likely consequences.* (9 marks)

Italy
1890–1945

INTRODUCTION

The problems of unification

Italian unification was only completed in 1870 when French troops left Rome and it became part of the New Kingdom. The unification process, or *Risorgimento*, left the new state with problems only partially resolved by 1890:

- many Italians still lived outside the borders of the new 'Italy': particularly in the Tyrol, Trentino and Istria. Since these regions belonged to the Habsburg Empire, this complicated relations with the Austro-Hungarian Government
- many Italians within Italy itself disliked the new central state. Unification brought new taxes and laws, and the poorer South resented the 'alien', richer North
- Pope Pius IX refused to recognise the new state. Resentful at losing control of Rome, the papacy discouraged Catholics from taking part in political life, further weakening internal unity
- much of Italy was poor, consisting as it did of a predominantly peasant population. Most Italians were hired labourers, and poverty was rife, especially in the South. Thousands of Italians emigrated annually, many to the USA. Poverty encouraged violence
- most Italian Governments were short-lived and unstable. They were elected on a very narrow franchise, and corruption was widespread.

Although Italian Governments between 1870 and 1914 made some progress in establishing a more democratic and stable state, many of the problems outlined above still persisted. Italy remained one of the weaker Great Powers of Europe.

> **KEY ISSUE**
>
> *What problems faced the newly united Italy?*

1 ✎ THE MINISTRIES OF CRISPI 1887–91 AND 1893–6

Francesco Crispi was Prime Minister, Foreign Minister and Minister of the Interior during this period. He carried out some reforms in local government and reduced the influence of the Church in education. However, when higher taxes led to violent protests in the South, Crispi responded with repression and a suspension of parliament.

1883	Crispi's ministry
1890	*Colonisation of Eritrea*
1896	*Italian defeat at Battle of Adowa*
1900	Assassination of King Umberto I
1903	Giolitti's ministry
1911	*Annexation of Tripoli*
1912	*Annexation of Dodecanese islands*
1913	'Red Week'
1915	*Italy joined World War I*
1919	Mussolini founded Fascist group in Milan *Italy evacuated Fiume D'Annunzio seized Fiume*
1921	*D'Annunzio left Fiume*
1922	March on Rome and Mussolini became Prime Minister
1923	New Electoral Law
1924	*Treaty with Yugoslavia over Fiume* Murder of Matteotti
1926	Right to strike abolished
1929	Lateran Treaties
1934	*Mussolini's first meeting with Hitler*
1935	*Invasion of Abyssinia*
1936	*Rome-Berlin Axis signed*
1938	*Munich Agreement*
1939	Council of Corporations replaced parliament *Invasion of Albania Pact of Steel with Germany*
1940	*Italy declared war and invaded France, British Somaliland, Egypt and Greece*
1941	*Italian defeats in East Africa*
1943	*Allied invasion of Italy and overthrow of Mussolini*
1945	Death of Mussolini

TABLE 28

Date chart of chief events in Italy 1890–1945 (foreign affairs in italics)

MAP 18 *Italy in 1890*

Crispi's principal concern was foreign policy. He was very aware of Italy's vulnerable strategic position and the fact that it was bordered by established Great Powers in France and Austria-Hungary, each hostile to the other. Italy had to tread carefully, but Crispi determined to strengthen links with Germany and Austria-Hungary, and joined them in the Triple Alliance of 1882. He also sought to create a colonial empire. In 1890 Eritrea was proclaimed an Italian colony. However, penetration into neighbouring Abyssinia (or Ethiopia) culminated in the disastrous battle of Adowa in 1896, when Abyssinian forces routed an Italian army – the first major defeat of a large European army by non-Europeans in modern times. Crispi resigned, and Abyssinia secured its independence. Italian humiliation was compounded by famine conditions in the next few years, accompanied by major outbreaks of violence throughout Italy. Weak Governments came and went, and King Umberto I was assassinated by an anarchist in 1900.

2 ⌐ THE MINISTRIES OF GIOLITTI 1903–14

In the decade before World War I Italy appeared to be recovering from some of its difficulties. Industrial production and foreign trade expanded considerably, whilst violence and the frequency of strikes declined. Much of the credit was due to Giovanni Giolitti, Prime Minister for most of the period 1903–14. The influence of the Left in parliament declined and the new Pope Pius X moderated the Church's stance, announcing its toleration of voting in elections where it was designed to keep Socialists out of power. Giolitti's reforms included laws to improve working conditions, an extension of the franchise in 1912 (although it was still confined to only 24 per cent of the population) and relaxing some of the restrictions on religious instruction in schools. However, poverty was not eradicated, and political corruption was still common.

Like his predecessors, Giolitti felt compelled to follow an active foreign policy in order to prove Italy's credentials as a Great Power. In 1911 Italy announced the annexation of Tripoli, part of the Turkish Empire. In 1912 Italy occupied the Dodecanese Islands. A weakened Turkey conceded Tripoli, but the war was costly for Italy and led to riots and strikes in 1913 and 1914. During the 'Red Week' of June 1914 several areas of Italy declared themselves independent communes or republics. Italy was still far from being a united country. Left-wing disaffection in particular was at its peak in 1914. Although moderate or reformist Socialists had joined Giolitti's Government, other Socialists refused co-operation and Giolitti's Government fell following a general strike in protest against heavy taxation. On the extreme Left there were also Syndicalists who sought to overthrow the political system through industrial violence.

KEY ISSUE

How stable was Italy in 1914?

3 ⌐ ITALY AND WORLD WAR I

From the outbreak of war until May 1915 Italy remained neutral. Prime Minister Salandra explained this on the grounds that Austria's action against Serbia was offensive, while the Triple Alliance was a defensive alliance and therefore Italy was entitled to remain neutral.

During 1914–15, Italians argued over the relative merits of continued neutrality. The war provided an opportunity for Italy to further its claim to those areas of Austria-Hungary with large Italian minorities. Foreign Minister Sonnino claimed that Article VII of the Triple Alliance promised Italy compensation to balance any Austrian gains in the Balkans, and he persuaded the German Government of this. In May 1915 Germany persuaded Austria to accept demands for the cession of Trentino, the South Tyrol and some Adriatic islands.

By this time, those who favoured Italy joining France and Britain had equally won considerable concessions in the case of Austria's defeat. By the secret Treaty of London (April 1915) the Allies agreed that, in return for Italian military assistance, they would help in the fight against Austria, and, when victory was won, Italy could have

Trentino, the South Tyrol, Gorizia, Gradisca, Trieste, Istria, parts of Dalmatia, the Adriatic islands, extensions to Libya (as Tripolitania was now known), Eritrea and Somaliland and a share of any war indemnity – all if Italy declared war within a month.

In May 1915 Salandra denounced the Triple Alliance and parliament voted in favour of war. Nationalist demonstrations were encouraged to ensure popular support. Three days later war was declared on Austria-Hungary but not on Germany until 28 August 1915.

See page 130

Italy's war record was not impressive, and both ministers and generals rose and fell fast. In December 1916 Salandra was replaced by Paolo Boselli, who himself resigned following the defeat of his army at Caporetto in October 1917, to be replaced by Vittorio Orlando. A total of 217 different generals were appointed in the space of two years, few victories of note were won, and by the time of the armistice the Treaty of London seemed less of a diplomatic triumph for the *Entente* than it had in 1915.

This became even more obvious during the Paris Peace Conference: the promises made in the Treaty of London conflicted with Woodrow Wilson's plans for national self-determination. Wilson, of course, had not been a signatory of the Treaty of London. Wilson publicly denounced Italian claims in April 1919. Orlando left the Conference, only to return uninvited within two weeks to make sure Italy got something.

Ultimately, Italy did gain a considerable amount of land from the Treaty of St Germain with Austria. Trentino, the South Tyrol, Trieste and Istria all became a part of Italy, but there were no colonies, no money and only some of the land Italy had hoped for: 9000 square miles of it, and a population of 1.6 million, in exchange for 600 000 dead, massive war debts and a huge increase in the cost of living.

4 ∽ POLITICAL HISTORY 1918–22

A *1919–21*

Italians had suffered considerable blows to their self-esteem during the war years. Discontent with the Government was shown in several ways:

- Orlando lost support and resigned in June 1919 when only 78 deputies, out of more than 500, voted for him
- in September 1919, Gabriele D'Annunzio, a poet and ardent nationalist, led an army of volunteers into the city of Fiume on the Dalmatian coast and claimed it for Italy since the majority of the population was Italian. D'Annunzio's supporters wore black shirts and used the straight arm salute, and proclaimed music to be the state religion. Their occupation of Fiume, which lasted for 15 months, showed both that there were groups of people prepared to take the law into their own hands, and that the Government would let them do so. The Government of Nitti chose to leave the rebels in Fiume and it was only in December 1920 that they were finally ousted by the army, leaving without a fight. The Fiume incident foreshadowed what was to come not only in the form of salutes and uni-

forms, but also in the attitude of the Government to lawbreakers. It became a commonplace of Italian political life in 1920–2 that the Government took no action against right-wingers who used violence to remove elected Governments and install their own

● the Socialist Party, the PSI, gained in strength 1919–20. The Party's membership grew from 50 000 before the war to 200 000 in 1919. Trade union membership in the Confederation of Labour rose from half a million to two million. With the increased membership came more strikes. Even more notably, the PSI controlled 26 of the 69 provinces and some 2000 town councils, flying the red flag of Socialism.

In the general election of November 1919, the Socialists won 156 seats. They were the largest and most organised political party in Italy. The 1919 party Congress at Bologna rejected reformism and chose instead to join the Third International, following the revolutionary line dictated by Moscow.

There were other indications of a leftward trend. In the confusion of 1919, many peasants returning to their homes after the war had taken land that had belonged to landlords. Sometimes there was a struggle, sometimes the land was simply taken because nobody seemed to own it. The Government officially recognised the seizures in the Visocchi Decree of September 1919 and the Falcioni Decree of April 1920. Respectable Italian society, used to the formality of elections in which their man always won and Governments were always conservative coalitions, not surprisingly wondered if revolution was just around the corner.

The old way of government was under attack elsewhere. Pope Benedict XV lifted the ban on Catholics participating in elections, thereby giving a tremendous boost to the newly formed Catholic Party, the *Popolari* or Christian Democrats. There was no official connection between the party and the Church but the leader was a Sicilian priest, Don Sturzo, and the party obviously won support from churchgoers. In the 1919 election, this new political force won over 100 seats. In fact the *Popolari* was never a united party as its members ranged from traditional, monarchical churchmen at one end to virtual Marxists at the other.

The one common ideal of *Popolari* supporters was opposition to anticlericalism, which was represented by the major coalition *bloc* in parliament, the Liberals and Democrats gathered around Giolitti. This opposition was to prove fatal in that it prevented the *Popolari* and the anticlericals uniting and forming a moderate alternative to either Socialism or Fascism.

The final, and apparently least important indication of opposition, was the foundation of the *Fascio di Combattimento* by some 50 malcontents on 23 March 1919. They were an assorted group, ranging from the syndicalist Bianchi to the monarchist de Vecchi via the futurist poet Marinetti, who suggested that the Pope should be dropped into the Adriatic. They won no seats in the 1919 elections. Even their leader, Benito Mussolini, won only 2 per cent of the vote in Milan, less than 5000 votes against 170 000 for the Socialists.

KEY ISSUE
Why was the post-war Government in Italy unstable?

Date of appointment	Name
March 1914	Antonio Salandra
June 1916	Paolo Boselli
October 1917	Vittorio Orlando
June 1919	Francesco Nitti
June 1920	Giovanni Giolitti
July 1921	Ivanoe Bonomi
February 1922	Luigi Facta
October 1922	Benito Mussolini

TABLE 29 *Italian Prime Ministers 1914–22*

BENITO MUSSOLINI (1883–1945)

Mussolini had had a difficult childhood before becoming a revolutionary Socialist and journalist in the early years of the twentieth century. He was rebellious and gained a reputation for violence and unpredictability. Mussolini was essentially against the Establishment, and as a good Socialist, condemned the war in 1914, but he soon changed his tune. He founded his own paper, *Il Popolo d'Italia*, and campaigned for Italy's entry into the conflict. When Italy joined the war in 1915, Mussolini enlisted, and had a brave but undistinguished record in the Army. After the war, he used his journalistic and oratorical skills to attract recruits to the new Fascist movement. Mussolini was an opportunist, with few consistent principles, only a desire for power, but his readiness to flout orthodox conventions and his skilful sloganising, which soon included promises to restore Italy's past greatness, had some appeal for those Italians terrified of a possible Communist or Socialist revolution. Mussolini was personally insecure but hid this in public, coming across as a confident, charismatic figure to Italians. This seemed more important than political consistency. Mussolini's early Fascism had few policies: it was based rather on sloganising on the lines of 'Believe, obey, do battle!' and 'We are not a party but are anti-Party and a movement.' In the context of the times, the way in which a politician appealed to popular sentiment was more important than a rational appraisal of what his party stood for.

However, 1920 and 1921 were to see the upsurge of this tiny group so that it rivalled the Socialists. This was partly due to Mussolini himself, despite unpromising beginnings.

In the summer of 1920 Giolitti's Government faced half a million workers sitting in factories following a lockout in the metallurgical industry in protest at low wages. Union leaders had been taken by surprise by this spontaneous revolutionary outburst and soon persuaded the workers to give in in return for higher wages. Yet such events and fear of revolution preoccupied the opponents of Socialism, many of whom now joined Mussolini's 'Fascist' party. In the winter of 1920–1 these men, organised into *squadre d'azione* (squads of action) by *ras* (local leaders) like Balbo in Ferrara and Grandi in Bologna, began a campaign of violence against Socialists that led to some 200 dead and 800 wounded in the period between December 1920 and May 1921.

The Government did little to prevent the violence and instead saw it as a cheap way of curbing the rise of Socialism, though by the spring of 1921 the clashes had reached riot proportions. Nonetheless the Government had succeeded in its aim of disrupting the progress of Socialism. At the party Congress at Livorno in January 1921 the PSI split into a revolutionary and a reformist wing, a move welcomed, if not actually forced, by the Fascists.

The increasing support for the Fascists was also reflected in the election of May 1921. Beforehand, Prime Minister Giolitti invited them to

How and why were the Fascists able to increase their support?

Extreme Nationalists	10		
Fascists	35	184	Government bloc
National Bloc (Giolitti)	139		
Radicals			
(Liberal Democrats)	68	175	Potential Centrist opposition
Popolari	107		
Reformists	29		
Socialists	123		
Communists	15	176	Left opposition
National minorities	9		

TABLE 30   *The May 1921 elections*

form a part of his right-wing electoral alliance, thereby promising them, for the first time, some influence in the Government as well as in the streets. The Fascists did well in these elections, as Table 30 shows.

From May to July 1921 Giolitti was able to govern on the basis of this coalition. Within a year there were to be 13 different groups in parliament. Since the deputies fell into three approximately equal groupings, the Fascists' 35 seats were crucial, as their defection to the opposition would make government very difficult. This situation took Mussolini by surprise. His immediate reaction was to become a respectable participant in government. He signed a 'peace treaty', 'the pact of pacification', with the Socialists to end their mutual violence. However, his lieutenants in the provinces disliked this curb on their power and protested against it, in reply to which Mussolini resigned as leader but in November accepted their demands for continued hostility, tore up the pact and resumed the leadership.

B *1921–22: The Fascists take power*

The economic conditions of the period did much to encourage support for extremist parties. As a result of Italy's war debts and problems of reconstruction, the *lire* was devalued and prices rose about 50 per cent while wages remained at their pre-war levels. In such circumstances, working-class voters were attracted to the left-wing parties in the hope of pressing for wage claims. In some cases, they took action on their own behalf by striking and occupying factories. In turn, this raised the spectre of revolution and increased the attractions of the Fascists for those who owned property and feared Socialism. The Fascists alone seemed to offer the firm action to prevent revolution that many Italians saw as the only alternative to Bolshevism. The party itself had relatively few working class members, as Table 31 shows.

From December 1921 to November 1922 both Fascist violence and short-lived Governments continued. Fascist thuggery became ever more efficient, and the Socialists claimed that in the two years before October 1922, 3000 of their supporters had been killed by the Fascist squads, who had suffered only 300 fatalities themselves. Giolitti, faced by Fascist opposition in parliament, was forced to resign in June 1921.

	%
Farm workers	24.3
Urban workers	15.4
Seamen	1.0
Students	13.0
Private sector employees	9.8
Public sector employees	4.8
Teachers	1.1
Members of professions	6.6
Tradesmen and artisans	9.2
Industrialists	2.8
Farmers and landowners	12.0

TABLE 31   *The social background of Fascist Party members, 1921 (of a Party membership of about 300 000). From* Italian Fascism and the Middle Classes *by R De Felice in* Who were the Fascists? Social Roots of European Fascism, *eds S Larsen and others (Bergen: Universitetsforlaget, 1980, page 314)*

His successor, Ivanœ Bonomi, was a reformist Socialist, and formed a Government with Radical and *Popolari* support, but it fell in February 1922. It was four weeks before the King could persuade Luigi Facta to take over. Mack Smith described Facta as '... a timid, ignorant provincial lawyer who had risen in politics by seniority alone. His appointment was at first taken almost as a joke ...'. His Government was defeated by the desertion of the *Popolari* in the summer of 1922, but on 1 August he again became Prime Minister when no other could be found. As Mussolini himself said: 'No one wanted or was able to seize power.'

On the day that Facta formed his new ministry, the unions began a general strike in an effort to force the Government to take some action against the Fascist violence. The Fascists had won control of a number of cities and had even driven the Communist town council of Bologna out of office in May 1922. Even worse, the Government had still failed to use the 240 000 armed forces, 65 000 police and 40 000 militia at its disposal to suppress the Fascists. When it did act, as at Sazana in June 1921 when 500 Fascists were put to flight by the police, the measures were effective.

Yet subsequent Governments had not bothered and even an order of December 1921 to provincial prefects to suppress the Fascists was ignored. However, the strike played right into Mussolini's hands, for yet again the spectre of Socialist revolution was raised. The Fascists promised that they would end the strike even if the Government would not. On 2 August they acted against the strikers in Ancona, Genoa and Leghorn. The next day they entered Milan and after three hours of street fighting occupied the offices of the Socialist newspaper, *Avanti*, smashed the presses and burnt the building to the ground. The Socialist administration of Milan was then attacked and the triumphant Fascists were addressed by D'Annunzio. When the transport workers continued their strike, the Fascists simply took over the trains and ran them themselves.

By the late summer, Mussolini had determined that the Fascists had the power to take over the Government, although he was undecided how. On 13 August the party congress gave its approval for his efforts to win power by peaceful rather than violent means.

Consequently, his first aim had to be new elections to increase Fascist representation in Parliament and so give greater weight to his demands for power. The incumbent Government of Facta looked fragile and it was expected that a new coalition would be formed under one of the accepted parliamentary leaders – Giolitti, Salandra or Orlando. Some of Facta's coalition favoured the inclusion of Fascists in the new Government. This latter group dominated the congress of liberal politicians held at Bologna on 8 October to form a new party which stated its intention to 'steer firmly to the right'. Consequently, there was in the Government itself a faction prepared to accommodate the Fascists.

There were still a number of potential obstacles to Mussolini:

- the most obvious were the King and the army. Victor Emmanuel had little time for the Fascists. However, many of his advisers, including the Queen Mother, Margherita, and his cousin, the Duke of Aosta, a general in the war and hero of the nationalist right, were known to be Fascist sympathisers. Mussolini himself tried to allay the King's fears, and in speeches explained that the King had nothing to fear from him. In the final analysis, the King's role was to prove decisive

● the loyalties of the army, whose support would be critical in the event of a Fascist uprising, were uncertain. Many young officers openly supported the party and one of its generals, De Bono, was a leading member of it. On the other hand, most soldiers had little time for Fascism and accepted that their loyalty was to Crown and State. To reinforce this, the Minister of War, Soleri, ordered the dismissal of officers who attended Fascist meetings in army uniform and started disciplinary action against De Bono

● D'Annunzio resented Mussolini's newfound support and still hoped to find a role as national saviour. He was a close friend of Facta with whom he discussed ways of keeping Mussolini out of power. The two decided on a national rally at which they would address a meeting of ex-servicemen, and appeal for peace, order and national unity. In this alliance of moderation and the hero of war veterans lay the greatest threat to Mussolini.

By mid-September much of north Italy was under Fascist control through their domination of local government. The problems of unemployment and strikes required immediate action that would be easier if the party also had control of the national Government, while the semi-military blackshirted 'squads' needed action to prevent disaffection. At the end of the month, Mussolini went on a tour of the north, in which he made his intentions clear: 'Our programme is simple: we intend to govern Italy', he told the crowds at Udine.

Under such a threat, Giolitti seemed the one politician with the support and experience to prevent a violent Fascist take over. All the moderate parties and Facta himself promised their support for him and by early October negotiations for him to form a new Government were almost complete. The plan was for a multi-party coalition including the Fascists, to be formed when parliament reassembled and prepared for fresh elections in the spring. Mussolini, however, made it clear that he would only join such a coalition if it were formed *before* parliament reassembled (before the planned rally of 4 November) and provided that elections were held sooner than the spring. Parliament was not due to meet again until 7 November, and Facta was concerned about his own ability to cope with the Fascist Party Congress planned for 24 October and the rally of 4 November. Both could easily result in violence, and Facta urged Giolitti to act quickly.

Both the Fascists and the Government prepared for the possibility of violence. On 16 October, the Fascist leaders met and drew up plans for a march on Rome. The *quadrumviri* – Balbo, Bianchi, De Vecchi and De Bono – were appointed to lead and co-ordinate these plans. Mussolini hoped that violence would not be needed, but that the threat of it would be enough to precipitate a crisis that would bring him to power

KEY ISSUE

Why was the March on Rome successful?

peacefully. On the same day, he met D'Annunzio and reached agreement over union recognition in the Genoa docks (a major cause of dissent between the supporters of the two men) and so reduced the likelihood of opposition from that quarter.

For his part, Facta sounded out the army leaders, Diaz and Badoglio, who assured him that 'the army will do its duty if it is necessary to defend Rome'. Badoglio thought that 'ten or twelve arrests' would be enough to crush the Fascists. Between 19 and 25 October the Rome garrison of 2500 was reinforced and plans for blocking the bridges and roads into the city drawn up. Police and troops guarded the stations as Fascist delegates passed through the city en route to the Party Congress in Naples.

On the first day of the Congress, Mussolini announced that the Fascists would join the Government only if they were given five cabinet posts, including the foreign ministry. At a march past of 60 000 supporters, Mussolini announced that it was only a matter of days and even hours before the Government was theirs. The plans for the march on Rome were finalised: three columns of marchers were to descend simultaneously on the city on 28 October. Mussolini repeated his pledge that they did not intend to confront the army but that Rome would be reached 'at all costs'.

Mussolini then returned to Milan, where he continued negotiations with Giolitti through the mediation of Lusignoli, the prefect of Milan. De Vecchi, Grandi and Ciano were sent to Rome to act as Fascist spokesmen in the capital, and the scene was set for Mussolini's final triumph.

On 26 and 27 October, the Fascist leaders in Rome told Facta, Salandra and the King that their party was on the point of seizing power by force. Facta's ministers urged resignation, but the King refused to appoint a new Prime Minister 'under threat of violence'. He was told of the defensive plans for the city and approved them. On the night of 27/28 October squads of Fascists seized control of town halls, post offices and stations in many towns of Northern Italy, unopposed by local officials or police. They did not, however, take possession of the major cities of Turin, Genoa and Bologna and their hold in Florence and Milan was not assured.

At 12.30 am on 28 October the military authorities were put in overall charge of public order throughout the country. Facta had an audience with the King at 2.30 am, in which the King approved a manifesto whereby the Government announced 'its supreme duty to defend the state at all cost, by all means and against all who violate its laws'. At 5 am the cabinet met and approved the manifesto and the firm measures taken to put down the uprising, so at 7.50 am a state of siege was announced, to commence at midday. By 9 am the Government's manifesto was appearing on buildings throughout Rome.

The trainloads of Fascist supporters were stopped at checkpoints and the main body of intending marchers – some 20 000 of them – was stopped 50 miles from the city when confronted by 400 policemen. Only two of the three columns, with a mere 5000 men between them, had reached their assembly points, where they waited for action, hungry, ill equipped and soaked by torrential rain. In Rome 28 000 troops and police awaited their arrival.

At 9 am Facta drove to the palace to get the King formally to authorise the state of martial law. He refused to sign it, a change of heart that was critical for the future of Italy but is difficult to understand, given that the Fascists stood little chance if they continued their attempt to win by force. After World War II, Victor Emmanuel explained that he thought there were 100 000 Fascists outside the city, and only 8000 troops to stop them. In fact, there were about 30 000 of each, but the King never asked the military commander of Rome, Pugliese, for an estimate. It is also possible that he feared his cousin, the Duke of Aosta, and thought that he might lead the revolution against him. Above all, he feared a civil war, especially as he was not convinced of the army's loyalty.

One account is that General Giraldi told him, when asked what the army would do, that 'the army will do its duty, but it would be better not to put it to the test'. This conversation took place between 5 am and 9 am. In addition, he certainly did not see a refusal to sign as tantamount to giving power to Mussolini. When Facta resigned, at 11 am on 28 October, Victor Emmanuel went through the motions of consulting all political parties, but by the evening had persuaded his old adviser, Salandra, to form a Government. Salandra agreed to this only on condition that Mussolini would join the Government.

At first it seemed likely that Mussolini would agree. Salandra negotiated with De Vecchi, Grandi and Ciano and agreed that there should be four Fascists in the new cabinet. However, in the early hours of 29 October, Mussolini rejected the offer. He had not gone to the trouble of organising a national insurrection for the reward of four

PICTURE 21 *Mussolini and the Fascist leaders*

cabinet posts. In the morning Salandra told the King that he was unable to form a Government, leaving Victor Emmanual with little choice. During the day Mussolini was contacted again, and that evening he caught the night train from Milan to become Prime Minister of Italy.

On 30 October the bedraggled columns of blackshirts, their numbers swelled by the scent of triumph, were allowed into Rome. There were some outbreaks of violence – 13 deaths were reported from the working class San Lorenzo district – but in general, the army prevented trouble. The blackshirts marched past the King on the balcony of his palace and then past Mussolini outside his hotel. Their 'March on Rome' had gone ahead, but it was of little significance. Mussolini had taken power at the end of a telephone while they were waiting around.

5 ⌁ POLITICAL HISTORY 1922–39

A *The consolidation of power*

Mussolini took power in the same way that many of his predecessors as Prime Minister had done, as the leader of a coalition of Fascists, Catholics, right-wingers and even Social Democrats. However, he did not intend that he should continue to follow in their footsteps, either in length of service or as part of a coalition.

His first steps towards establishing greater power were taken in November 1922. On the 16 November the Chamber gave him a vote of confidence by 306 votes to 116 in a massive reversal of his previous fortunes and on the 25th the King gave him dictatorial power to restore order and introduce reforms. As this power was due to last only until 31 December 1923, Italians could still believe that they were living in a constitutional democracy, since after that date Mussolini's Government would again be accountable to parliament.

However, 1923 saw the further erosion of constitutional government. In January the Fascist squads were transformed into the 'MVSN', a volunteer militia for national security, which took its oath to the state, and not to the King, as its predecessor, the now disbanded Royal Guard, had. This provided Mussolini with what amounted to a private army of 300 000. Throughout the year, there were changes of personnel in key jobs, like the police force, the prefectures and local government, while in March a new group of senators, including several leading Fascists like De Bono, was created.

Then in November, a month before the emergency powers expired, the Accerbo electoral law was debated. It was brought before parliament rather than introduced by decree because of its importance and because it affected parliament's composition. While it was debated black-shirted troops strolled ostentatiously around the building, armed with pistols and daggers.

By this law, the party that received the highest number of votes in an election, provided that it won at least 25 per cent of the votes, would automatically receive two-thirds of the seats in the Chamber, while the rest of the seats would be divided proportionally. In theory, it would put an end to the succession of weak coalition Governments that had for so long plagued Italian politics, and for this reason it was supported by parliamentarians like Giolitti and Salandra. In practice, since it was the blackshirts and the Ministry of the Interior that ran elections, it gave massive power to the Fascist party.

The elections of April 1924 showed just this. A number of right wing and liberal politicians, such as Orlando and Salandra, joined the Fascist electoral alliance, thereby adding respectability to the movement. The Communist Party attempted to organise a united opposition alliance but the other parties suspected it of underhand methods, so that there were six different opposition groups. In the election, the Fascists and their supporters won some two-thirds of the votes (4.5 million) and the divided opposition one-third (2.5 million).

With such a majority, it was not only hard to prevent Mussolini and the Fascists doing as they liked, but also it provided the King with an excuse to take no action against the Fascists, whatever they did. After all, had not the people shown their overwhelming support for them?

The murder of Giacomo Matteotti on 10 June 1924 at first threatened Mussolini's power but was then used to further consolidate it. Matteotti was a Socialist deputy who had openly criticised Fascism in a book, *The Fascists Exposed*, in which he gave details of case histories and acts of violence by the blackshirts. In the Chamber, he asked why it was that the Fascists were proud of the fact that Italians alone were incapable of running their own affairs and had to be ruled by force. Shortly afterwards, he was murdered by the Fascists, with the most obvious complicity of the leadership. The moment to question Mussolini's leadership seemed to have arrived. The King again refused to act, seeing that the only possible alternative was Socialism, which he disliked and which would lead to violence. Some politicians, but few of the leaders like Giolitti or Orlando, led by Ancola, who made a final 40 minute speech listing the crimes of Fascism (he too was murdered in 1925), walked out of the Chamber and set up their own assembly. This was known as the 'Aventine Secession'.

Mussolini himself denied all knowledge of Matteotti's murder and dismissed all those remotely implicated. Having done so, he turned on the opposition, introducing press censorship on 1 July and banning

> **KEY ISSUE**
>
> *How was Mussolini able to consolidate his power after the March on Rome?*

> **KEY ISSUES**
>
> *What was the significance of Matteotti's murder?*

Government supporters		Opposition parties	
Fascists	375	Popolari	39
Independent Liberals	15	Reformists	24
Social Democrats	10	Socialists	22
Peasant Party	4	Communists	19
	404	Sardinians	2
	107	Dissident Fascist	1

TABLE 32 *The 1924 Chamber*

meetings by all opposition parties on 3 August. When the deputies who had walked out tried to return to parliament in 1926 they were told that they had forfeited their seats by 'an unconstitutional and clearly revolutionary secession'. What might have been a genuine opportunity to attack Mussolini's position turned out to be no more than a momentary setback.

From then on, it became increasingly difficult to oppose the Fascist regime. In 1925, the *Legge Fascistissime* was passed, by which further press controls were imposed, Freemasonry and other secret organisations forbidden and local government controlled through Fascist appointed *podestas*. The constitution was altered by a new fundamental law, by which the Prime Minister became Head of State and responsible only to the King, and not to the Chamber. This position was made unchallengeable by the law of 31 January 1926 by which government by decree (by Mussolini) was authorised, thus destroying any existing myth of constitutional democracy. Over 100 000 decree laws were to be enacted in the next 17 years.

A new electoral law was brought in in May 1928 by which universal suffrage was abolished and the franchise restricted to those over twenty-one who paid taxes of more than 100 *lire*. The electorate was reduced from 10 million to 3 million. In elections, the names of potential candidates would be submitted by unions and employers to the Fascist Grand Council, which would then choose 400 candidates. Their names would then be submitted to the electorate which would either support or reject the whole 400. The first election held on these terms was in March 1929. Surprisingly, 136 000 voted against the listed candidates, but the remaining 2 864 000 voters were obedient to the cause. By the 1930s, *Il Duce* (The Leader), as Mussolini now called himself, was unstoppable.

Why was there so little opposition to Mussolini?:

● many Italians had considerable reason to like him. After all, had he not brought them stability, money, jobs and a new pride in their country? And if they were among his supporters, did they not get a uniform, a belief in something and even entertainment? As Albertini, a Liberal senator, said: 'Mussolini has given the government freshness, youth and vigour, and has won favour at home and abroad ... . He has saved Italy from the Socialist danger which has been poisoning our life for 20 years'

● even abroad he was admired. Winston Churchill, after an hour's interview in 1927, spoke highly of him and Lloyd George admired the Corporate State

● such parliamentary opposition as there was, was divided and weak. Many of the old-style liberals, who had generally provided the ministries from 1870 to 1922, readily confessed that he seemed better able to govern the country than they had been. These political leaders failed to oppose him until it was too late, and then too ineffectively. Giolitti and Orlando only joined the opposition in November 1924, while Nitti had taken refuge in Paris in 1923

● the rest of the opposition generally regarded each other as more of a threat than Fascism. Reformist Socialists vied with the majority Socialists, while both were suspicious of the Communists. When they did act collectively – in the Aventine secession – they merely provided the King with an excuse to ignore appeals against Mussolini on the grounds that the Chamber gave no lead.

For those who did oppose Mussolini the penalties were severe. There were several assassination attempts – three in 1926 alone. Mussolini's person was then declared inviolable and the death penalty was used even for contemplating an attempt on his life. For anyone considered a possible opponent, there was, in the first instance, the unofficial action of the squads, whose treatment ranged from the standard dose (one litre) of castor oil, to eating live toads in public or having one's head shaved and painted in the national colours.

KEY ISSUE

What methods did the Fascists use to reinforce Mussolini's dictatorship?

There was an enormous police force which included the *OVRA* or secret police. Known enemies of the regime, if left alive, were kept under surveillance in remote villages, or sent to the camps on the Lipari islands. The most notable active opponent was Carlo Roselli, who was stirred into action by Matteotti's murder. After escaping from the Lipari Islands, he edited the leading opposition paper *Justice and Liberty* from Paris, where there were a number of voluntary exiles. Roselli, though, after a brief excursion to the Spanish Civil War in 1936, was assassinated.

It is difficult to gauge the true measure of opposition to the regime, which was efficient at disguising it, as this description illustrates:

'The crowds which cheered Mussolini's speeches in Tuscany and Lombardy last summer are quoted as evidence of his popularity among the masses; the reports did not mention that 15 train-loads of blackshirts followed him to swell the ranks and overawe the crowd, that workshops were closed and the men driven to his meetings under pain of dismissal, that his arrival at each town was preceded by the arrest of suspects by the hundred.'

B *Fascism in theory and practice*

The Manifesto of the Fascist Party of 6 June 1919 and the programme adopted by the Fascist Party Conference at Rome in November 1921 throw interesting light on the programmes and ideas of the Party.

In 1919, the Party's political and economic proposals were radical and socialist:

● the monarchy was to be abolished and a constituent assembly called to draw up a new constitution
● the workers were to be brought into industrial management and a wealth tax to be introduced
● Church property was to be confiscated
● an 85 per cent tax was to be levied on war profiteers.

These proposals were clearly left wing, while the party's foreign policy was openly nationalist. Like Hitler's, Mussolini's first declaration of principles was a mixture of Socialism and nationalism.

Why did Fascism triumph in Italy?

Historians have disagreed over the reasons for the eventual triumph of Mussolini and Fascism. Some could not understand how a supposedly liberal state like pre-war Italy had succumbed to such a regime, although it was easy to forget the corruption that had existed in the old political system, and the political, economic and social problems that had dogged Italy since unification. However, some writers, such as the Marxist Antonio Gramsci, did blame the old liberal Governments, which, they claimed, had done little to give the ordinary people a real stake in pre-war Italy. This view was echoed by some non-Marxist historians like the British Denis Mack Smith, who also emphasised the shallow roots of democracy in Italy. He also pointed out that the old liberal Governments had neglected the needs of ordinary people. This, coupled with the hostility of the Catholic Church, and disillusionment heightened by dashed expectations from the war, presented great opportunities to a movement which had the advantage over its opponents in being prepared to adopt any tactics, legal or illegal, to seize power. Mussolini learned the potential of a strategy which involved helping to promote disorder, and then claiming to have the only remedy for restoring order, namely, the coming to power of his own supporters.

However, the party programme of 1921 was very different. There were no proposals about the constitution, no wealth tax mentioned, no attack on the Church ('the freedom of the Church must be guaranteed') and the representation of the workers was to be restricted to 'personnel matters' only.

Two years later, when in power, the Fascists halved death duties and ended a commission of enquiry into war profiteers. In other words, Mussolini had discovered that the appeal of his party was not to the working class, but to men of property, who owned something and were frightened by talk of revolution. Fascists therefore posed as the defenders of this property and had, apparently, become conservative nationalists.

Neither Mussolini nor his supporters attached much importance to political manifestos. As Mack Smith has written:

KEY ISSUE

How consistent were Fascist policies?

Fascist policy was built up by a wholesale borrowing of ideas, the intention being to make the regime look progressive and yet sound. Measures and ideas did not need to be consistent, so long as they were popular, showy, easy to administer, preferably non-committal, and pre-digested enough to need no extra thought or definition.

In his first speech to the Chamber as Prime Minister, Mussolini told the deputies that there was no lack of programmes, but rather a lack of the will to put those programmes into action. This, then, was Mussolini's promise – action, not words, by a man strong enough to implement them. Hence Fascist propaganda concentrated not on what they were going to do about the economy, the constitution or whatever, but on the strength and power of the party and its leader. The result was pictures of Mussolini working in the fields, Mussolini's 'hypnotic stare' and his autobiography with its emphasis on virility and the ability to 'will' things to happen. Mack Smith again summarised this:

... any reception in Mussolini's gigantic marble study was always carefully staged to humble the visitor. His most important quality was that of being a stupendous poseur. His mixture of showmanship and vulgarity appealed to the common people, who liked to hear of his adulterous relationships and illegitimate children because he then became more human and virile. They were not allowed to know about his ill health or use of eyeglasses, and foreign journalists would be expelled if they mentioned his ulcer, let alone if they hinted at syphilis.

PICTURE 22 'Il Duce'.
Mussolini as he liked to be seen

Consequently, historians cannot expect to see in Mussolini's Italy a clear-cut programme being put into action. As Hitler was to promise simply to make Germans proud and employed, so Mussolini promised only to make Italy great again.

Once the Fascist Party was established in power, there was little that could be strictly described as 'political policy', since most of what needed to be done to make Italy great lay in the economic or imperial sphere. There was, however, a spate of legislation in the period 1936–8. As Mussolini became increasingly under Hitler's influence, a number of Nazi-style measures were introduced in Italy. Hitler returned to Germany from a visit to Italy in 1937 promising that he would 'Prussianise Italy'. Soon afterwards the Italian army began marching the goose-step (renamed the *passo Romano* or Roman step), although, as Marshal De Bono pointed out to the *Duce*, it was not best suited to make Italian soldiers look fearsome, as their average height was only 5'4" (1.6 m).

The following year saw the introduction of anti-Semitic laws, by which foreign Jews were barred from Italian schools, all Jews who arrived in Italy after 1919 were to leave within six months, Jewish teachers lost their jobs and marriage between Italians and Jews was forbidden. These laws were enforced despite the fact that there were only 56 000 Jews in Italy (0.1 per cent of the population), many of whom were members of the Fascist Party. It was not surprising that Hitler referred to Mussolini as his 'Italian *gauleiter*'.

C *Relations with the Church*

The Lateran Treaties of 11 February 1929 were a major achievement of Mussolini's Government, since they ended the long-standing hostility of the papacy to the united kingdom of Italy. The actual Lateran Treaty restored to the Pope the right to rule over the 108.7 acres of the Vatican City, an area carved out of the centre of Rome, in full sovereignty; there was to be no challenge to any laws or powers he might create within the boundaries of that City. Previously, he had had all his temporal power – that is, his right to rule as a king over an area, as opposed to his spiritual power over men's hearts and minds – removed.

> **KEY ISSUE**
>
> *How significant were the Lateran Treaties for Church–State relations?*

Added to the treaty was a 'Concordat', or agreement, which theoretically defined the role of the Church in the Fascist State. Catholicism was to be the state religion, Church marriages were to be recognised as legal by the State, and religious instruction was to be given in both primary and secondary schools. For its part, the papacy gave up any claims to rule temporally over any area beyond the Vatican City, and agreed that the State could object to any bishop or archbishop on political grounds. To seal the agreement, the papacy was paid 750 million *lire* in cash and 1000 million *lire* in government bonds.

In theory, the agreements should have been a triumph for both sides. For the Pope, it gained a restoration of temporal power, albeit limited, a large amount of money and an important place for the

Church in society, as a result of its continued importance in education and religion. For the Fascists, it won international prestige as the only Government which could solve a 60-year-old dispute, and it won the support of traditional Catholics who had been opposed to all constitutional Governments of Italy.

In fact, relations between the two did not remain friendly. It soon became obvious that the agreements about marriage, education and the appointment of bishops were merely conveniences to win over the Pope, and in fact the State did much as it liked. Pius XI did his best to reassert the role of the Church in education, as it came more and more under the wing of the Fascists. In 1931, a Catholic youth organisation, *Catholic Action*, was set up, and through this the Church was able to wield some influence over the young. Ultimately, however, the Church did benefit from the 1929 arrangements, for they at least protected it from the kind of persecution that Hitler meted out to its German counterpart.

D *Education and leisure*

At first, Italian schools maintained considerable freedom over their curricula and methods. The 1923 Education Act stressed the importance of a humanist education and suggested that philosophy be taught at all levels. Thereafter Mussolini stressed the need for reforms of a Fascist nature with more emphasis on discipline and loyalty to the State, less on individual differences.

To these ends there were several educational reforms:

● 'Fascist culture' became a compulsory subject, and mixed schools were ended

● textbooks came under the scrutiny of the Party. History, in particular, suffered. In 1926, 101 out of 317 history texts were banned, and in 1936 a single history textbook became compulsory. Dates started at 1922 (*anno primo*) and the section on World War I described how Italy had saved Britain and America from imminent defeat. Introductory reading books were also suitable cases for treatment, as these extracts from books for eight-year-olds illustrate:

> The eyes of the Duce are on every one of you. No one can say what is the meaning of that look on his face. It is an eagle opening its wings and rising into space.
>
> How can we ever forget that Fascist boy who, when near to death, asked that he might put on his uniform and that his savings should go to the party?

Even so, results were not what they might have been, for the 1931 census still reported 20 per cent illiteracy (48 per cent in Calabria), while the 1936 census gave no figures on this at all.

Equally, children's leisure time was considered an important area for Fascist activity, and in 1926 a youth organisation, the *Balilla*, was founded. The movement's symbols were the book and the rifle and new members took its oath, '... to follow the orders of the *Duce* and to serve the cause of the Fascist revolution with all my might, and, if necessary, with my blood.' The organisation also had a creed, which ran as follows:

> I believe in Rome the Eternal, the mother of my country, and in Italy her eldest daughter, who was born in her virginal bosom by the grace of God; who suffered through the barbarian invasions, was crucified and buried, who descended to the grave and was raised from the dead in the nineteenth century, who ascended into heaven in her glory in 1918 and 1922, who is seated on the right hand of her mother Rome; who for this reason shall come to judge the living and the dead. I believe in the genius of Mussolini, in our Holy Father Fascism, in the communion of martyrs, in the conversion of Italians and in the resurrection of the Empire.

The *Balilla* was only for boys. Girls joined the 'Little Italian Girls'. Then, as the *Child's Guide to Fascism* explains:

> From the age of eight to fourteen the boy as a member of the *Balilla* is trained both physically and morally; on reaching fourteen he passes into the *Avanguardisti*, while as a youth of 18 he can take his place with the Fascist Levy in the ranks of the National Fascist Party.

The leisure-time of adults was considered equally important, for when not at work they might be tempted to think about or even criticise the

Interpretations of Mussolini and Fascism

Historians of Fascist Italy have had a natural interest in examining this period in a broader context, for example considering the extent to which Mussolini's Italy was a model for other varieties of European Fascism, or the extent to which Fascism can be divorced from the personality of Mussolini himself. Liberal Italian historians, even whilst Fascism was still in control, were anxious to emphasise that Fascism in Italy was a 'mistake', born mainly out of post-war problems in 1918, rather than reflecting some flaw in the Italian character. Exponents of this view had an optimistic view of Italian development that emphasised Italy's progress towards becoming a modern parliamentary democracy, a progress rudely shattered, or at least interrupted by, the disruption of war and the apparent threat of Socialist Revolution which made Fascism acceptable to people who in more 'normal' times would not have been seduced by such an extreme movement.

One of the more controversial interpretations was that of the Italian historian Renzo De Felice, who published a massive several volume biography of Mussolini between the 1960s and the 1990s. Unlike the British historian Denis Mack Smith, who tended to emphasise Mussolini's opportunism and reliance on propaganda, De Felice appeared to take more seriously Mussolini's ambitions to be a statesman with the mission of restoring Italy's greatness. De Felice believed that Mussolini's regime did essentially rest upon consent, at least before World War II, and he was anxious to distinguish between Fascism and German Nazism. For example, De Felice argued that Mussolini's foreign policy was relatively moderate, and that his alliance with Hitler was purely tactical.

Not surprisingly, this approach was criticised by many other historians. Probably the more conventional view of Mussolini and his regime was that of Mack Smith, who tended to interpret Fascism in terms of the inadequacies of the unification process in Italy, a process which had left behind many unsolved problems. Mussolini the opportunist appeared to give Italians hope, but ultimately anything he achieved was superficial and short-term.

Most historians, whatever their interpretations of Mussolini's role, accept that the differences between Nazism and Italian Fascism were at least as great as the similarities: for example, for all Mussolini's wish to make the Italians 'great', and the fact that Italy adopted some of Hitler's anti-Semitic policies, race was never an important part of Fascist philosophy. The German-Jewish historian G. Mosse recalled travelling through Italy by train in 1936, in order to emphasise the differences:

Every train had a *carabiniere* on it with a machine gun. The people in my compartment were telling anti-Mussolini jokes. The *carabiniere* of course walked up and down the train corridor and

I, coming from a German ambience, was terrified. But what happened in the end was that the *carabiniere* came into the compartment, not to arrest us, but to tell other Mussolini jokes ... Such an episode could never have happened in Germany.

Extract from *Nazism: A Historical and Comparative Analysis of National Socialism* by G Mosse (1978). Copyright © (1978) by Transaction Publishers. Reprinted by permission of Transaction Publishers.

regime. To avoid this, the *Dopolavoro* organisation was founded. This was an umbrella organisation for recreation, and in 1932 it controlled 1350 theatres, 8265 libraries, 2208 dramatic societies, 3324 brass bands and 2139 orchestral societies. It also organised holiday cruises, authorised football referees (under the chief referee with his gold whistle) and licensed players. Even the Olympic Games Committee had to be affiliated to the Party, while in 1939 the Italian lawn tennis association ordered its international players to wear the Fascist uniform and make the Fascist salute when their opponents offered to shake hands.

6 ↪ ECONOMIC HISTORY

The Italian economy was reorganised by Mussolini to increase the influence of the State without destroying capitalism. Since Mussolini discovered that his support came from those with property and wealth (rather than, as he originally expected, those *without*), his economic policy had to satisfy them. At the same time he realised the need for increased state intervention if the economy were to make any real progress.

The economy was therefore organised into what was known as the 'Corporate State'. Each occupation was to form two syndicates, one for workers and one for employers, which would meet both separately and jointly to create agreements on wages, hours and conditions of work, rights of dismissal and the like. Such agreements would be binding on both sides and thus, hopefully, put an end to the appalling record of wage disputes that had so beset the Italian economy both before and after World War I. To further this end, the Vidoni Palace Pact of 1925 forbade strikes.

In all, there were 21 separate categories of syndicate for trade and industry. All metal workers, for example, were grouped in the ninth category while the sugar beet industry was represented by the fifth category. A 22nd category was set up to represent professional people and artists. Each of the syndicates was under the control of a representative of the Fascist Party, and all were under the Ministry of Corporations founded in 1926 with Mussolini himself as Minister.

In 1930, a National Council of Corporations was set up, wherein workers, employers and the Party were represented. The Council was to plan, regulate and control production. In 1933, Mussolini announced plans for it to become a legislative assembly to replace the Chamber so that the laws of the country would be determined by representatives of the economic interests directly, rather than by political representatives of those economic interests. The Corporate State and its development were closely studied by other European Powers, who seriously saw it as an alternative to total state control, with its links to Communism, and the wayward boom and bust nature of capitalism.

KEY ISSUE

What were the principal features of the Corporate State?

The Corporate State had both advantages and disadvantages for Italy and Italians. Certainly, the workers lost their right to free collective bargaining, and the use of the strike as a weapon in this. Equally, the chaos of the post-war years was avoided. Close state control helped to save the *lire* from devaluation after the Wall Street Crash. Instead, Mussolini simply ordered all workers to take a cut in wages. On the other hand, the new system created an enormous and often-inefficient bureaucracy, which may have helped to ease unemployment, but cost a great deal for what it achieved. The *Economist* commented in 1935:

'The new corporative state only amounts to the establishment of a new and costly bureaucracy, from which those industrialists who can spend the necessary amount can obtain almost anything they want, and put into practice the worst kind of monopolistic practices at the expense of the little fellow who is squeezed out in the process.'

Equally, corruption increased as time went on. Even mock factories were built in order to get a state subsidy, while Mussolini's friend with interests in the Carrara marble mines made a healthy profit from the new public building programme.

In the field of agriculture, Mussolini's economic policy achieved much:

- the great propaganda campaign, the 'Battle for Grain', featured pictures of the *Duce* in the fields or at the wheel of a tractor and on 21 April, which was made into a public holiday to rival May Day, he distributed gold, silver and bronze stars to the most productive farmers. New land, notably the Pontine Marshes and the Volturno Valley, was brought under cultivation
- the overall result was that the production of wheat increased by 50 per cent between 1922 and 1930 and doubled in the whole period 1922–39, so that wheat imports could be reduced by 75 per cent between 1925 and 1935. Even so, wheat remained the third largest import, with over 500 million *lire* being spent on it in 1933, while the cost remained high because of the subsidies to farmers. In addition, much of the marginal land given over to wheat production was not actually suitable for it (e.g. hillside terraces) and would have been better suited to olives or fruit
- little attempt was made to alter the traditional pattern of landholding so that a small number of very wealthy landowners remained in control of a huge number of very poor labourers. In 1930, about 15 families held a total of over one million acres, while more than half of the land cultivated was owned by less than 20 000 estates.

Nonetheless, considering Italy's backwardness up to this time, some credit must be given to Mussolini's agricultural policy.

Something was also done for Italian industry:

● at first, industry was left in private hands though it was encouraged and partly controlled by the State through subsidies. The Fiat Company, for example, produced 80 per cent of Italian cars, and involved itself in mining, cement, smelting and the newspaper business. Electrification, subsidised by the Government, proceeded apace, increasing fivefold between 1917 and 1942. Modern industries, notably the Edison Electric Company, Montecatini Chemicals and the Pirelli Rubber Company, also thrived, while new oil refineries were built at Bari and Leghorn

● in 1933, the Institute for the Reconstruction of Industry was set up and the State took over direct control of many banks and heavy industries, in an attempt to help the economy through the depression. As with agriculture, much was achieved but Italian industry still remained comparatively backward. Table 33 illustrates the dependence on imported raw materials and the failure to export industrial products, except for textiles.

Communications were greatly encouraged by the Fascist State, partly because of their prestige value. The well-known boast of Mussolini that he had at least made the trains run on time was supported by the electrification of 5000 kilometres of railway. The building of the mighty *autostrade* (motorways), carving their way through mountains and over valleys, was also encouraged, though many minor roads were neglected as a result. This was a good example of priority being given to a project that could be used for military purposes, and could be seen by all the world, taking priority over what was most beneficial economically. Two mighty ocean liners – the *Rex* and the *Count of Savoy* – were also built to ensure that Italy could hold her own in international shipping. Equally, great pride was taken in the achievements of Major de Bernardi, who set world speed records in a Macchi seaplane powered by a Fiat motor in 1927 and 1928.

Another aspect of Mussolini's economic policy was the 'Battle for Births', launched in 1927. Mussolini was convinced that a populous nation was a powerful nation and pointed to Germany before the Great War as an example. He therefore determined to increase the population to 60 million, from 37 million in 1920. To this end, high taxes were introduced for bachelors and prizes were given to the most prolific

TABLE 33 *Main Italian imports and exports 1933*

Imports (in million lire)		Exports (in million lire)	
Raw cotton	737	Fruit and garden produce	1091
Coal and coke	685	Raw and artificial silk	820
Wheat	504	Cotton fabrics and yarn	676
Machinery	365	Cheese	241
Wool	361		

mothers. 93 of those who had between them produced 1300 children received the *Duce*'s personal congratulations in 1933.

The net reproduction rate (the number of live births per every thousand women of childbearing age) did rise, reaching 1.131 in 1935–7. However, in 1932 there were less than one million live births in Italy for the first time since 1876, and by 1940 the population had only reached 43.8 million. Much of this increase was due to a decline in emigration, mainly the result of a change in policy by the American authorities. In 1920, 350 000 Italians had emigrated to America; in 1921 the USA introduced limits on immigration and by 1924 only 4000 Italians went to the USA each year.

The major trend in population was the shift to the cities from the countryside. The population of Rome increased between 1921 and 1931 from 690 000 to over one million. It is equally notable, though, that the shift in population led primarily to an increase in bureaucrats and professional people, rather than industrial workers, for heavy industry remained backward throughout the period, as Table 34 illustrates.

Although, therefore, both agriculture and industry were improved under Mussolini's rule, Italy remained well down in world terms. In addition:

- like his predecessors, Mussolini did nothing to solve the traditional problems of the Italian economy – the dualism and the overwhelming poverty of the south. If anything, his policies accentuated the dualism

See page 157

- as the depression lifted, the emphasis in the economy shifted to military and semi-military production, primarily to help with the imperial missions described below, but in the process disrupting the normal growth of the economy.

	1900	*1918*	*1930*	*1940*	
(a) Pig iron output (annual production in million tons)					
Italy	–	0.3	0.5	1.0	
USA	14	39.7	32.3	43	(world leader)
Germany	8.5	11.9	9.7	13.9	(European leader)
Belgium	1.0	–	3.4	1.8	
Luxembourg	1.0	1.3	2.5	1.0	
(b) Steel output (annual production in million tons)					
Italy	0.1	0.3	0.5	1.0	
USA	10.4	45.2	41.4	60.8	
Germany	6.6	15.0	11.5	19.0	
Belgium	0.7	–	3.4	1.9	
France	1.6	1.8	9.4	4.4	

TABLE 34
Italy's place in the world economy 1900–40

7 ⌐ FOREIGN POLICY 1922–39

A *European policies 1922–35*

'My objective is simple, I want to make Italy great, respected and feared', said Mussolini, thus providing the only real guidelines to his aims in foreign policy. Italy's humiliation in and after World War I, and the nationalist wave on which he climbed to power, were bound to make for a nationalist foreign policy, wherein any available means would be used to demonstrate Italy's return to greatness. He did, however, face the traditional problems of Italian foreign policy of powerful and hostile northern neighbours.

See page 158

KEY ISSUE

What were Mussolini's aims in foreign policy?

Although Mussolini would never have admitted this to be a problem, it did require him to protect his country against possible French or German hostility, which involved the subsidiary aim of securing influence in the Balkans to ensure that he could at least balance the influence of these potential enemies there. As these first two aims were, to some extent, achieved during the 1920s, Italian foreign policy became increasingly expansionist in the 1930s, aiming not only at control of the Mediterranean, but also at an African empire.

Italy's 'renewed greatness' was first demonstrated soon after Mussolini became Prime Minister. In August 1923 General Enrico Tellini and four other Italians on his staff were assassinated while working for the boundary commission of the Conference of Ambassadors – a body set up to complete the detailed territorial arrangements of the treaties of 1919 – on the border of Greece and Albania, while actually in Greece.

Without waiting for further news or explanation, Mussolini demanded from the Greek Government a full apology and 50 million *lire* compensation. Greece appealed to the League of Nations, which referred the matter to the Conference of Ambassadors. In the meantime, on 31 August, as soon as the Greeks had rejected Italy's demands, Mussolini ordered his navy to bombard the island of Corfu, on which marines were then landed. The Conference of Ambassadors tried to push Greece into apologising and, if a commission of enquiry found evidence to support Italy's claim that the assassins were Greek, pay the compensation. Under pressure from Britain, Mussolini agreed on 27 September to withdraw his forces and in exchange received the 50 million *lire*.

The exercise had not been wholly successful; for example, Italy had responded to pressure from the Conference of Ambassadors and had not received the full apology. But the Italian press made much of it as the triumphant return of Italy to the international scene as a nation that got its way.

During the 1920s Mussolini was also able to secure influence in, and prestige from, the Balkans. In 1924 the Pact of Rome was signed with Yugoslavia, by which Italy received the long-disputed town of Fiume, though a part of it, the suburb of Susak, went to Yugoslavia, along with Port Barros. Two treaties with Albania, in 1926 and 1927, firmly established Italian influence, which was extended thereafter by loans, military agreements and arrangements for Italy to receive Albanian oil.

This marked the first stage in Mussolini's efforts to establish Italy in the Balkans, where the 'Little *Entente*' of Czechoslovakia, Romania and Yugoslavia was so closely tied to France, Italy's likely enemy .

See page 281

Further to this end, and in order to maintain an independent state between himself and his other possible enemy (Germany), Mussolini cultivated the friendship of Austria and Hungary. In 1927 a treaty of friendship was signed with Hungary and in 1930 a similar treaty with Austria. Relations with Austria became even closer after Hitler came to power in Germany, and it was Mussolini who provided the arms and money for the Austrian Chancellor's private army, the *Heimwehr.*

In March 1934 Mussolini achieved his objective of creating a counter to the French-backed 'Little *Entente*' with the signing of the Rome Protocols, when Dollfuss of Austria and Gömbös of Hungary visited Rome. The Protocols arranged for increased trade links and a common foreign policy between Italy, Austria and Hungary. Shortly afterwards, in July 1934, Mussolini's Austrian policy was put to the test when Dollfuss was murdered by Nazis. Mussolini acted quickly, sending troops to the border with Austria as an obvious threat to Hitler not to intervene. When Hitler backed down, Mussolini could claim a minor triumph. The friendship of Bulgaria was also cultivated, reaching a peak in 1929 when the daughter of King Victor Emmanuel, Princess Giovanna, married King Boris.

During the 1920s Mussolini realised that he could not yet attempt to have the Versailles settlement revised in his favour and needed the friendship (or at least an absence of hostility) of France and Britain. Therefore in 1925 he went to Locarno and signed the treaties guaranteeing the Franco-German and Belgo-German frontiers, and in 1928 was a signatory of the Kellogg-Briand Pact.

KEY ISSUE

How successful was Mussolini's foreign policy before 1935?

In particular, he drew closer to Britain, seeing it as a possible friend in any future conflict, though privately resolving to end British power in the Mediterranean. Agreement was reached over the frontier between Libya and Egypt, and discussions were held on the possibility of British aid for railway building in East Africa. During the 1920s, therefore, Italy remained a member of the League of Nations, and acted as a good citizen of Europe.

See page 289

Hitler's advent to power in Germany altered things considerably. Mussolini was delighted to see a fellow traveller in power, and saw the potential of a German alliance against Britain and France to revise the 1919 settlement. On the other hand, he was wary of having Germany too close, that is, in Austria. In April 1933 Göring and Papen visited Rome, but all the visit achieved was German agreement to the Four Power Pact – Mussolini's brainchild to have a pact of the four Great Powers, Italy, Germany, France, Britain to keep the peace in Europe, thus replacing the League. It was only ever signed by Germany and Italy, on 15 July 1933.

Hitler and Mussolini first met in June 1934, in Venice. The meeting got off to a bad start as Hitler had been told that Mussolini would be in civilian clothes. He was therefore infuriated to be welcomed by Mussolini in full dress uniform when he was in a suit. Then Mussolini refused to have an interpreter, despite his German being very poor, so it is likely the meeting meant little to either.

The crisis following the death of Dollfuss a month later worsened things further, so that in 1934–5 Mussolini was far from being an ally of Hitler. Indeed, in April 1935, Mussolini even attended the Stresa Conference, called by France to consider what action to take over German rearmament and to guarantee the independence of Austria. Italy joined the declarations and protests, largely to avoid British and French hostility to Italian imperialism but partly in genuine hostility to Germany.

B *The Abyssinian crisis*

'We have a right to empire as a fertile nation which has the pride and will to propagate its race over the face of the earth, a virile people in the strict sense of the word', said Mussolini.

In the 1920s, the Italian Empire was hardly promising. Libya was territorially the heart of the Empire, but only some 2000 Italians had settled there, and by 1930 it was costing over 500 million *lire* per annum, compared with 107 million in 1921. The two smaller Italian colonies, Eritrea and Italian Somaliland, looked more promising, for they bordered on to Ethiopia (Abyssinia), one of the few remaining independent kingdoms of Africa.

See Map 19 on page 186

During the 1920s, therefore, Italy took a special interest in Abyssinia, sponsoring its membership of the League in 1923 and signing a treaty of friendship in 1928. However, it became clear that the ruler, Haile Selassie, did not intend to allow his country to be dominated by one modern Power, and Mussolini considered the possibility of war to force Abyssinia under Italian control.

Mussolini used the excuse of an incident in December 1934. Some Italians in the border area of Ual-Ual were fired on and killed in December 1934. Mussolini demanded an apology and compensation from Abyssinia. The Abyssinians in turn insisted on an investigation, to which the League of Nations agreed in May 1935. In the meantime, Mussolini made preparations for his attack, both by building up forces and sounding out the attitude of Britain and France. Already, in 1906, Britain and France had agreed that a part of Ethiopia should be a minor sphere of Italian influence. In January 1935, Pierre Laval, the French Foreign Minister, while on a visit to Rome, gave part of French Somaliland to Italy and sold to Italy France's shares in the Abyssinian Railway. Clearly, France was not going to oppose Italy although later Laval claimed he had given his support only to Italy's economic plans, not military ones.

Similarly, the British made no mention of Abyssinia when they met Mussolini for the Stresa Conference in April. In June, Eden, on behalf of the British Government, offered the Abyssinians a corridor to the sea through British Somaliland if they gave Mussolini part of Ogaden, an offer rejected by Mussolini. In the summer, Italian troops arrived in

Eritrea. In July, the League's investigators reported that neither side was to blame for the incident at Ual-Ual since both believed the other was on its territory.

This did not satisfy Mussolini, who continued to make noises about his intentions, as a result of which a meeting between the British, French and Italians was held in Paris on 16 August. At this meeting, Italy was offered the opportunity to develop Abyssinia, provided that the Abyssinians agreed. The Italians rejected the offer, since they were unlikely to get that agreement, and by now Mussolini had decided on war.

On 3 October 1935 Italian troops attacked from Eritrea and on 6 October captured Adowa, thus avenging the defeat of 1896. The next day the Council of the League condemned Italy as the aggressor and arranged for economic sanctions to be imposed on Italy. No arms were to be carried to Italy, and no goods to be bought from it. Oil, coal, iron and steel were all excluded from the ban, and the Suez Canal was not closed to Italian shipping.

See page 158

Nonetheless, the Italian press made much of this 'harsh' measure, and Italians were persuaded to give up their wedding rings and other valuables to provide much-needed cash. By the time the sanctions were brought in on 18 November, the Italian Army was already making progress . Marshal Badoglio reorganised his troops to take advantage of the mountainous countryside and brought in air support and introduced poison gas.

During the winter, Britain and France made various efforts to end the fighting. In December, the British Foreign Secretary, Sir Samuel Hoare, discussed the affair with Laval, his French counterpart. They proposed the partition of Abyssinia, with Italy receiving the northern and southern thirds to add to Eritrea and Italian Somaliland respectively, and a rump state being left in the middle. This was known as the 'Hoare–Laval Pact'.

Before the plan was put to either of the protagonists, the press found out about it. There was a great outcry in both countries, for here were the two leading countries in the League of Nations, which was based on the principle of opposing aggression, prepared to give way to the aggressor country. The plan got no further and on 18 December Hoare resigned, prompting King George V to remark 'No more Hoares to Paris'.

At the same time, a British naval squadron was sent to Alexandria, and France, Greece, Turkey and Yugoslavia all promised to support, diplomatically at least, any action that Britain took against Italy. However, the British were indecisive, for to act against Mussolini was to drive him into the arms of Hitler, and before any action was taken, the attention of Europe was refocused on the Rhineland, wherein Hitler sent his troops in March 1936.

With the rest of Europe far more interested in the *Führer*, the *Duce* proceeded in Abyssinia. In April the Abyssinian Army was heavily defeated at Lake Ashangi, and Haile Selassie fled to Britain, knowing that his country was beaten. On 5 May the Italian Army entered Addis

KEY ISSUE

What was the importance of the Abyssinian crisis for Italy and for European relations generally?

MAP 19
Italy and its Empire

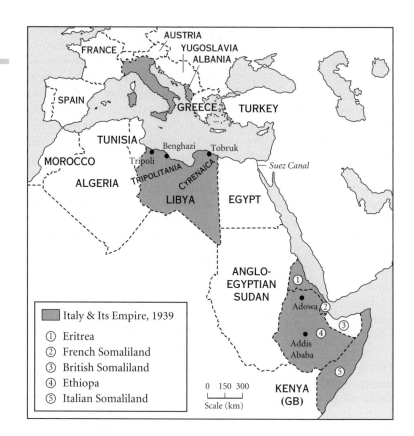

Italy & Its Empire, 1939
① Eritrea
② French Somaliland
③ British Somaliland
④ Ethiopa
⑤ Italian Somaliland

Ababa and four days later Abyssinia was formally annexed and became, with Eritrea and Italian Somaliland, Italian East Africa. The King of Italy became Emperor of Abyssinia. To the *Duce*'s chagrin, only 1537 Italians died in the conquest – not nearly enough for the purposes of national sacrifice or to 'harden the national character'.

The conquest complete, the Italians then began the process of pacification, building forts and roads and suppressing native attacks, on the basis of 'ten eyes for an eye'. On 19 February 1937 the Viceroy, General Graziani, was the subject of a failed assassination attempt, which was followed by a brutal round-up of all possible opponents, including Ras Desta Demtu, the leading native opponent, who was captured and publicly executed. Thereafter, the colony was reasonably peaceful and in 1938 even Britain and France recognised Italy's ownership.

The conquest of Abyssinia was regarded as a major triumph in Italy, ranking alongside the Concordat of 1929. Mussolini had said 'the Italian character has to be formed through fighting', and fighting it had had. Nonetheless, little else was gained, for the party officials and bureaucrats moved in, making the colony as corrupt and profitless as the mother country. In 1939, only 2 per cent of Italy's trade was with its colonies. The Italian population of New York was still 10 times greater than the Italian population of Italian colonies.

C *European policies 1935–39*

When the Spanish Civil War broke out in July 1936, Mussolini immediately provided Franco and the Nationalists with men and equipment, on the grounds that he could not allow a Communist government to be formed in the Mediterranean. At first, volunteers were sent and their presence kept secret, but then a film of the capture of Malaga by the Spanish Fascists was shown in Rome and the audience did not take long to recognise the Italian number-plates!

Italian involvement in Spain was expensive and also produced considerable tension with Britain, as Mussolini was supplying submarines to attack shipping carrying Russian goods in the Mediterranean. As a result British, French, Greek and Danish cargo ships had all been sunk. In 1937 the Nyon Conference was held to discuss patrolling rights and Italy was granted a zone to patrol. This allowed Mussolini to provide Franco with what he required fairly freely. Yet again Britain paid a heavy price in trying to woo Italy away from Germany.

Italy was inevitably drawing closer and closer to Germany. On 25 October 1936, the two agreed to maintain Austria's independence. Mussolini referred to this as the 'Rome-Berlin Axis, around which can revolve all those European states with a will to collaboration and peace'. Thereafter, relations became closer and closer. In September 1937, Mussolini visited Germany, where he was suitably impressed by the massive displays, the 800 000 crowd that applauded him and Hitler's flattery in referring to him as his 'teacher of Fascism'. In November Italy joined the Anti-Comintern Pact, and in December withdrew from the League.

Even the *Anschluss* was not opposed in March 1938. Hitler sent a special envoy, Prince Philip of Hesse, a son-in-law of Victor Emmanuel, to explain his actions to Mussolini. Hitler thanked the latter suitably after Austria had, to the annoyance of many Italians, been swallowed by Germany. In May 1938 Hitler visited Rome and Mussolini, determined to impress, had the houses *en route* whitewashed and 6000 possible opponents arrested. Hitler was not at first impressed, finding the King, with whom he stayed, tiresome, but later mellowed as the navy put on a display in Naples harbour and the crowds roared their approval in Florence.

Again, in September 1938, Mussolini triumphed in Europe when he brought together its leaders at the Munich Conference to settle the Czech crisis without resort to war. Nonetheless, it was increasingly clear that he was little more than Hitler's sidekick.

Partly to correct this impression and show his independence, Mussolini organised the invasion of Albania in April 1939. The invasion had little other purpose since Albania was all but controlled by Italy anyway, but it might show the world that Italy was still a 'virile nation'. In fact, the invasion was a shambles. There was no Albanian army to stop the four divisions of Italian troops, and King Zog fled before they reached the capital, Tirana, which they then proceeded to loot. The Italian press were not even sure whether it was supposed to report that

> **KEY ISSUE**
>
> *How successful was Mussolini's foreign policy between the Abyssinian crisis and the outbreak of World War II?*

See page 310

their men had overcome fearful odds or that they had been welcomed as liberators from the vile dictator Zog.

The chief effect of the episode was to show Mussolini how unprepared he was for a real war. He admitted as much to Göring, who attended Victor Emmanuel's coronation as King of Albania. Nonetheless, in May 1939, apparently infuriated by an American paper's report that Ribbentrop had been booed by a crowd in Milan, he suddenly decided to draw closer still to Germany, and ordered the Foreign Minister, his son-in-law Ciano, to conclude a formal alliance. This treaty, known as the 'Pact of Steel', tied the two so closely that Italy was committed to join Germany in any war, be it aggressive or defensive.

Unknown to Mussolini, German plans for the attack on Poland were already advanced. When Hitler informed him of these plans on 25 August, Mussolini replied that Italy was not ready for war, and when asked what he needed, asked for an enormous quantity of supplies, including 10000 tons of lead and 150 anti-aircraft batteries, enough to ensure Hitler would not want to call on Italy's help. When Poland was invaded, therefore, Mussolini was in a quandary. Italy was not prepared for war, yet 'the Italian character has to be formed by fighting'. He could not admit to being neutral, so he called Italy 'a non-belligerent power' until June 1940, by which time Hitler had convinced him of the need to fight and could see the advantages of using Italian troops in North Africa.

Mack Smith has argued forcibly that Mussolini's foreign policy was inconsistent and haphazard. 'Mussolini's violent changes of policy', he writes, 'were sometimes accepted on his own valuation as brilliant strokes of Machiavellian deceit, part of a superplan which the fullness of time would reveal, but Ciano's diary now confirms that they were rather a pathological symptom. At one moment he vetoed the *Anschluss* and began to fortify the Brenner; at the next he struck an attitude and announced to the world that he was standing beside Germany in shining armour. At one moment he was ranting against Hitler and hoping that the Russians would beat Germany; then in a matter of days he suddenly changed when a recollection of Chamberlain reminded him how contemptible were the pluto-democracies.'

This is perhaps to exaggerate, for Mussolini's policies were consistent in their ends, if not their means. It would, though, be true to say that his policies were extravagant, both literally – by 1939, annual expenditure exceeded income by 28 039 million *lire* – and metaphorically – who else could claim that 'by a single order and in a few hours I can mobilise eight million bayonets'? Incidentally, in June 1940, only one and half million could be mobilised!

Since Mussolini's main aim was to increase his own power, he was ultimately a failure, although it was only Italy's disastrous performance in World War II which brought Fascism down. Even before 1939 the propaganda was more impressive than the substance, and Fascism did not have the efficiency or widespread support to dominate Italian society in the way that its leaders might have hoped. Nor did Italy have the economic or military strength to compete as a Great Power on equal terms with Germany or even Britain and France. Although Mussolini achieved a measure of stability for Italy by remaining in power for over 20 years, he never convinced even his own people that Italy could be a successful world Power, and his alliance with Germany, and even his attempts to emulate Hitler, were ultimately disastrous.

8 ∽ ITALY DURING WORLD WAR II

Mussolini attacked France in June 1940 and Greece in October 1940 in a 'parallel' war to that of Hitler. Neither attack was particularly successful and Germany had to bale out Mussolini in Greece. Mussolini then turned his attention to capturing British Somaliland in August 1940, followed by an attack on Egypt and the Suez Canal. None of these attacks was well planned, but seemed to be simply attempts to pre-empt further German successes. The crippling of the Italian fleet by Britain in the autumn even prevented Italy from securing control of the Mediterranean. By the end of 1940 Italian forces in Libya had been defeated by a much smaller British army; whilst by May 1941 the whole of Italian East Africa was in British hands. Mussolini became increasingly dependent on Hitler's support. He followed Hitler's lead in declaring war on the USA, and provided some Italian troops for the disastrous Russian campaign. Before 1942 was over most Italians were already sick of a war that few had wanted in the first place.

The Allied invasion of Sicily in July 1943 effectively marked the end of Mussolini's power. Some of his own colleagues conspired against him. Mussolini was arrested, and without their leader, few Fascists knew what to do. The King asked Badoglio to form a Government and continue the war. Full of distrust for their unreliable ally, the Germans occupied Italy. The Italian Government announced its surrender in September, as Allied troops invaded the Italian mainland. However, stiff German opposition ensured that the fighting in Italy was to continue well into 1945, even though Italy now fought on the Allied side. Hitler secured Mussolini's rescue in a daring operation, and the wretched *Duce* was installed in North Italy as head of a puppet Fascist state, effectively under German control. In April 1945 Mussolini was captured by Italian partisans fighting on the Allied side, and he was killed without ceremony. However, Mussolini's Fascist regime was already effectively long dead, and although Italy had fought the final stages of the war on the Allied side, its post-war future remained uncertain.

9 ∽ BIBLIOGRAPHY

Useful surveys of the whole period are *Italy: Liberalism and Fascism 1870–1945* by M Robson (Hodder and Stoughton, 1992) and *Italy From Liberalism to Fascism: 1870–1925* by C Seton-Watson (Methuen, 1967). A readable biography is *Benito Mussolini* by C Hibbert (Longmans, 1962). *Fascist Italy* by A Cassells (Routledge, 1969), *Italian Fascism,*

1919–1945 by P Morgan (Macmillan, 1995) and *A History of Italian Fascism* by F Chabod (Cedric Chivers, 1974) are also useful.

Detailed studies include *The Seizure Of Power-Fascism in Italy 1919–1929* by A Lyttelton (Weidenfeld and Nicolson, 1973); *The Italian Dictatorship* by R Bosworth (Arnold 1998); and *Mussolini's Roman Empire* (Penguin paperback, 1976), by D Mack Smith. A useful short study is *Italian Fascism* by Giampiero Carocci (Penguin paperback, 1974); and *Mussolini And Fascist Italy* by M Blinkhorn (Lancaster Pamphlets, Methuen, 1984), is a short and concise book written for students. A good survey for students is *Italy 1915–1940* by P Morgan (Sempringham, 1998).

10 ⌐ STRUCTURED QUESTIONS AND ESSAYS

1. (a) To what extent was Italy a unified state in 1870? (10 marks)
    (b) What achievements did Crispi and Giolitti have as leaders of Italy? (15 marks)
2. To what extent did Italian Governments succeed in solving Italy's problems in the period 1890 to 1914? (25 marks)
3. (a) Explain why Italy entered World War I on the *Entente*'s side in 1915; (10 marks)
    (b) What contribution did Italy make to the *Entente* cause in World War I? (10 marks)
    (c) What did Italy gain from its participation in the war? (10 marks)
4. (a) Explain the meaning of the 'March on Rome' in the context of 1922; (3 marks)
    (b) Explain briefly why Mussolini was able to seize power in 1922; (7 marks)
    (c) To what extent had Mussolini succeeded in establishing a dictatorship in Italy by 1929? (15 marks)
5. (a) Explain the meaning of the Corporate State as it existed in Fascist Italy; (3 marks)
    (b) How successful was Mussolini's economic policy? (7 marks)
    (c) To what extent were Mussolini's policies 'stronger on propaganda than substance'? (15 marks)
6. To what extent had Mussolini succeeded in carrying out his objectives within Italy by 1939? (25 marks)
7. (a) Explain briefly why Italy invaded Abyssinia in 1935; (3 marks)
    (b) Explain why Italy drew closer to Germany in the years between 1935 and 1939; (7 marks)
    (c) How valid is the assessment that Italy's entry into World War II was 'the most crucial mistake in Mussolini's foreign policy'? (15 marks)
8. Did Mussolini bring any lasting benefits to the Italian people? (25 marks)

11 ～ SOURCE-BASED EXERCISE ON FASCIST ITALY

Study the sources below and answer the questions which follow.

SOURCE A
Proclamation by the Quadrumvirate 26 October 1922 (Source: B Mussolini, My Autobiography *(1939)). This was the order given to the Fascists to embark on the March on Rome. The Quadrumvirate was a committee of four generals presided over by Mussolini himself*

Fascisti! Italians!

The time for determined battle has come! Four years ago the National Army loosed at this season the final offensive, which brought it to victory (the battle of Vittorio Veneto). Today the army of the Blackshirts again takes possession of that victory, which has been mutilated, and going directly to Rome brings victory again to the glory of that capital. ... The martial law of Fascism now becomes a fact. By order of the Duce all the military, political and administrative functions of the party management are taken over by a secret Quadrumvirate of Action with dictatorial powers.

The Army, the reserve and Safeguard of the Nation, must not take part in this struggle. Fascism renews its highest homage given to the Army of Vittorio Veneto. Fascism, furthermore, does not march against the police, but against a political class both cowardly and imbecile, which in four long years has not been able to give a Government to the nation. Those who form the productive class must know that Fascism wants to impose nothing more than order and discipline upon the nation and to help to raise the strength which will renew progress and prosperity. The people who work in the fields and in the factories, those who work on the railroads or in offices, have nothing to fear from the Fascist Government. Their just rights will be protected. We will even be generous with unarmed adversaries. Fascism draws its sword to cut the multiple Gordian Knots which tie and burden Italian life. We call God and the spirit of our five thousand dead to witness that only one impulse sends us on, that only one passion burns within us – the impulse and the passion to contribute to the safety and greatness of our country.

Fascisti of all Italy! Stretch forth like Romans your spirits and your fibres! We must win! We will.

Long live Italy! Long live Fascism!

Our programme is simple: we wish to govern Italy. They ask us for programmes, but there are already too many. It is not programmes that are needed for the salvation of Italy, but men and willpower ...

Our political class is deficient. The crisis of the Liberal State has proved it ... We must have a State which will simply say: 'The State does not represent a party, it represents the nation as a whole, it includes all, is over all, protects all.'

SOURCE B
Speech by Mussolini in Udine, September 1922

SOURCE C

*From Mussolini's book
'La Dottrina del Fascismo'
(The Doctrine of Fascism),
1932*

Fascism is today clearly defined not only as a regime but as a doctrine ... Above all, Fascism, in so far as it considers and observes the political considerations of the moment, believes neither in the possibility nor in the utility of perpetual peace. It thus repudiates the doctrine of Pacifism-born of the renunciation of the struggle and an act of cowardice in the face of sacrifice. War alone brings up to their highest tension all human energies and puts the stamp of nobility upon the peoples who have the courage to meet it ...

Such a conception of life makes Fascism the precise negation of that doctrine which formed the basis of so-called Scientific or Marxian Socialism: the doctrine of historical Materialism, according to which the history of human civilisations can be explained only as the struggle of interest between the different social groups and as arising out of changes in the means and instruments of production ... Fascism believes, now and always, in holiness and in heroism, that is in acts in which no economic motive – remote or immediate – plays a part ... and above all it is denied that the class struggle can be the primary agent of social changes ...

After Socialism, Fascism attacks the whole complex of democratic ideologies and rejects them both in their theoretical premises and in their applications ... Fascism denies that the majority, through the mere fact of being a majority, can rule human societies ... it affirms the irremediable, fruitful and beneficent inequality of man ... By democratic regimes we mean those in which from time to time the people is given the illusion of being sovereign ... democracy is a regime without a king, but with very many kings, perhaps more exclusive, tyrannical and violent than one king, even though a tyrant ...

A party that governs a nation in a totalitarian way is a new fact in history. References and comparisons are not possible. Fascism takes over from the ruins of Liberal Socialistic democratic doctrines those elements which still have a living value ... it is to be expected that this century may be that of authority, a century of the 'Right', a Fascist century. If the nineteenth century was the century of the individual, it may be expected that this one may be the century of 'collectivism' and therefore the century of the State ...

For Fascism the State is an absolute before which individuals and groups are relative. Individuals and groups are 'thinkable' in so far as they are within the State ...

The Fascist State organises the nation, but it leaves sufficient scope to individuals; it has limited useless or harmful liberties and has preserved those that are essential. It cannot be the individual who decides in this matter, but only the State.

If every age has its own doctrine, it is apparent from a thousand signs that the doctrine of the present age is Fascism.

SOURCE D
Speech by Mussolini to the Italian General Staff, printed in The Times, *28 August 1934*

It is, therefore, necessary to be prepared for war not tomorrow but today. We are becoming – and we shall become so increasingly because this is our desire-a military nation. A militaristic nation I will add, since we are not afraid of words. To complete the picture, warlike – that is to say, endowed ever to a higher degree with the virtues of obedience, sacrifice, and dedication to country. This means that the whole life of the nation, political, economic, and spiritual, must be systematically directed towards our military requirements. War has been described as the Court of Appeal, but pursue the course dictated by their strength and by their historical dynamic nature, it falls that, in spite of all conferences, all protocols, and all the more or less highest and good intentions, the hard fact of war may be anticipated to accompany human kind in the centuries to come just as it stands on record at the dawn of human history.

Q

Having carefully read and discussed Sources A–D above, answer the following questions.

1. *Compare and contrast these four Sources in terms of tone and what they show of Mussolini's ability as a propagandist.* (10 marks)

2. *What is Mussolini's justification in Source A for the Fascist take-over of power?* (5 marks)

3. *What was there in Sources A and B which might have appealed to many Italians in 1922?* (8 marks)

4. *What can you deduce from Sources B, C and D about the principles of Fascism?* (9 marks)

5. *According to Source C, what was new about Fascism as a political movement?* (6 marks)

6. *Compare the usefulness to an historian of these four Sources as evidence of Fascism as a political creed and system of government.* (12 marks)

KEY ISSUE

*What was the
significance of
the Locarno Treaties?*

See page 289

KEY ISSUE

*How successful was
Stresemann's foreign
policy?*

was accepted as a member of the League. Germany was also given a permanent place on the League's Council. In 1927 the Allied Commission of Military Control left Germany (it had been posted to guard against German rearmament) and the Rhineland occupation forces were reduced by 10 000.

In 1929 Germany signed the Kellogg–Briand Pact and in 1930 the Allies left the Rhineland. Stresemann's policy had achieved much – Germany was once again a free agent in European affairs and there was a good chance of further concessions and revision.

The policy of fulfilment also raised questions. It was generally popular in Germany, although the Nationalists were hostile to anything that smacked of co-operation with the League of Nations, which they regarded as nothing more than an instrument for imposing the terms of the Treaty of Versailles. Others argued that it was not possible to pursue a policy of friendship with both the Western Powers and Russia, and that an alliance with Russia was a more profitable route to treaty-revision in the East.

However, Stresemann has been also criticised for double-crossing. On the one hand he supported a policy of friendship to the Western Powers, willingly accepting their loans, while on the other, he sent men and money into the Soviet Union for military purposes. Given that his aim was treaty revision, he was pursuing his end by the two means best open to him, for the forces in preparation would give Germany the teeth it required to force some concessions.

German preparations in Russia were significant. More than 100 fighter pilots a year were trained, while a tank school was opened at Karma in 1929. A considerable number of men were trained, but little equipment was made; for example, there were only some ten tanks and less than 70 planes available in 1931. Nevertheless, a start had been made, and enough men trained to provide the basis of a fighting force.

THE NAZI STATE 1933–45

1 ⌐ POLITICAL HISTORY

A *The capture and consolidation of power*

It is not possible to speak of Hitler's 'seizure of power', nor of 'the end of the Weimar Republic'. Hitler did not seize power, but was appointed Chancellor, constitutionally, by President Hindenburg. The 'end' of the Weimar Republic can be dated as early as May 1932, when von Papen became Chancellor responsible only to the President, or as late as August 1934, when Hitler became President. On 30 January 1933 Hindenburg appointed Hitler as head of a cabinet that contained only two other Nazis, had a majority of Nationalists, including Hugenberg and Seldte, and was dependent on others for a majority in the *Reichstag*. Hitler's immediate priority was to secure power for himself and the Nazi Party and end the dependence on other parties.

By refusing to co-operate with the Centre Party, Hitler precipitated *Reichstag* elections, which were to be held in March 1933. The election campaign was used to extend Nazi power and influence. Göring, as Prussian Minister of the Interior, recruited 50 000 'police' auxiliaries to assist in the maintenance of law and order. These recruits, most of whom were attached to one of the Nazi private armies, the SA (*Sturm Abteilung*) and the SS (*Schutz Staffel*), had only to don a white arm band to assume authority. Among the orders they received from Göring was the following: 'Police officers who make use of firearms in the execution of their duty will, without regard to the consequences of such use, benefit from my protection: those who, out of a misplaced regard for such consequences, fail in their duty will be punished ... failure to act will be regarded more seriously than an error due to taking action'. The new era had arrived.

On 27 February 1933 the *Reichstag* building in Berlin was burnt to the ground. Hitler blamed it on the Communist Party, and argued that an uprising was planned. President Hindenburg therefore allowed a decree that suspended or adjusted many civil liberties:

> restrictions on personal liberty, on the right of free expression of opinion, including freedom of the press, on the rights of assembly and association; violations of the privacy of postal, telegraphic and telephonic communications ... are permissible beyond the limits otherwise prescribed.

The young Dutchman, van der Lubbe, who started the fire was tried and executed. Many KPD members were arrested and the party's efforts in the elections severely hampered. It was claimed that the fire was a KPD (Communist) plot. Subsequently, it was believed that the Nazis

1933	Hitler appointed Chancellor
	Reichstag Fire
	Last Reichstag elections
	Enabling Law
	Boycott of Jewish shops
	Trade unions dissolved
	Nazis became only legal Party
	German withdrawal from League of Nations
1934	*German–Polish Non-Aggression Pact*
	Night of the Long Knives
	Hitler became Führer
1935	Saar voted for return to Germany
	Conscription reintroduced
	Anglo-German Naval Agreement
	Nuremberg Laws
1936	*Remilitarisation of Rhineland*
	German involvement in Spanish Civil War
	Four-Year Economic Plan
	Rome–Berlin Axis
1938	*Anschluss: annexation of Austria*
	Munich Agreement over Czechoslovakia
	Krystallnacht: action against the Jews
1939	*Occupation of Czechoslovakia*
	Nazi-Soviet Pact
	Invasion of Poland and start of World War II
1941	*Invasion of Russia*
1944	Bomb Plot
1945	Death of Hitler and German surrender

TABLE 38

Date chart of events in Germany 1933–45 (foreign affairs in italics)

in that area. The occupation was, therefore, quite in contrast with Hitler's victory in the Saar. It is important to realise that the move did not involve 'winning' land, or reuniting Germans, for the Rhineland had never been 'confiscated' – it was simply to be kept free of troops.

There seems little doubt that in sending troops there Hitler was testing his enemies. The men he sent were by no means crack divisions and could well have been forced to retreat by a show of strength by the British and French, although Hitler's orders were that they should resist on the Rhine if France moved against them. But France was 'between governments' and was not prepared to act without British backing. The troops went in during the week-end, and the British, as Hitler well knew, were not prepared to act until the Monday, by which time any action would be that much harder.

The eventual reaction was as Hitler had hoped. There were official protests followed by debate about the validity of the original treaty terms that banned German forces from a part of their own country. These seeds of doubt about the morality of the Versailles settlement were to prove invaluable to Hitler.

See page 187

While progressing towards the achievement of one aim, the renunciation of Versailles, Hitler continued to prepare himself for others by the formation of alliances and agreements with friends and neighbours. On 11 July, he agreed to respect Austrian independence in return for 'policy befitting a German state'. On 25 October, following the visit of the Italian Foreign Minister, Ciano, to Berlin, the Rome–Berlin Axis was signed. On 18 November Hitler recognised Franco's regime in Spain and a week later signed the Anti-Comintern Pact with Japan, technically an agreement to join together to stop the spread of Communism, but in effect an extension of the alliance with Italy, since Italy joined the Pact in November 1937.

With these allies at his side, Hitler seemed increasingly invincible, especially in view of the continued isolationism of the United States and the position of the Soviet Union. Britain and France realised the difficulty of their position, and in 1937 Lord Halifax visited Berlin in the hope of discovering Germany's objectives and suggesting a peaceful settlement, while France tried to strengthen the resolve of its eastern allies (Poland, Romania, Yugoslavia and Czechoslovakia).

See pages 151 and 310

After 1937, Hitler achieved each of his first three aims before 1939, while his efforts to achieve the fourth – *Lebensraum* – led to the outbreak of war in September 1939. In March 1938 he succeeded in uniting Germany and Austria by the *Anschluss*, thereby reuniting German people and extending Nazism. During the summer he campaigned for the German-speaking Sudetenland area of Czechoslovakia, which was finally won in September and October of that year after the Munich Conference. Once again, the German *Reich* had been extended and the Versailles settlement overturned. In March 1939 the rest of Czechoslovakia was taken and Memel re-attached to Eastern Prussia.

Each of these achievements helped to fulfil the original aims, and each was completed without going to war but rather with the agreement or the compliance of the Western Powers. In the case of both

Austria and the Sudetenland, they were again ready to reconsider the terms of the Versailles settlement and see in them the unfairness of applying the principle of self-determination to other powers but not to Germany. In the case of Czechoslovakia itself, the British and French were defeated not by argument but by what their Governments regarded as the sheer impossibility of taking action against a Power that had already entrenched itself in the country. It is significant that it was after this, in March 1939, that Britain and France offered guarantees to Poland to help protect its frontiers.

After his success in Memel, Hitler made new demands on Poland and, significantly, found new justifications for his actions. On 28 April, in reply to a letter from President Roosevelt asking for assurances that Germany would not attack 31 named countries and for discussions on disarmament, Hitler denounced his naval agreement with Britain of 1935 and his agreement with Poland of 1934. He claimed that the British guarantee to Poland threatened to 'encircle' Germany and was contrary to his existing agreements.

He now began detailed preparations to put into practice his aim of *Lebensraum*, which would be most difficult and face most opposition. In May he signed bilateral non-aggression pacts with Denmark, Latvia and Estonia, and strengthened the alliance with Italy. He continued to demand Danzig and the right to construct a road and railway across Pomorze (the 'Polish Corridor'), and by late June German 'volunteers' arrived in Danzig and set up a *freikorps*.

Then, on 23 August 1939 a Non-Aggression Pact with Russia was signed. This was a complete contradiction of principle for both sides, since Hitler's stand against the Communist threat had been a crucial factor in his success in the early 1930s, and he had been the architect of the Anti-Comintern Pact. Self-interest overrode principle for both sides. Agreement with Russia gave Hitler freedom of action in the east, since he no longer had to fear Russian aid for Poland. Consequently, on 1 September he launched his attack on Poland, hopeful that, yet again, the British and French would not stand by their international agreements and let him have his way. This time he was proved wrong.

For the Soviet point of view, see pages 269 and 312

Interpreting Hitler's foreign policy

ANALYSIS

There is a danger in examining Hitler's foreign policy of imposing on it a pattern that did not exist in Hitler's mind. He certainly had the aims outlined in mind, and he had expressed them in detail in *Mein Kampf* in 1924. However, whether he still saw them as realistic ten years later, or whether he had a definite plan for their achievement, is less certain.

Some historians, including the German Hildebrand and the British Trevor Roper, tended to concentrate on Hitler's expansionist aims, and looked for consistency in his thoughts and actions from the early days of the Nazi movement. For example they pointed out that already in 1924 Hitler was writing about a war for *Lebensraum* against Russia.

One of the most controversial opposing views was put forward by AJP Taylor in 1961. He argued that Hitler did not have a pre-determined programme, and tended to wait on events and then exploit them, rather than initiate an expansionist foreign policy himself. There was particular controversy about the so-called Hossbach Memorandum of 1937, the record of a meeting between Hitler and his generals in which Hitler outlined his determination to acquire *lebensraum* and his plans to prepare for war in various circumstances in the next few years. Although some historians took this as evidence of a 'blue print for aggression', Taylor and some other historians depicted this as evidence of daydreaming, or a domestic manoeuvre to settle arguments about the pace of rearmament, rather than a plan for precise action.

Others have emphasised that it is possible to have fairly consistent aims, whilst at the same time following opportunist or flexible tactics. There were further arguments about the extent to which Hitler was following in the footsteps of earlier German statesmen from before World War I, and the extent to which his foreign policy was different and more radical.

In some respects Hitler was certainly the great opportunist, whose skill lay in his ability to exploit a situation and to time his actions to perfection. His timing was well illustrated by the Rhineland crisis of 1936, his opportunism by the *Anschluss* of 1938. Yet whether he planned to take Austria in that way at that time, or whether he planned to reoccupy the Rhineland before looking to the south and the east, is to surmise.

Certainly, he realised that the winning of *Lebensraum* would be the hardest aim to achieve, and would have to wait till he had achieved a position of strength, but here again he completed and perfected the means to the end at the last minute. The agreement with Russia was not a long-held plan, but an opportunity created by the inability of France and Britain to come to agreement with the Communist USSR. Like his other opportunities, Hitler exploited it to the full. He was particularly adept at exploiting any psychological weaknesses in his opponents, for example in correctly assessing, at least up to 1939, the reluctance of the Western democracies to go to war.

See also discussion on pages 313–14

4 ⌒ GERMANY DURING WORLD WAR II

The Nazi regime maintained its hold on the German population until the end of the war. This was partly due to the Allied demand for 'unconditional surrender', which made most Germans, Nazi and non-Nazi alike, feel that they had little choice but to fight to the end. Hitler had not planned for a long war, and the German economy was certainly not geared to the demands of a long conflict. This was in contrast, for example, to Britain and the USSR, both of which changed almost overnight to total war production from the beginning of their involvement in the conflict. Nevertheless, certain trends in Nazi Germany were evident as the war progressed:

- there was increased oppression as the concentration camp system was extended and the powers of the authorities over people's lives increased
- certain individuals and offices increased their powers: for example Göring's Office of the Four-Year Plan extended its sphere of operations. The *gauleiters* also had their authority increased. Nevertheless, the lack of co-ordination from the top persisted, and indeed was perpetuated by Hitler, so that ultimately everything continued to depend upon himself, or the few like Martin Bormann, Head of the Party Chancellery, who controlled access to Hitler
- from 1942 onwards Hitler reluctantly agreed to give more priority to war production, and limit the production of consumer goods. In February 1943, following the Stalingrad disaster, Goebbels did announce 'Total War'. Albert Speer was able to radically improve the efficiency and productivity of German industry, with the assistance of millions of slave labourers brought to Germany, so that war production was actually at its peak in 1944, despite Allied bombing of Germany
- there were many acts of resistance to the regime, from individuals and groups such as the conservatives, idealists and army officers who failed to assassinate Hitler in the July 1944 Bomb plot. However, there was no single unified resistance movement in Germany.

The Allied invasion of Germany from East and West culminated in the inevitable destruction of Hitler's regime in 1945. The country was devastated and occupied, although it was to remain at the forefront of European and world affairs for the next 40 years as World War gave way to Cold War, with Germany still very much in the firing line.

> **KEY ISSUE**
>
> *How were Germany's economy and society affected by the experience of World War II?*

> See pages 217–18

5 ⌒ BIBLIOGRAPHY

There are now several studies of the Weimar Republic, a topic once comparatively neglected in English. *The Weimar Republic* by J Hiden (Longman Seminar Studies, 1974) contains some documents, although the long introduction is more useful in analysing the issues. *Imperial and Weimar Germany* by J Laver (Hodder and Stoughton, History at Source, 1992) contains many written and visual sources, together with a commentary and advice on how to tackle essays and sources questions in this topic. *From Bismarck to Hitler: Germany 1890–1933* by G Layton (Access to History series, Hodder and Stoughton, 1995) and *Germany 1916–1941* by E Feuchtwanger (Sempringham Publishing, 1997) are useful. *The Weimar Republic* by E Kolb (Unwin Hyman, 1988) and *The Weimar Republic* by D Peukert (Penguin paperback, 1993) are both detailed and useful. An unusual and readable book, detailing how one small German town experienced the events of the 1920s and 1930s, is *The Nazi Seizure of Power* by W Allen (Penguin paperback, 1989). *Years of Weimar and the Third Reich* by D Evans and J Jenkins (Hodder and Stoughton, 1999) contains a wealth of material.

There is a wealth of material on the Nazi period itself. Just a few can be mentioned. *The Third Reich* by D Williamson (Longman Seminar Studies, 1982), is better for its introduction than the documents. *Nazi Germany 1933–1945* by J Laver (Hodder and Stoughton, History at Source, 1991), contains written and visual sources, plus a commentary and advice on how to answer essays and sources questions on this topic. *Germany: The Third Reich* by G Layton (Access to History series, Hodder and Stoughton, 1992) and *Hitler and Nazism* by D Geary (Routledge, Lancaster Pamphlets, 1993), are accessible books. A controversial view of Hitler is to be found in *The War Path: Hitler's Germany 1933–1939* by D Irving (Papermac, 1983). A biography of Hitler, written for students at this level and including an analysis of various interpretations, is *Adolf Hitler: Germany's Fate or Germany's Misfortune?* by J Laver (Hodder and Stoughton, 1995). There are several studies of the different interpretations of the Nazi period: one of the most useful is *The Nazi Dictatorship: Problems and Perspectives of Interpretation* by I Kershaw (Edward Arnold, 1989). A useful overall study is *The Third Reich, a New History* by M Burleigh (Macmillan, 2000).

6 ⌐ STRUCTURED QUESTIONS AND ESSAYS

1. (a) Outline the main features of the Constitution of the Weimar Republic; (10 marks)
   (b) What threats to its existence did the Weimar Republic face in the period 1919–24? (15 marks)
2. (a) Briefly explain why the Ruhr was occupied in 1923; (3 marks)
   (b) Outline the effects of the great inflation of 1923–4 on Germany; (7 marks)
   (c) To what extent, by 1929, had Germany recovered from the crisis of 1923–4? (15 marks)
3. (a) Outline the main terms of the Treaty of Versailles; (5 marks)
   (b) Explain Stresemann's aims in foreign policy; (10 marks)
   (c) How successful was Stresemann in restoring Germany's position as a Great Power by 1929? (10 marks)

4. (a) Explain why the Nazi Party was able to increase its support in the period 1930–January 1933; (10 marks)
   (b) Assess the validity of the statement that 'Hitler came to power by backstairs intrigue rather than popular support'; (15 marks)
5. Why did the Weimar Republic fall to the forces of the Right rather than of the Left? (25 marks)
6. (a) Briefly explain the importance of the Reichstag Fire in the consolidation of Nazi power in Germany; (3 marks)
   (b) Explain why Hitler moved against the SA in 1934; (7 marks)
   (c) To what extent had Germany become a 'Nazi' state by the end of 1934? (15 marks)
7. How and to what extent were Nazi racial policies implemented in Germany between 1933 and 1938? (25 marks)
8. To what extent had the Nazis carried out a social and economic revolution in Germany by 1939? (25 marks)
9. (a) Outline the main aims of Hitler's foreign policy; (10 marks)
   (b) To what extent had he succeeded in carrying out these aims by 1939? (15 marks)
10. Why was opposition to the Nazis within Germany not more successful between 1930 and 1945? (25 marks)

7 ⌁ AN INTERPRETATION OF HITLER'S RISE TO POWER

The following is intended to offer one interpretation of Hitler's rise to power, and should be used as a discussion document rather than as a definitive interpretation. Obviously, there are many omissions and inadequacies, and it is hoped that readers will identify and expand these for themselves.

The birth of democratic government in Germany in 1919 was the culmination of a trend that had developed throughout the life of the German Empire. Between 1871 and 1912 the nationalist and imperialist parties lost support, while the left-wing parties, especially the Social Democrats, won increasing support. By the time of the outbreak of World War I, the Right wing was still in power only by virtue of its close connections with the *Kaiser* and its dominance at the Imperial Court. This trend towards the Left, and with it support for a less autocratic form of government, continued in the elections for the Constituent Assembly of 1919. This is illustrated in Table A, in which the parties have been amalgamated and the percentage vote for each group simplified to the nearest whole number.

The democratic Constitution of the Weimar Republic was not therefore a historical aberration, imposed upon an unwilling German people by the bullying allies, but the clear culmination of a long-term trend.

However, the new Republic, and democracy, lost support rapidly and considerably in the early years of its life. Saddled with responsibility

	1871	1912	1919
Right	53%	26%	15%
Centre	35%	29%	39%
Left	3%	35%	45%

TABLE A
Percentage of votes cast for different groups for the Reichstag and Constituent Assembly

for the Treaty of Versailles and faced with political extremists on the Left and Right, the Weimar Republic was soon in difficulty. This was reflected in the elections of 1920, when the two right-wing parties, the DNVP and DVP, won almost 30 per cent of the vote. There followed even more problems for the new Government – inflation, the Franco-Belgian invasion of the Ruhr and the continued political violence that resulted in nearly 400 political murders between 1919 and 1923. The elections of May 1924 well reflected the electorate's disillusion with the Weimar Republic. In particular, as Table B shows, the extremist parties did far better than before, the Nazis winning over 6 per cent of the vote and the Communists over 12 per cent. After only five years, the future for democracy in Germany looked bleak, and the Kremlin concluded that Germany was, again, ripe for revolution.

Yet the period after 1924 saw a considerable recovery in the fortunes and popularity of the Weimar Governments. Industrial output recovered, in some fields regaining the pre-war levels even though Germany was 13 per cent smaller. In the diplomatic field, the Locarno Treaties were signed and Germany was accepted as a member of the League of Nations. These achievements were again reflected in the elections of the period, as Table B demonstrates.

TABLE B

Election results 1920–8, expressed as percentages of the votes cast

	1920	May 1924	Dec 1924	1928
Nazis	—	6.5%	3%	2.5%
Right (DNVP, DVP)	29%	29%	31%	23%
Weimar coalition (DDP, Z, BVP, SPD)	48%	42%	49.5%	50%
Communists	2%	12.5%	9.5%	10.5%

This new-found stability was destroyed by the Depression. Because of its dependence on foreign loans, Germany was worse hit than any other country, with unemployment reaching a high point in 1932, when about one in three of the adult male population of Germany was unemployed. The future for Germany seemed hopeless – what country was going to lend money to Germany in such circumstances? Germans looked from their immediate economic grievances to their other grievances. Why was Germany so hard hit? Because of the dependence on foreign loans. Why were they so dependent on others? Because of the crisis of 1923. Why had there been a crisis then? Because of the reparations charged through the hated *Diktat*, the Treaty of Versailles, that all patriotic Germans so hated. To many ordinary Germans, all the old wounds that had apparently healed in the 1920s had been opened up once again.

These circumstances gave rise to massive new support for the Nazi party, although it was still not in a majority when Hitler became Chancellor. Table C illustrates this final change.

The Communists maintained a fairly steady support, if anything gaining slightly from the SPD, as Table 36 on page 196 demonstrates. Support

	1930	July 1932	Nov1932
Nazis	18%	37%	33%
Right	11.5%	7%	10%
Weimar coalition	43%	35%	36%
Communists	13%	14%	17%

TABLE C
Election results 1930–2, expressed as percentages of the votes cast

for the Nazis came from two chief sources. One group was those who had not bothered to vote before: the turnout in 1930 was 7 per cent higher than in 1928, and another 2 per cent up in 1932. Secondly, those who had previously voted for the right-wing and moderate right parties – the DNVP, DVP and DDP – shifted their allegiance. Again, this is better demonstrated by the more detailed Table 36. Between 1928 and 1930 the DNVP lost 7 per cent and the DVP 4 per cent of their votes. Those who were already dissatisfied with the Weimar Republic now crossed to the Nazis. Who exactly were these voters, and what was it that particularly attracted them away from their parties to the novelty of the Nazis?

Firstly, it is clear that Hitler's support did not come from where he expected. His original power base, and the scene of the attempted *putsch* of 1923, was Munich, the capital of Bavaria. In the early 1920s, this had indeed been the centre of his support. In the 1924 election, the Nazis had won more than 10 per cent of the vote in only four constituencies, three of which – Upper Bavaria, Lower Bavaria and Franconia – were in Bavaria. Yet between 1930 and 1933, when the Nazi vote averaged well over 30 per cent, not one of these three recorded an average vote of over 40 per cent for the Nazis. Only Franconia averaged over 35 per cent, while in Lower Bavaria the Centre Party won 47 per cent of the votes. Hitler's supporters at the time of his rise to power were to be found away from Bavaria, the original power base.

Equally, he found little support in the cities. Until 1928, Hitler assumed that he would win votes among unemployed and threatened factory workers. But that year the Nazis won only 1.4 per cent of the vote in Berlin, and did little better in other major cities. Significantly, after the 1928 elections, Hitler ordered his touring speakers to brush up on their knowledge of farming problems and get out into rural areas.

For it was in the countryside that the new support for the Nazis lay. An analysis of voting figures shows five constituencies where the Nazis won a consistently high percentage of the votes in all the elections between 1928 and 1933. These were Schleswig-Holstein, East Prussia, Mecklenburg, East Hanover and Frankfurt (Oder). All were predominantly agricultural areas, with few major cities, and situated well away from the major industrial area. They were inhabited mainly by middle-class – *Mittelstand* – farmers, the owners of middle-sized farms with few workers outside the family and largely dependent for a living on the sale of agricultural products in local markets. They were likely therefore to be hard hit by the national cash shortage that the Depression produced.

A second group of enthusiastic Nazis was the young. In 1931, 60 per cent of the 118 000 students supported the Nazi Student Movement, and in 1932 the students of Berlin University – traditionally a left-wing centre – voted for a majority of Nazis. It was the young who provided many of the members of the SA and SS, both of which expanded rapidly during the depression period. Membership of the SA rose from less than half a million in the late 1920s to one-and-a-half million by 1933, while it is recorded that the SS had ten applicants for every vacancy, and that a quarter of its members held doctorates. Again, it is easy to see a link between the young and the Depression. The lack of jobs made the future hopeless for them, and their qualifications would prove worthless; at least the Nazis offered the prospect of a change.

Thirdly, Hitler's support came from Protestants rather than Catholics. In predominantly Catholic areas, Bavaria and the western borders, the Centre Party and the Bavarian People's Party (BVP) recorded consistently high support, even in the elections of 1932. This resulted partly from traditional Catholic hostility to the central Government – a hostility that was born out of the *Kulturkampf* – but also from the high degree of organisation among Catholics. Two million Catholics were members of either the 'People's League for Catholics' or the 'Catholic Youth Organisation' in 1930. In contrast, Protestants were less well organised and tended to fall easier prey to Nazi charms.

Having established *who* gave their support to Hitler, either through the ballot box or membership of party organisations, it is worth examining briefly *why* they did so. His supporters were more likely than most Germans to have suffered the effects of the Depression, and therefore were likely to be disenchanted with the existing moderate alternatives. They were unlikely to be attracted by the Communist alternative. In the case of farming people, there was the risk that their land would be lost if the Communists came to power and in the case of students Communism offered little special reward for their extra qualifications. In addition, they were often already supporters of right-wing parties and therefore likely to be attracted to the nationalist aspects of Nazism. They were disillusioned with their own parties' links with Weimar democracy: the DNVP had had members of the Government since 1925. Yet even accepting all these factors, how could they come to support such a plainly 'nasty' party as Hitler's?

Hitler himself was by no means 'nasty' in their eyes, but rather, an attractive and intelligent leader. Much of our analysis of his rise to power has been prejudiced by our moral outrage at what he later did, and by the evidence that has been used to produce a picture of his early life. It is now clear that much of this evidence about his days as a down-and-out was gathered by a journalist called Heiden from a tramp called Hanisch, who had met Hitler in a Viennese dosshouse while he, Hitler, was trying to avoid conscription in the Austrian Army. Hanisch was prosecuted by Hitler for theft, so it is hardly surprising that he painted an unflattering picture. There is little doubt that in the circumstances of the Depression Hitler's simple explanation of Germany's ills and the simple solution that he offered, were exactly what the bulk of German people felt was needed in 1930.

The ideology of the Nazi Party blended many traditional German beliefs and ideas. It included the *völkisch* tradition of Austria and southern Germany, which asserted not only the racial superiority of the people but also the right of Germans to dominate others. It also took on the Prussian traditions of militarism and discipline that promised firm leadership and an established order, both values that held special attractions in the early 1930s. To these traditional German ideas was added anti-Semitism, but this, as Abel's survey of 1934 showed, was not a major factor in attracting people to the party. Nazism rather offered an apparently cogent alternative to the existing confusion, an alternative that not only promised different policies but also a return to the traditional Germanic values that had been deserted by Weimar.

See page 213

8 ⌁ SOURCE-BASED EXERCISE ON ANTI-SEMITISM IN NAZI GERMANY

Study the sources below and the questions which follow.

... The action committees must at once popularise the boycott by means of propaganda and enlightenment. The principle is: No German must any longer buy from a Jew or let him and his backers promote their goods. The boycott must be general. It must be supported by the whole German people and must hit Jewry where it is most vulnerable ...

The boycott must be co-ordinated and set in motion everywhere at the same time, so that all preparations must be carried out immediately. Orders are being sent to the SA and SS so that from the moment of the boycott the population will be warned by guards not to enter Jewish shops. The boycott ... will be continued until an order comes from the Party leadership for it to stop.

SOURCE A
Nazi Orders for a boycott of Jews in Franconia, 29 March 1933

The Jewish laws are not taken very seriously because the population has other problems on its mind and is mostly of the opinion that the whole fuss about the Jews is only being made to divert people's attention from other things and to provide the SA with something to do. But one must not imagine that the anti-Jewish agitation does not have the desired effect on many people. On the contrary, there are enough people who are influenced by the defamation of the Jews and regard the Jews as the originators of many bad things. They have become fanatical opponents of the Jews. This enmity often finds expression in the form of spying on people and denouncing them for having dealing with Jews, probably in the hope of winning recognition and advantages from the Party. But the vast majority of the population ignore this defamation of the Jews; they even demonstratively prefer to buy in Jewish department stores and adopt a really unfriendly attitude to the SA men on duty there, particularly if they try and take photographs of people going in.

SOURCE B

The report of a Social Democrat in Saxony on the effects of anti-Semitic propaganda, September 1935

On the evening of 9 November 1938, Reich Propaganda Director and Party Member Dr. Goebbels told the Party leaders assembled at a social evening in the old town hall in Munich that in the districts of Kurhessen and Magdeburg-Anhalt there had been anti-Jewish demonstrations, during which Jewish shops were demolished and synagogues were set on fire. The *Führer* at Goebbels' suggestion had decided that such demonstrations were not to be prepared or organised by the party, but neither were they to be discouraged if they originated spontaneously ...

The oral instructions of the Reich Propaganda Director were probably understood by all the Party leaders present to mean that the Party should not appear outwardly as the originator of the demonstrations but that in reality it should organise them and carry them out ... At that time most of the killings could still have been prevented by a supplementary order. Since this did not happen, it must be deduced from this fact ... that the final result was intended or at least was considered possible and desirable.

SOURCE C

A secret Nazi Report on 'Crystal Night', 9–10 November 1938

Next morning – I had slept well and heard no disturbance – I went into Berlin very early ... I alighted at the Alexanderplatz ... I had to go down a rather gloomy alley containing many small shops and inns. To my surprise almost all the shop windows here were smashed in. The pavement was covered with pieces of glass and fragments of broken furniture.

I asked a patrolling policeman what on earth had been going on there. He replied: 'In this street they're almost all Jews.'

'Well?'

'You don't read the papers. Last night the National Soul boiled over.' ...

For the space of a second I was clearly aware that something terrible had happened there. Something frighteningly brutal. But almost at once I switched over to accepting what had happened as over and done with and avoiding critical reflection. I said to myself: 'The Jews are the enemies of the New Germany. Last night they had a taste of what this means ... If the Jews sow hatred against us all over the world, they must learn that we have hostages for them in our hands ... .'

But in any case I forced the memory of it out of my consciousness as quickly as possible.

SOURCE D

A German girl recalls her reactions to 'Crystal Night' (Melita Maschmann in 'Account Rendered')

SOURCE E (PICTURE 25)

A cartoon from a German children's book, 1938

1. *What evidence is there in Sources A and C that*
    (a) anti-Semitic measures were initiated by the Nazi Party or government;
    (b) the Nazis were concerned about the impact of the measures? (6 marks)

2. *Compare Sources B and D as evidence of the impact of anti-Semitic measures on the German population. How reliable are these two Sources as evidence?* (6 marks)

3. *Comment on the message and tone of Source E.* (4 marks)

4. *Using these five Sources, and your own knowledge, estimate the extent to which anti-Semitic measures in Germany during the 1930s were foreshadowed in the Nazi programme and propaganda before Hitler came to power.* (7 marks)

5. *Use these five Sources, and your own knowledge, to comment on the view that 'Anti-Semitism was one of the main features of National Socialism, and one which commanded popular support.'* (7 marks)

Russia and the USSR 1914–45

10

1 ～ THE REVOLUTIONARY PERIOD

A *Russia in World War I*

Russia was even less prepared for the rigours of the Great War than the other European Powers. The general staff had anticipated a 12-week campaign. There were no reserve officers, the artillery available was out of date. Communication and co-ordination problems abounded. There were 72 different aircraft types, 12 of them Russian-made, but a lack of suitable trained officers and fuel. Some mechanics, in an effort to make the fuel lighter, even watered it down. Aircraft from France arrived at Murmansk and were taken across the snow in parts by dog sleigh. Railways were such that in many places there were several lines arriving at a town but only one leaving it.

The result was hundreds of thousands of soldiers sitting on station platforms, quite content with their daily ration of a pound of meat and endless supplies of vodka, but doing little for the war effort. In Western Russia, few lines ran north/south (though plenty east/west), making communication between the different sections of the front difficult.

Moreover, the economic requisites for modern warfare were lacking. There were only some three and a half million industrial workers in a population of 115 million. Statistics of production for key industries like iron, steel and coal illustrate the likely weaknesses of the economy. It was to prove almost impossible to provide the quantities of such goods that were to be needed for shells, weapons, uniforms, transport, radio and all the vast and complex needs of a mass army. In addition, Russia's dependence on foreign loans to provide the finance for industry inevitably left a gap of capital during wartime. The omens were not good.

Militarily, the war proved to be a disaster. In three months of 1914 the Russian army experienced huge losses: 151 000 men killed, 683 000 wounded and 895 000 prisoners. Equipment frequently failed to arrive in the right place at the right time, giving rise to the tales of one rifle between three soldiers and German advances being held up by the mounds of Russian dead.

During 1916 some of the supply problems were overcome and the army fared better, but the underlying weaknesses remained. For example, no NCO (non-commissioned officer) class had been created, largely for fear of its potential to organise opposition, so all depended on the officer class, many of whom had been promoted for their wealth and connections rather than efficiency. Equally, the Russian dependence on its Western allies left it lacking not only in military support campaigns,

KEY ISSUES

Why did the Russian army perform poorly in the war?

See page 128

See page 131

TABLE 39

Date chart of events in Russia 1914–24

1914		Russian defeats at Tannenberg and Masurian Lakes
1915		Progressive Bloc formed in Duma
		Tsar took command of army
1916		Brusilov offensive
1917	Feb/March	Revolution in Petrograd
		Provisional Government set up
		Abdication of Tsar
	April	Return of Lenin to Russia
	July	July Days – demonstrations against Government
		Kerensky became Prime Minister
	Sept	Kornilov Revolt
	Oct/Nov	Bolshevik Revolution
1918		Dissolution of Constituent Assembly
		Treaty of Brest-Litovsk
		Outbreak of Civil War
		Execution of royal family
1920		Russo-Polish War began
1921		Kronstadt Revolt
		New Economic Policy introduced
		Famine in Volga region
1922		Stalin became General Secretary
		Formation of USSR
1923		Soviet Constitution introduced
1924		Death of Lenin

most notably Gallipoli, but also supplies: in 1916 the French were able to deliver only 56 planes of an order of nearly 600.

If the war went badly at the front, it went even worse at home. The industrial needs of an army of millions necessitated economic reorganisation. Some 80 per cent of factories were taken over and run by the State, and extra men drafted in from the countryside to operate them. Unfortunately, the men brought in were not trained for the necessary tasks and output actually fell by about 50 per cent. At the same time, as a result of military service and moving men, the area of land under cultivation fell by 20 per cent.

A vicious circle of economic problems confronted the Tsar's Government: labour shortages, food shortages, increased demand for goods, an inadequate transport system, the disruption of foreign trade and the decline in Government revenue, caused in part by the prohibition on the sale of alcohol, a Government monopoly. Each problem was of itself sufficient to threaten a Government. Together they were overwhelming.

Moreover, Nicholas II seems to have been quite unable to control the situation, and actually worsened it by wrong decisions. In 1915 he dismissed his uncle, Grand Duke Nicholas, and assumed the post of Commander-in-Chief for himself. This identified him directly with the failures of his forces, so that he bathed in their reflected failure. It also took him away from Petrograd, as St Petersburg had been renamed because of its Germanic sound, and left the court in the hands of his wife, Alexandra. She in turn relied for advice on Gregory Rasputin, the 'holy man' who was able to alleviate, at times, the haemophilia of her son,

Alexis. He took the opportunity, until his assassination in December 1916, to promote himself and his own circle. Some of Rasputin's advice was sound, but his interference in affairs of state, along with rumours of his dissolute lifestyle, made him a hated figure and adversely affected the reputation of the royal family with which he was closely associated.

In addition the Tsar appointed aged and incompetent ministers from this circle. In February 1916 the 75-year-old Ivan Goremykin was replaced as Prime Minister by the 69-year-old Boris Stürmer, who also took over the foreign ministry. He was widely rumoured to be pro-German, giving people and army little faith in their Government during 1916.

By this time prices had reached astronomical proportions, especially as wages did not keep pace. Table 40 details some of these. Overall, food prices increased more than five-fold between 1914 and 1917. In 1916 the secret police even discovered that banks were storing sugar in their vaults, such was its value. By 1917, less than 10 per cent of factory workers in the Novy Lessner district of Petrograd received what was regarded as the minimum living wage of 200 roubles a month, while more than half of them received less than 100 roubles a month. Not surprisingly, workers became increasingly discontented and strikes increasingly common, as Table 41 illustrates.

Pre-war price	Price in January 1917	
Bag of rye-flour	6 roubles 50 kopecks	40 roubles
1 pud (3.1 lbs) wheat flour	2 roubles 50 kopecks	16 roubles
Bag of potatoes	1 rouble	7 roubles
1 lb meat	10–12 kopecks	60–70 kopecks

TABLE 40
Price inflation in wartime Russia

Year	Number of strikes	Number of strikers
Aug–Dec 1914	68	34 752
1915	928	553 094
1916	1284	1 086 345
Jan–Feb 1917	1330	

TABLE 41
Strikes in Russia 1914–17

KEY ISSUE

To what extent were the Tsar and his Government responsible for Russia's problems?

B *The March Revolution (or February according to the old Russian calendar)*

A police report in Petrograd of early 1917 read as follows:

> The impossibility of obtaining goods, the loss of time spent queuing up in front of stores, the increasing mortality rate because of poor housing conditions, the cold and dampness resulting from lack of coal ... – all these conditions have created such a situation that the mass of industrial workers is ready to break out in the most savage of hunger riots.

> Forbidding changes of employment from one factory to another and from one job to another has reduced the workers to a chattel state, good only for common fodder. Restrictions on all meetings, even for the purpose of organising co-operatives or canteens, and the closing of unions are the reasons why the workers led by the more educated and perhaps the more revolutionary among them, adopt an openly hostile attitude to the government and protest against the continuation of the war.

KEY ISSUE

What caused the February/March Revolution?

In such conditions, the outbreak of a series of strikes culminating in bread riots on 8 March was no great surprise. The surprise was the failure of the forces of law and order to curb the riots, and the support for the strikers that came from the respectable elements of society – the white-collar workers, the liberals, the *zemstvo* men. Herein lay the difference between 1917 and 1905. Then they had been ready to follow and obey. Now, when a Cossack officer ordered his men to fire on demonstrators on one of the bridges, they refused, and turned on their officer.

Why did these groups now oppose the Tsar? For the soldiers, nearly three years of war had been enough. They no longer had faith in their officers to lead them to any kind of victory. Moreover, many of them had for the first time been brought together with other men and trained in the ways of soldiering. As a result, they at last had the ability to make a meaningful stand against the Tsarist regime, when before their lack of training and weapons made them easy prey.

Inflation had done more than anything else to convince white-collar workers of the need for change. Few knew what they did want, but many knew what they did *not* want – Tsar Nicholas.

The wealthy were less affected by the economic rigours of the time, but had other, powerful, reasons for deserting the Tsar. They were certainly disillusioned by the court circle that had power, if for no other reason than that they were excluded from it. They had expressed their views in the *Duma* in 1916, but had then been ignored, winning only the dismissal of Stürmer. In addition, some realised that the likelihood of a revolution increased daily. If there were to be a change their best place was at the head of it. Hence, in 1917 there was a serious plot to replace the Tsar by either Prince Lvov or Milyukov, hatched by a wide range of wealthy men, like the industrialist, Terschenko, *Duma* leaders like Guchkov and Kerensky, generals like Brusilov and Alexeyev. Only the turn of events prevented it reaching fruition.

KEY ISSUES

What part did the Bolsheviks play in the February/March Revolution?

The revolutionary parties played little part in the March Revolution. The Bolsheviks were weak in both numbers and influence. There were probably no more than 10 000 of them. When they called for a strike in Petrograd in February 1917 to commemorate the opposition of Social Democrats to the war, few followed them. Almost all the leaders were in exile – Lenin and Radek in Switzerland, Litvinov in London, Stalin in Siberia, Bukharin and Trotsky in the United States. Only when the new Provisional Government declared an amnesty did they begin to return to Russia. As Ferro has written, 'paralysed by their differences, the revolutionaries were unable to bring about the downfall of Tsarism, and it was finally the state itself which contributed most effectively to fulfil the revolutionaries' dreams'.

Nevertheless, when Nicholas II abdicated on 15 March, his brother, Michael, declined to take the throne, leaving a power vacuum that was in part filled by the revolutionaries. The official government was taken over by the Provisional Government, intended to last only until a new constitution was drawn up by an elected constituent assembly. The Provisional Government led by Prince Lvov contained predominantly liberals, such as the new Foreign Minister, Milyukov, but also three right-wingers and a single Socialist Revolutionary, Alexander Kerensky, as Minister of Justice.

However, the new Government was no more able to deal with the overwhelming problems than its predecessor had been. Consequently, local organisations and groups tried to deal with them. Among these were the re-formed *soviets* elected by workers, soldiers and ordinary people. In places they organised food supplies and controlled the post and telegraph. The Petrograd *Soviet* was the largest and best known, but it did little at first to oppose the Provisional Government, since much that the Government did – granting the political amnesty and Finnish independence– was its own policy. It did, however, attempt to ensure its own power by the issue of 'Order No. 1', which instructed soldiers to obey itself rather than their officers, if there were a conflict between the Government and the *Soviet*.

KEY ISSUE

What was the importance of the Soviet after the Revolution?

C *The summer of 1917*

The identity of interest between *Soviet* and Government did not last long. In April Lenin returned from Switzerland, via Germany, whose Government foresaw that Lenin could disrupt the Russian war effort to the extent of surrender. He would have no compromise, and on the day he returned he announced his plans for the future, known as the 'April Theses', to the assembled ranks of Bolsheviks.

Lenin said that the war must be ended by the overthrow of the capitalist system, co-operation with the Provisional Government ended, the *soviets* controlled by Bolsheviks and banks, land, factories and transport taken over by those *soviets* in the name of the State. At first, his colleagues were opposed to this new line, given that they had promised conditional support to the Provisional Government, but by the end of April his policies had been endorsed by a conference of the party.

In the meantime, the Provisional Government struggled. At first, it continued to take part in the war. When a letter from Milyukov to Russia's allies explaining this policy was made public, Milyukov was forced to resign and the reformed Cabinet, which now contained six Socialists of various hues, pursued a less decisive policy. Russian troops continued to fight but nothing was said of how long or to what end this would go on.

KEY ISSUE

What problems did the Provisional Government encounter during its existence?

See page 132

The Provisional Government's land policy proved even less success-ful. The expropriation of Tsarist estates was announced but nothing was done about the other estates. Consequently, many families in the coun-tryside simply took the law into their own hands and took over the estates. By July over 1000 had been seized. This in turn affected the army. Soldiers heard of what was happening at home, and, anxious not to be left out, simply deserted the army and went off to stake their claim.

First Lvov and then Kerensky as Minister of War were trapped. Rus-sia's promises to its allies were such that military obligations could not be ignored, yet the soldiers had little desire to fight, and every desire to get home. Hence the Galician offensive, despite its initial success, failed and the German army simply rolled the Russians back.

This failure, combined with continued inflation, unemployment and desertion, led to demonstrations in Petrograd on 16 July. The outbreak was not Bolshevik-inspired, but, seeing the possibility of chaos again, they tried to take over the leadership of the movement as a way of toppling the Provisional Government. Instead, Kerensky was able to command enough support to suppress the riots and show the Bolsheviks to be unpatriotic and pro-German. The Bolshevik paper, *Pravda*, was banned and most of the Bolshevik leaders fled or were imprisoned. Lenin himself went to Fin-land. If Kerensky, now Prime Minister, could rally support for genuinely non-tsarist policies, his chances of keeping the Bolsheviks out were bright.

Paradoxically, it was the right wing that gave the Bolsheviks new strength and hope. In September, General Kornilov, Army Comman-der-in-Chief, attempted to march on Petrograd, end the *Soviet* and cleanse the Provisional Government of Socialist elements. His march from Moscow failed miserably, largely because many of his men desert-ed en route, partly in response to a continued Bolshevik, Menshevik and Socialist Revolutionary propaganda campaign.

In the capital, Kerensky released Trotsky and other Bolshevik leaders in an effort to unite his supporters against the threat of a counter-coup from the Right. Its effect was to restore the Bolsheviks as patriots in the eyes of the people. They alone were 'unsullied' by connections with tsarism and the war, and soon after the Kornilov episode had won con-trol of both the Petrograd and Moscow *Soviets*.

Lenin now returned from Finland to the border town of Viborg, and encouraged his colleagues to plan for the uprising called for in the 'April Theses'. The Central Committee of the party approved the plan on 20 October and a Military-Revolutionary Committee of the Petro-grad *Soviet* was established to draw up detailed plans, under the chair-manship of Trotsky.

KEY ISSUE

What was the importance of the Kornilov Revolt?

D *The November Revolution (or October by the old Russian calendar)*

During the last weeks of October, plans for the *coup* were carefully made and 6–7 November fixed as the date. On the evening of the 6th, Lenin arrived at the party's headquarters, the Smolny Institute in Petro-grad, to find everything carefully organised and ready. Early the next morning sailors on the battleship *Aurora* opened fire on the Winter Palace across the river Neva, to give the signal for the revolution.

More than 20 000 troops were committed to the Bolsheviks. They now occupied the important strategic points of the city – stations, electrical power stations, main roads, the banks – almost without opposition. Only the Winter Palace remained untaken that day, guarded as it was by 100 cadet officers. During the night of the 7–8, Bolshevik troops moved up to surround it and entered the grounds. Early the next morning they moved in, again without a struggle, and arrested the ministers of the Provisional Government, apart from Kerensky who had already fled. To all external appearances, little had happened and little changed. Key points in the city were still guarded by troops, and the problems of prices and the war remained.

The evening of 7 November saw the first significant change. The second 'All-Russian Congress of Soviets' met and recognised both the end of the Provisional Government and the legality of the new 'Council of People's Commissars' (as the Bolshevik leadership called itself) as the Government. This recognition was opposed by some of the Congress, especially the Mensheviks, who walked out, but the Bolsheviks and leftist Socialist Revolutionaries were now able to command a majority.

KEY ISSUE

Why was the Bolshevik coup successful?

Having won approval for his Government, Lenin, as its President, addressed the Congress. He told it of his Government's first two decrees. The first asked 'all the warring peoples and governments to open immediate negotiations for an honest democratic peace'. The second abolished all private property in the form of landowners, Church and Royal estates and took it into State ownership. It was to be distributed to the peasants by local *soviets*. At a stroke, Lenin had, apparently, fulfilled two of his three promises to the people – peace and land. The third promise – bread – was less simply achieved.

In reality, the pronouncements of the leadership could have little effect on events, so far as peace was concerned. Lenin had asked for peace involving no exchange of land or reparations and negotiations for this would take time. In the meantime, he had offered an armistice, and this came into force in mid-December.

With regard to the land decree, Lenin was doing no more than acknowledging what had already, in many areas, happened: that is, the peasants had taken the land. Nevertheless, it was a significant move in two respects. Firstly, it seemed to assure the Bolsheviks the support of the peasantry, since their opponents were unlikely to win favour for a land policy that promised the return of landlords or the removal of their newly won land. Therein lay the Bolsheviks' problem for the next 20 years. They were now stuck with a land-owning system in which the peasants *owned* their plots, but, because of the population, those plots were tiny and therefore inefficient. The struggle of the Bolsheviks and their successors to promote a productive agricultural sector without offending the peasants was to prove a continuing and insoluble problem.

Moreover, the distribution of the land did not win the Bolsheviks votes in the elections for the Constituent Assembly in mid-November.

The Council of People's Commissars could not avoid holding these elections, since the Assembly had been a major policy aim throughout the year. Some 90 millions were enfranchised for the elections but less than half voted. Their votes confirmed the fears of the Bolshevik leadership. They won 175 seats. Their allies, the Left Socialist Revolutionaries, got a further 40.

KEY ISSUE

Why was the Constituent Assembly dissolved?

However, opponents of the Bolsheviks were in a large majority – 370 right-wing Socialist Revolutionaries, 15 Mensheviks, 17 Cadets. The rest of the seats – about 80 – were won by representatives of the various minority nationalities, few of whom supported the Bolsheviks. There was no way the Bolsheviks would win a majority in a democratic vote.

Consequently, the Assembly was broken up by Red Guards, the Bolsheviks' main military force, the day after it met. Lenin explained it away as representing 'true democracy', since the Bolsheviks knew genuinely what the people wanted and had no need of elected assemblies to tell them. To others, it went against all they had fought for and objected to in Tsarism. All the parties except the Left Socialist Revolutionaries were confirmed and determined in their hostility to the new form of dictatorship.

Soviet historiography, after 1917, presented the events of that year as a great achievement for the Bolsheviks, representing the most politically conscious elements of the Russian working class, and led with great skill by Lenin. Trotsky's crucial role in events was ignored, once he had fallen out of favour in the 1920s. The reality was that there was a power vacuum in Russia following the March Revolution. The Bolsheviks were able to fill that vacuum, because although a small conspiratorial group, they alone appeared to have a leader with the will to act decisively, and were not associated with the existing Government. This gave them an advantage over other larger revolutionary groups which agonised over theoretical arguments about the right time to initiate the next Socialist stage of revolution, following the overthrow of the autocracy in March – which according to the orthodox Marxist analysis, had initiated merely the first or 'bourgeois' stage of revolution. Lenin's analysis was less complicated: he persuaded his colleagues that if the moment to strike presented itself, it should not be passed up.

2 ∽ LENIN'S RUSSIA

A *The Civil War 1918–22*

By early 1918 the Bolsheviks controlled only the NorthWestern area of the Russian Empire, that is, the two great cities, Petrograd and Moscow, together with the areas between and around them.

Elsewhere, a confusion of opponents and governments existed. Some of these were based on the minority nationalities, many of whom, such as the Lithuanians, Moldavians and Ukrainians, declared their independence. In other areas, leaders of the anti-Bolsheviks, or

'Whites', formed armies with the aim of establishing a power base and advancing from it to the Bolshevik stronghold.

In addition, Russia's former allies sent troops to Russia with two aims in view – initially to continue the Eastern Front against Germany and protect their war supplies; but also to help to defeat Bolshevism, which they saw as a potential threat (did it not promise 'world revolution'?) and which had told them it would not repay Russia's debts.

Another anti-Bolshevik force was the Czech Legion, 30 000 men originally captured by the Russians in the war against Austria-Hungary, and then used to fight for the Allies against their former employers, but who were now in central Russia.

The 'Civil' War was therefore the efforts of these varied and disparate forces to defeat the Bolsheviks, and their success in withstanding those attacks and eventually defeating them.

The first attack came from the South, from the area of the Don Cossacks. In December 1917, Generals Kornilov, Denikin and Alexeyev, formed a White Army there. They launched their first attacks in early 1918, but Kornilov was killed in battle and they made little headway.

In the spring of 1918 the Caucasian states of Georgia, Armenia and Azerbaijan declared their independence and held off a Bolshevik attempt to conquer them and win control of the oil fields there. In early 1919 Denikin's White Army advanced northwards but was then pushed back to the Black Sea where, during the summer of 1919, he won control of Kiev and Odessa and was within 250 miles of Moscow before a new Bolshevik attack forced him to resign.

His successor, General Wrangel, won back control of much of Southern Russia during 1920, and only after the defeat of Polish forces

> ## KEY ISSUE
>
> *Why did the Civil War break out in Russia?*

> See Map 20

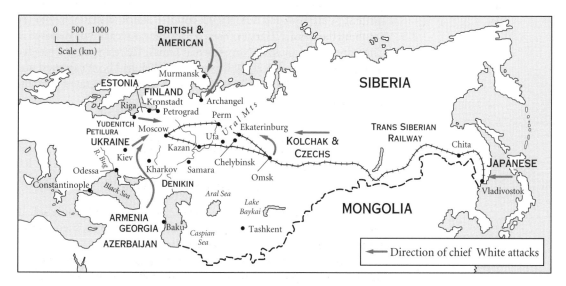

MAP 20 *The Russian Civil War, showing places mentioned in text and directions of main White attacks*

in October 1920 was a new Bolshevik offensive launched, which forced him to abandon Southern Russia and take his army to Constantinople. Thereafter, Soviet Republics were set up in Georgia and Armenia. In 1922 these, together with Azerbaijan, were combined to form the Transcaucasian Soviet Socialist Republic.

This Southern front saw confused and intermittent action. Denikin's army had at first been popular with the peasants, but his troops were ill disciplined and too ready to take advantage of the chaotic conditions to benefit themselves. They were also equipped by the British and French, thus giving them the label of being unpatriotic. Nor was this the only force – there were also local partisan groups and a Ukrainian nationalist army. Given this confusion, the Bolsheviks were to some extent able to ignore this southern area until it genuinely threatened them.

The same could not be said of the east. Here, the Czech Legion posed a major threat to the Bolsheviks. The Legion had been formed before the Revolution and planned to get to Vladivostok and then back to the west. It asked the Bolsheviks for help in this scheme but when none was forthcoming turned against them, and thereafter received financial help from the Western *Entente* and joined local White groups. By June 1918 the Legion controlled the Trans-Siberian Railway and all the towns along it from Vladivostok to the Volga.

In November the independent Siberian Government that had been set up at Omsk by rightist Socialist Revolutionaries and Mensheviks was ousted by the Whites, whose leader, Admiral Kolchak, previously commander of the Black Sea Fleet, was declared 'supreme Ruler of Russia'. His White army, together with the Czechs, advanced westwards taking Perm and Ufa and threatened both Kazan and Samara.

This forced Trotsky, the Bolshevik Commissar for War, to hurry to Kazan to organise the defences. By April 1919 they had reached their furthest point west, and a Bolshevik counter-attack was launched to the South by the former Tsarist officer, S Kamenev. Kolchak was defeated at Chelyabinsk and then, in November, at Omsk. He resigned and handed over to General Semenov. By February Kolchak had been captured and executed by the Reds, while his armies simply disintegrated into the countryside.

The Whites' hopes in the Far East were left in the hands of the Japanese, who kept control of Vladivostok throughout the war, leaving it only in October 1922, by which time it had become the last city in White hands. In fact, for almost two years the Reds had simply left Vladivostok alone, setting up a buffer state, the 'Far Eastern Republic', based at Chita, between themselves and the Japanese.

The Civil War in the North and West was even more confused. In January 1918 the British had landed troops at Murmansk, theoretically to keep an eye on German troops in the East. In August, British and French forces took Archangel and set up a government there under Chaikovsky. During 1919 there was considerable fighting between Red troops and these Allied forces, but neither Britain nor America were prepared to send more troops or money to Russia. This was hardly sur-

See Map 20

prising, since the armistice to end four years of war had only recently been signed. Consequently, in the autumn, the allies abandoned both Archangel and Murmansk, which were quickly taken by the Reds.

To the south of this, German troops occupied the Baltic States and White Russia until mid-1919. Then a White force, backed by the British, was set up in Estonia under General Yudenitch. In October 1919 this army launched an attack on Petrograd and reached the suburbs of the city. For a time Petrograd was virtually cut off, but Yudenitch had neither the forces nor the equipment for a long siege. Trotsky again arrived to inspire the defence of the capital and Yudenitch, unable to either besiege Petrograd or advance, was forced to retreat, in the process of which his forces dispersed. During 1920, the Soviet Government recognised the independence of Finland and the three Baltic States, ending possible hostility from those areas.

In January 1918 the Ukraine had declared its independence from Russia and a moderate Socialist Government had been set up. In February 1918 this Government had signed a separate peace treaty with Germany and Austria-Hungary. Immediately, the Bolsheviks had attacked but had been defeated by German forces, which then took control of the Ukraine themselves. They established a more right-wing Government led by General Skoropadsky, who was himself displaced by the Ukrainian Socialists under General Petliura in November 1918.

In February 1919 the Red Army took Kiev, only to be removed by Denikin in August, recapture it in December and then be attacked by a Polish Army under Pilsudski. In May 1920 he captured Kiev but the support he had hoped for from the Ukrainians was not forthcoming and by December the Bolsheviks had retaken the city and driven the Polish forces back across the River Bug. On 28 December the Soviet Government recognised the independence of the Ukrainian Soviet Government, which two years later joined the Union of Soviet Socialist Republics.

The victory of the Reds over the multifarious groups that attacked them was sometimes presented almost as a military miracle. In early 1918 the Reds controlled a minute proportion of the country and lacked the troops and equipment to fight a many-fronted war against enemies receiving aid from the west. The Tsar had himself depended on allies for his equipment; where were the Reds now to get theirs? By their control of the industrial centres, they were able to utilise the factories to provide arms and equipment.

At the same time, Trotsky, as Commissar for War, organised the Red Army. It had started as a volunteer force, but was converted into a regular army of conscripts with strict discipline. 30 000 former officers of the Tsarist army were brought in by Trotsky to provide expertise and leadership.

In contrast, the various enemies were divided in their intentions. The nationalities, many of whom were Socialists, wanted only what they had always wanted – independence from the centre. The White leadership, on the other hand, wanted to win control of that centre. The hopes of the Allies were at first grandiose. In December 1917 Britain

KEY ISSUE

How were the Reds able to win the Civil War?

and France had divided Russia into spheres of influence for their future control. Yet once the war with Germany was ended, there was little desire or incentive to continue a war in the farthest and coldest parts of Europe. In addition, the participation of the Allies and the behaviour of the White Armies undoubtedly gave the Reds additional support among ordinary people – were they not defending the homeland from acquisitive foreigners? Peasants did not love the Bolsheviks, but they loved the Whites even less, especially when the latter were suspected of aiming to restore land to the former owners.

B *The Treaty of Brest-Litovsk 1918*

Following Lenin's offer of peace in November 1917, an armistice with Germany was signed on 15 December 1917. The peace treaty that followed was finally ratified by the Congress of Soviets only in March 1918. In the meantime, Trotsky, who acted as the chief negotiator, had delayed the final terms for as long as possible, in the hope that either revolution in Germany and Austria-Hungary would topple the Emperor or that the Allies would come to Russia's aid. Both hopes proved illusory.

Negotiations opened on 3 December 1917 at Brest-Litovsk. On Christmas Day, German and Austrian delegates accepted the original Russian request for a peace with no annexations of land and no financial indemnities, if the Western Allies agreed to the same principle within ten days. Trotsky appealed to the West to agree, but no reply came.

The German delegation therefore put forward the demands of its Government. These had been formed by the general staff and demanded extensive annexations in the hope that the extra land would provide the military needs for food and equipment. Trotsky balked at the prospect and for ten days refused to negotiate. Then, on 9 February 1918 the new Ukrainian Government signed a separate treaty and Trotsky left Brest and declared the war ended with no peace being signed.

The Germans responded by a fresh declaration of war. They advanced to within 100 miles of Petrograd when Lenin ordered a resumption of negotiations. On 3 March 1918 Trotsky signed the Treaty of Brest-Litovsk.

By it, the Russians surrendered the Western part of their country. Estonia, Latvia, Lithuania and Poland were given up to Germany and Austria, and areas in the Southern Caucasus to Turkey. Finland, Georgia and the Ukraine were to have their independence recognised. A total of 6000 million marks was to be paid as reparations. Since the areas surrendered represented the wealthiest regions of Russia, more than a third of the population and farming land and 80 per cent of its coal mines were lost. All the gains that the Russian Empire had made in the West over several hundred years were given up.

Unsurprisingly, the peace treaty created splits in the Government. The Central Committee of the Bolshevik Party accepted it by seven to

KEY ISSUE

How severe was the Treaty of Brest-Litovsk?

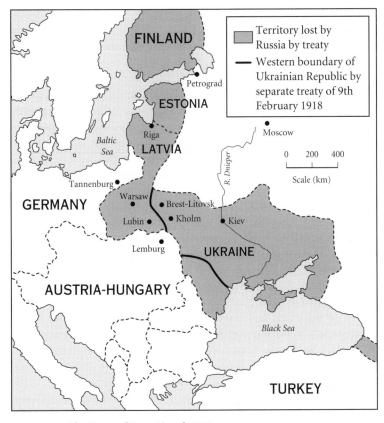

Territory lost by
Russia by treaty

Western boundary of
Ukrainian Republic by
separate treaty of 9th
February 1918

MAP 21 *The Treaty of Brest-Litovsk 1918*

four, and the left-wingers, led by Bukharin and Radek, resigned to pursue a more revolutionary line. The Left Socialist Revolutionaries ended their support for the Bolsheviks. Lenin's answer was that Russia could take no more war. Moreover, he said, the treaty was only a temporary measure, since the inevitable and promised revolution in Germany would soon come and, in its aftermath, all comrades would renounce their gains ill gotten by war.

C *Economic policy*

'WAR COMMUNISM'

The early economic measures of the new Government were the result of practical rather then theoretical considerations. That is to say, they were less inspired by Marxist doctrines about State ownership than a practical desire to alleviate the acute economic problems and satisfy the military requirements of the Civil War. The Bolsheviks had come to power without a detailed blueprint for the creation of a Socialist society, and therefore had to improvise. The land decree of 1917 has already been mentioned.

Among the other early measures was the nationalisation of the banks and of war industries, together with a State monopoly of the

See page 239

KEY ISSUES

What were the principal features of War Communism and what was its impact on Russia?

grain trade. Each of these resembled measures that other countries involved in the war had taken. During 1918 other industries were nationalised, first sugar, then oil and in June a decree that legally made all industries nationalised, though it was some time before this was actually, and gradually, undertaken.

As the Civil War progressed, the problems for the Bolsheviks, or the Communists as they were now known, increased. Paper money, already worth about a tenth of its pre-war value, lost all value, and wages were for a time paid in kind. In their desire to keep up the war effort, the commissars took power to send workers wherever they were needed, be it in the army or industry. Private wealth and trade were banned.

The overwhelming problem was food. The peasants had just taken land for the very first time. Now the Government urgently needed their grain to feed the workers and fighters. To this end a decree of 1919 ordered the peasants to hand over to the State any grain surplus to what was needed for subsistence.

In response, the peasants simply reduced their production so there was no surplus. By 1921 only about half as much stock was kept and half as much land cultivated as there had been in 1913. Little food arrived in the cities, and the only prospect of a livelihood lay in the countryside. City workers in their thousands simply left and went into the country, to join the thousands of soldiers returning from their wars.

The Government had been alarmed by reports of discontent, and Lenin had already decided on a change of course before the dramatic events of March 1921. Yet the events of this month were significant. Shortly before the Tenth Communist Party Congress opened in Petrograd, the sailors of the Kronstadt naval base outside the city, joined by some of the Red Army, refused to obey their officers and called for a new revolution to give genuine freedoms – of speech, of assembly, of private trade.

KEY ISSUE

What was the significance of the Kronstadt Revolt?

Trotsky decided firm action was needed and sent his men across the frozen Bay of Finland to bring the rebels to order. There followed ten days of fighting in the midst of snowstorms before the rebels surrendered. Most were killed or imprisoned. It was to be the last organised revolt against Communist rule.

This outburst, together with the peasants' active refusal to take part in grain requisitioning, simply emphasised the need for change. Agriculture lay at the heart of the problem. The peasant farmers had somehow to fulfil four functions. They had to provide food enough for both themselves and the workers in the cities. They had to grow enough to export and so provide foreign capital to finance the purchase of machinery for industry. They had to provide raw materials like flax and cotton for industry, and, finally, they had to become the consumer class, the sector of the population with enough cash to stimulate demand for industrial goods. Such were their functions in the eyes of the Government.

Yet to the peasant farmer the only function was to provide himself and his family with enough to eat, and something to spare to sell. The extra money thus earned would help him to enlarge his farm and improve life for his children. The Communist Government had done the one and only thing it could to win the peasants' support in giving them land they could own and farm for themselves. Any other policy, especially anything likely to give the peasants less control over their own property, would lose that new support.

'NEW ECONOMIC POLICY'

Lenin's new policy of March 1921 was primarily aimed at keeping the peasants' support and giving them an incentive to produce more:

- the requisitioning of surplus grain was ended and instead an agricultural tax introduced, to be paid in kind until 1923 and thereafter in cash. The amount to be paid was a fixed proportion of the surplus, hence the more that was produced, the greater the peasant's share of his own surplus
- any surplus could be privately traded, at first only at local markets but then through middlemen, known as *Nepmen*, to the towns. By 1923, some three-quarters of trade was controlled by private individuals, 14 per cent by the State and 10 per cent by co-operatives
- the 'New Economic Policy' (NEP) was not restricted to agriculture. Industry and trade were restored in part to private enterprise although the types of works and businesses in private hands tended to be small and local. The State retained control of what Lenin called 'the commanding heights' – heavy industry, the transport system and banking. Thus the average number of workers in State-owned firms was over 150, in private firms only two.

NEP had considerable success in its immediate aim of restoring the economy to something like its pre-war level. In 1920–21 there was a great drought in the Volga region to add to the ravages of war and civil war that had all but destroyed the economy. Thereafter, though, there was a considerable recovery in living standards and production levels. Table 42 illustrates this recovery. However, these figures should be taken as very approximate, since both Tsarist and Soviet statistics are prone to

	1913	1921	1922	1923	1924	1925	1926
Grain (million tons)	81.6*	37.6	50.3	56.6	51.4	72.5	76.8
Pig iron (million tons)	4.2	0.1	0.2	0.3	0.75	1.5	2.4
Electricity (million Kwh)	1.9	0.5	0.8	1.1	1.5	2.9	3.5
Steel (million tons)	4.2	0.2	0.4	0.7	1.1	2.1	3.1
Cotton fabrics (million metres)	2582	105	349	691	963	1688	2286
Sown area (million hectares)	105.0	90.3	77.7	91.7	98.1	104.3	110.3

TABLE 42
Production figures in Russia, 1913–26

(*1913 had been a particularly good year for the harvest.)

exaggeration and it was obviously extremely difficult to obtain accurate figures of production during the years of war and civil war.

Table 42 illustrates not only the achievement of NEP but also the desperate state that Russia had fallen into by 1921. For example, the grain harvest of 1921 was only 46 per cent of that of 1913 – by 1926 it had recovered to be 94 per cent of the pre-war level. Pig iron had fallen to less than 5 per cent of its pre-war level; by 1926 it was back to 57 per cent. Electrification was the one area in which a positive advance was made, due largely to Lenin's personal interest and enthusiasm: 'Soviets plus electrification equals Communism' was an oft-quoted phrase of his.

Nevertheless, NEP was not without its problems or faults. Above all, it shelved rather than solved the agrarian crisis. Undoubtedly, as long as farms remained small, uneconomic units, the levels of production needed for a genuine advance would never be reached. By returning to a private trade system the immediate problem had been solved but at some time a fundamental reorganisation would be needed. Equally, all other sectors of the economy were under State control, so that the town worker could still be ordered where to go, and how much he could be paid and so forth, while his country colleague was free to produce as he liked. This paradox was unsatisfactory, not only on economic but also ideological grounds.

NEP was strongly criticised by many within the Party who had welcomed the drastic measures of War Communism on ideological grounds, regarding it as representing a pure form of Socialism, whereas the new policy, by allowing a degree of private enterprise and increasing income differentials, seemed to be a compromise with capitalism. Lenin himself was ambiguous in his attitude: sometimes he referred to NEP as a desperation measure to preserve Communist rule, at other times he gave it ideological justification as a form of 'State capitalism', a half-way house to full Socialism.

D *The Soviet Constitution and the Communist Party*

The Constitution was drawn up in 1918 and adopted by the fifth All-Russian Congress of Soviets in July of that year. Diagram 3 illustrates the chief components of the governmental system.

The All-Russian Congress met for only about one week in each year and was therefore far too cumbersome a body to act as a genuine executive body. Equally, its Central Executive Committee was too large to meet regularly. Therefore, genuine executive power lay primarily with the Council of People's Commissars.

The franchise was universal although, as Diagram 3 shows, the factory workers received more generous representation than country dwellers. The 'non-labouring' *bourgeois* classes, including the clergy, were disenfranchised. All elections were open: there was no secret ballot.

The crucial factor in this democratic Constitution was the role of the Communist Party, as the Bolshevik Party renamed itself in March

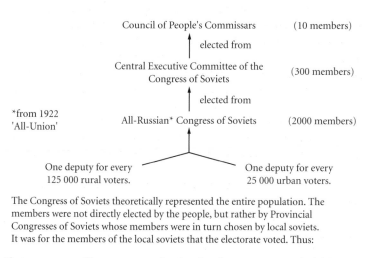

Council of People's Commissars   (10 members)

↑ *elected from*

Central Executive Committee of the
Congress of Soviets   (300 members)

↑ *elected from*

*from 1922
'All-Union'

All-Russian* Congress of Soviets   (2000 members)

One deputy for every
125 000 rural voters.   One deputy for every
25 000 urban voters.

The Congress of Soviets theoretically represented the entire population. The
members were not directly elected by the people, but rather by Provincial
Congresses of Soviets whose members were in turn chosen by local soviets.
It was for the members of the local soviets that the electorate voted. Thus:

Electorate → Chooses → Local soviets choose → Provincial Congress
members of   delegates to Provincial   chooses delegates to
local soviets   Congress of Soviets   All-Russian Congress.

DIAGRAM 3 *The Soviet
Government*

1918. The Party had, at the time of the Kronstadt mutiny, banned not
only all other political parties, but also any opposition or discussion
within itself, such as Bukharin and Radek had shown over the peace
treaty. Lenin was determined that the economic concessions made in
1921 should not be paralleled in the political sphere – far from it. Until
1921, too, the Mensheviks and the Socialist Revolutionaries had both
functioned.

Not only was the opposition banned (a ban enacted by the *CHEKA* –
the secret police) but also the Party was enlarged and restructured.
From being an *élite* in 1917 it had 431 000 members by 1920 and over
half a million by 1921. It now took additional powers in the army, in
factories and in local government, where Party members not only
voiced the views of the Party but also took the action to put them into
practice. The Party too had a structure that parallelled the official governmental structure of the State, as Diagram 4 shows. At each level of
government, therefore, there was an equivalent organ of the Party. Not

See pages 244–5

KEY ISSUE

*What were the main
features of the Soviet
Constitution?*

Political bureau (*Politburo*)

↑

Central Committee of the Communist Party (*Praesidium*)

↑

Party Congress

↑

Local Communist Party groups

DIAGRAM 4 *The Soviet
Communist Party*

surprisingly membership of the two was frequently identical, especially in the higher echelons.

The Communist Party ensured its own authority by a campaign of terror beginning in July 1918. In that month, the Tsar and his family were murdered in the cellar of the house where they were kept at Ekaterinburg by local Bolsheviks fearful of the advance of Kolchak's White Army.

The next month two attacks by opponents led to the full counter-attack by the Communists. A Jewish girl, Dora Kaplan, attempted to assassinate Lenin himself while Uritsky, the head of the *CHEKA* in Petrograd, was shot dead. In retaliation 1500 people in Petrograd were shot. This led to a widespread terror campaign, which formed merely one aspect of the Civil War. Prisoners in that war, on both sides, were killed as a matter of course, while the *CHEKA* singled out more obvious opponents – landlords especially – as one way of encouraging the compliance of others.

The Kronstadt mutiny led to a renewed terror. All those taken prisoner there were executed and others suspected of similar sympathies were imprisoned. Again, the resolution of March 1921 to forbid dissension within the Party resulted in over 100 000 expulsions from the Party. Only with the ending of the Civil War and the start of the economic recovery in 1922 did the 'Red Terror' relax.

The final touches to the political organisation of the Soviet Union came in December 1922 when the Union of Soviet Socialist Republics – the Russian, Ukrainian, Byelorussian (or White Russian) and Transcaucasian Republics – joined together. In government, the 'All-Russian' Congress of Soviets now became 'All-Union' Congress, and in the Party organisation a similar 'All-Union' structure was formed. The separate Republics maintained some control, especially in the social and cultural fields, and each had its own congress, but in practice the important decisions were still made at the centre. At the centre, an increasingly important role was played by the small *Politburo*, functioning like a sort of cabinet, and the *Orgburo* and the *Secretariat*. Local party organisations were subordinated to the centre, and the powers of local *soviets* reduced. A bureaucratic state was quickly developing.

E *Foreign Policy 1920–4*

See page 243

The conclusion of the Civil War did not mean the end of war for the new State. The Polish invasion of the Ukraine in 1920 was repulsed and Lenin then decided to continue his advance into Poland. The Russo-Polish border had constantly been in dispute and it was in the Russian tradition to land-grab from Poland whenever and wherever possible. More importantly, Lenin hoped that the time had come for the advance of Communism beyond the boundaries of Russia, as had been hoped and promised for so long. The new states of Eastern Europe were relatively unarmed, while Germany was weaker than ever – surely the time was ripe to at least sow the seeds of international revolution?

The Polish armies were swiftly pushed back and in August 1920 the Red Army was outside Warsaw. Here, with considerable French aid and the guidance of General Weygand, the Poles fought back and the Russians were forced to retreat and leave their new conquests. The gamble had failed, and the West had had its only victory in Russia. In March 1921 the Treaty of Riga was signed defining the frontier and leaving resentment on both sides of it.

See page 243

See page 151

Before 1924, the Soviet Union could look for little help, trade or friendship from the Western Powers. Their participation in the Civil War had left each suspicious and convinced that the war between Communism and the West was not over. In March 1919 the Third Communist International (*Comintern*) had been founded with the express intention of spreading Communism around the world and organising the overthrow of the Western Governments. For their part, the Soviets could fear the West's intentions following the construction of the *cordon sanitaire* and the signing of treaties between France and the new East European countries.

KEY ISSUE

Why were the Soviet Union and the Western Powers mutually suspicious?

Nevertheless, given its perilous economic condition, the Soviet Union needed trade with the West to help build up industrial expertise. The first step in this direction was taken in March 1921 when an Anglo-Russian trade treaty was signed. In May a similar treaty was signed with Germany. Then in April 1922 Soviet delegates attended the Genoa conference on economic problems, a sign that the Bolsheviks were prepared to co-operate with the West.

However, the French demanded that the Soviet Government should repay the debts of Tsarist Russia to France. The Soviets refused. For two years there was little contact, until on 1 February 1924 – after Lenin's death – Great Britain recognised the Communist Government and it was followed shortly afterwards by Italy and France.

Soviet policy was not, however, aimed simply at friendship and trade. Lenin certainly hoped the great international revolution would still come. In the meantime it had been postponed and therefore all that could be done was to foster the most favourable conditions for the future. To this end, the Western Powers should be divided so that they should not unite against revolution. Lenin was remarkably perceptive in seeing that a Russo-German alliance would be the way to uphold these divisions. He realised that the Versailles Treaty had alienated Germany from the rest of Europe and that agreement with Russia would, for Germany, be a way of maintaining the divisions of the capitalist West.

The Treaty of Rapallo (6 April 1922) was the basis of Russo-German friendship. By it, the two 'pariah nations' as Lloyd George called them, agreed to cancel all territorial claims against each other and to co-operate economically. A supplementary commercial treaty of 1925 and a treaty of friendship and neutrality (the Treaty of Berlin) of 1926 further consolidated the alliance.

See pages 204 and 284

By secret agreements German factories producing military goods were built inside Russia, thus enabling the Germans to get round the military terms of Versailles and the Russians to see Western military technology. By earlier arrangements, several German companies worked in Russia, especially in mining. Until the early 1930s Russo-German friendship proved of considerable mutual advantage, but it also provided the Western Powers with severe embarrassment.

3 ⌐ STALIN'S USSR

A *Ideological conflict and the emergence of Stalin*

The mid-twenties were a time of ideological reassessment among the Communist leadership. The revolution had been won in Russia and the

TABLE 43

Date chart of events in the USSR 1924–45. (Foreign affairs in italics)

1924	Death of Lenin
1925	Trotsky dismissed as War Commissar
1926	Trotsky and Kamenev expelled from Politburo
1927	Trotsky expelled from Party
	Party resolved to collectivise agriculture
1928	Bukharin opposed collectivisation policy
	Beginning of First Five-Year Plan
1929	Trotsky exiled to Turkey
	Start of forced collectivisation and dekulakisation
	Expulsion of Bukharin and Rightists from Party
1930	Stalin's 'Dizzy with Success' article
1932	Beginning of famine in Ukraine and other areas of the USSR
1933	Start of Second Five-Year Plan
1934	Secret police reorganised as NKVD
	USSR joined League of Nations
	Assassination of Kirov
1935	Stakhanovite programme launched
1936	Show Trial of Zinoviev, Kamenev and others
	Yezhov appointed head of NKVD
	New Constitution adopted
1937	Show Trial of Radek and others
	Purge of Red Army leadership
1938	Start of Third Five-Year Plan
	Show Trials of Bukharin, Rykov and others
	Beria became head of NKVD
1939	*USSR proposed alliance with Britain and France*
	Molotov replaced Litvinov in charge of foreign affairs
	Nazi-Soviet Pact
	USSR invaded Eastern Poland
	Baltic States signed treaties with USSR
	Beginning of Russo-Finnish War
1940	*Treaty of Moscow ended war with Finland*
	USSR occupied Baltic States
1941	*Non-Aggression Pact signed with Japan*
	Germany invaded USSR
1942	Battle of Stalingrad
1943	*Dissolution of Comintern*
	Teheran Conference
1944	Siege of Leningrad lifted
	Red Army entered several Eastern European countries
1945	*Yalta Conference*
	Capture of Berlin and end of war
	Potsdam Conference

state reorganised. What of the future? Lenin himself was increasingly disturbed by what he saw around him.

Much of the idealism of the movement was gone. For example, the minority nationalities were no better treated than they had been by the Tsars. Far from being a state in which people *wanted* to help each other and work for the creation of a Socialist utopia, the Soviet Union had become a state in which people were bullied into working for the State. An enormous bureaucracy had been created to bully them.

In an article of January 1923, *On Co-operation*, Lenin wrote of the 'uselessness' of 'the machinery of state' and the paradox of revolution occurring first in the least-industrialised European state. He wrote of the need for a 'cultural revolution' to educate the people into the need for the revolution that had already happened. Then, in his last article, *But Fewer But Better* (March, 1923), he wrote that the 'state apparatus' was 'deplorable not to say disgusting'. This was an attack on the *Rabkrin*, a body of workers and peasants established to inspect the civil service, and by 1923 under Stalin's control. Yet Lenin's disillusion with his new state was ultimately of less importance than the conflict between his successors.

In March 1923 Lenin suffered his third major stroke as a result of which he lost the power of speech. From then until his death in January 1924 the struggle between his likely successors was the real issue, although the infighting was already going on before his death. Four men were genuine candidates for the succession:

- Trotsky, organiser of the Revolution, victor of the Civil War and Lenin's right-hand man, was thought by some to be the most likely successor
- Zinoviev, also a close colleague of Lenin and head of the Comintern
- Kamenev, one-time President of the Central Executive Committee
- Stalin, General Secretary of the Party Central Committee, Commissar for Nationalities and *Rabkrin*, was immensely powerful within the Party, and was already the most powerful man in the USSR by 1924. However, he had not been one of the leaders in 1917 and had been verbally attacked by Lenin for his ruthlessness.

Between 1923 and 1925 Kamenev, Zinoviev and Stalin were united in their opposition to Trotsky. There were many issues that divided them and were debated in private and semi-public (party congresses) in these years. The size of the bureaucracy, the extent that dissent should be allowed within the Party, and the solution to the continuing agricultural problem were all key issues on which it was possible to see the case for several alternatives.

Above all, what of the promised world revolution? To Trotsky, a revolt in Russia alone was a contradiction of the theses of both Marx and Lenin – the revolution had to be both permanent and worldwide if the Soviet Union were to be secure. All resources and efforts should be directed to that end. Only then could the Soviet Union itself be safely built up. In contrast, Stalin argued for 'Socialism in one country'. Russia had to be established as a powerful Socialist country, strong enough to defend itself from attacks and to lead the attack to the rest of the world.

KEY ISSUE

Why did Stalin emerge as leader of the USSR?

LENIN (1870–1924)
(VLADIMIR ILYICH ULYANOV)

Lenin excited little interest outside a relatively small group of Russians and foreign Socialists before 1917. Although he had written much, and was recognised as a Marxist, few were clear about what he really stood for. Yet soon after the Revolution he became a notorious figure worldwide, and soon became important as much as a symbol as a human being, exciting both adulation and hostility in different quarters. In the USSR itself, Lenin was virtually deified soon after his death, Stalin in particular using the cult of Lenin as a tactic to gain support in his own rise to power.

Serious analyses of Lenin began to appear soon after his death. Trotsky, despite his own prominence in the Russian Revolution, generously praised Lenin's contribution to the establishment of the first Socialist State, in a biography published a year after Lenin's death. Lenin was beyond criticism for all Soviet writers until the first serious relaxation of censorship in the mid-1980s, in Gorbachev's USSR. Even then there was no overt criticism of Lenin, but it became acceptable to state that some of the excesses associated with the Stalinist period were already present to some extent in Lenin's Russia, although responsibility was ascribed to Lenin's colleagues rather than to the man himself. Reformers in the 1980s USSR were keen to point out that despite Lenin's insistence on a disciplined Party organisation, he was prepared to debate issues with colleagues, and did not share Stalin's automatic suspicion of anybody who did not immediately agree with him. Only in the 1990s were Russian historians prepared to really delve into the differences between the myth and the reality of Lenin, and point out his faults and excesses as well as his achievements.

Non-Marxist historians outside the USSR never had such susceptibilities when writing about Lenin. They were sometimes prepared to praise Lenin's qualities of determination and, for example, his contempt for the type of personality cult characteristic of many modern dictators. Nevertheless they were inclined to blame him for developments such as the growth of the bureaucratic one-party state which enabled more ruthless individuals like Stalin to exercise what was seen as virtually unlimited power. Typical of the more modern critical assessment of Lenin is the work of Richard Pipes, who analysed documents hidden in the Soviet archives until after the break-up of the Soviet Union, and which demonstrated a previously less well publicised side of Lenin's activities. Pipes, for example, emphasised Lenin's ruthlessness in personally authorising the execution of hostages after gaining power. Extract from *The Unknown Lenin* by Richard Pipes (1996). Reproduced by kind permission of the Yale University Press.

Lenin was, not an idealist, but a mass murderer, a man who believed that the best way to solve problems – no matter whether real or imaginary – was to kill off the people who caused them. It is he who originated the practice of political and social extermination that in the twentieth century would claim tens of millions of lives.

JOSEPH STALIN (1879–1953)

Stalin was not typical of the early Bolshevik revolutionary leaders. He was an outsider, a Georgian and not from the middle class background of Lenin and other Bolshevik intellectuals. He became a professional revolutionary, but one who carried out active tasks such as robbing banks in order to get funds for the Party, rather than engaging in intellectual debate. Unlike other leading Bolsheviks, he spent little time outside Russia. Stalin played an active role in both the revolution and the Civil War, when his alienation from Trotsky began. Although given various posts by Lenin, who realised too late that he might not be the best man to succeed him, it was as General Secretary of the Party that Stalin was able to develop and wield powerful influence.

Apart from the political arguments about Russia's future after Lenin's death, there was also the personal conflict. Stalin was often portrayed as the unimaginative official, who had worked his way up from humble beginnings to the top by hard work and loyalty. Trotsky was the Jewish intellectual who had spectacularly thrust himself forward and brought honour to himself. The two had little liking for each other. Stalin's reputation as a 'grey blur' was partly due to Trotsky's contempt for him. In fact Stalin showed considerable political skill in the 1920s, presenting himself as a moderate figure in the centre, whilst those around him intrigued. His strength was that he controlled the Party machine and could pack congresses with his supporters. In contrast Trotsky, for all his oratorical skills, had no power base within the Party, was widely distrusted for his ambition, and made several tactical mistakes.

Once Stalin was in power, Soviet interpretations of his role and importance bordered on adulation for the remainder of his life. Only in 1956, three years after his death, did his successor Khrushchev criticise, although not publicly, Stalin's repressive policies in the 1930s. In 1959 there were the first inklings of public criticism: the official *History* of the Party criticised the excesses of Stalin' personality cult as it was developed in the 1930s, although the man himself was praised for destroying the Party's enemies, and of course for his leadership in the war. The *History* concluded by commending Stalin's overall contribution to the world Communist movement. Only in the 1980s did serious criticism of Stalin begin in the USSR, and then Stalin himself rather than the Party was the target.

Historians and commentators in both Russia and the West have been influenced in their assessments of Stalin by their own attitudes towards the Soviet Union generally. Those like the writer Alexander Solzhenitsyn, who was imprisoned for years in a Soviet labour camp, had no time for the system and had a low opinion of both Lenin and Stalin. Those historians who were more sympathetic to Lenin, for example Marcel Liebmann, emphasised that the 'bureaucratic tyranny' which characterised Stalin's USSR was of a very different order from that of Lenin's State. Others, conscious that the economic revolution of the 1930s was a gigantic experiment directed by the Party, explained Stalin's methods without excusing the bloodshed: 'The "revolution from above" ... required hierarchical subordination, in suppression of discussion; therefore there had to be an unquestioned commander-in-chief' (A Nove, Was Stalin really necessary? *Encounter*, April 1962.) On the whole, modern assessments of Stalin have been very critical, emphasising that Stalin even more than Hitler probably deserves the title of 'the greatest mass murderer in history'.

During 1924 and 1925 Stalin and his allies openly attacked Trotsky. In October 1924 Stalin publicly referred to Trotsky's correspondence of 1913 in which he referred to Lenin as 'a professional exploiter of everything that is backward in the Russian workers' movement'. In 1925 Trotsky fell ill and, partly voluntarily, resigned as Commissar of War and took a less important post in the Council of National Economy.

The next dispute was between Stalin and his former allies on the agricultural issue. There was still a grain shortage and the peasants demanded more concessions. Stalin supported the motion at the 14th Party conference to cut the tax on grain by 25 per cent and make it easier for farmers to lease land and employ labourers. Again, agriculture had won a concession from Communism. Kamenev and Zinoviev opposed the motion. It was carried by 559 votes to 65. The elections for three new members of the *Politburo* also went Stalin's way. All three new men, Molotov, Voroshilov and Kalinin, were his supporters.

During 1926 and 1927 a new alliance of Trotsky, Zinoviev and Kamenev made a final effort to oppose Stalin, on the grounds that he led the bureaucracy against the interests of the peasants. This alliance of former enemies smacked of opportunism. Zinoviev and Kamenev had also not completely lived down their tactical mistake of 1917, when they had advised Lenin against a seizure of power.

The 15th Party Conference of October 1927 endorsed Stalin's policy of 'Socialism in one country'. All three opponents were removed from the *Politburo*. In December 1927 they planned to circulate a memorandum to the Conference. Fearing it would not be allowed, they had it printed secretly. Members of *OGPU*, as the *CHEKA* had become, found the presses. All three, together with 75 colleagues, were expelled first from the Central Executive Committee and then from the Party. Subsequently, Trotsky was expelled from Russia in 1929, while Zinoviev and Kamenev remained in Russia until the purges and show trials of the 1930s.

Stalin's power was not yet unchallenged. The winter of 1927 and 1928 saw further grain shortages that convinced Stalin of the need for an end to NEP and a new agricultural policy. However, some leading

Party members, with whom he had allied in 1925, were wedded to the moderate idea of a wealthy peasantry. Prominent among these were Bukharin, editor of the Party paper *Pravda*, Tomsky, head of the unions, and Rykov, Chairman of the Council of People's Commissars. They believed that the development of a wealthy peasant class of *kulaks* should be encouraged. Such a policy, they claimed, would stimulate consumer demand and thereby industry also. In contrast, the Leftists or hard-liners, believed that the peasants should be squeezed; in other words, they should be heavily taxed, and the revenue raised used to finance industrialisation. All Communists believed that the USSR must industrialise in order to achieve Socialism. The debate was simply about the best way to achieve this goal.

During 1928 the Comintern Conference condemned reformism. A debate on agriculture in the columns of *Pravda* followed, in which rich peasants were condemned. Bukharin wrote in their defence, but in February 1929 he and the others were accused, with Kamenev, of plotting against Stalin's campaign against wealthy peasants. All three nominally supported Stalin but by the end of the year had left the Party. Stalin's 50th birthday at the end of that year was celebrated with massive demonstrations and huge street portraits.

Stalin's emergence as unchallenged leader was primarily the result of his manipulation of his official posts and his ability to identify himself as a genuine successor to Lenin. As General Secretary, Stalin controlled an enormous power machine. Directly under him, he had over 700 officials and local party secretaries were appointed directly by him. The secret police came under his authority, as did the youth movement, the *Komsomol*, founded in 1927. There were separate sections in the Secretariat for press, statistics, village affairs, education and the like. Thus the General Secretary, largely through his power of appointment, could build up vast local and national bases of support. If his appointees and supporters voted for him in the Party Conference, he was likely to win.

Lenin had written against Stalin before his death, saying that he should be removed as General Secretary and replaced by someone 'more tolerant, more loyal, more polite and more attentive to the needs of comrades'. Stalin ignored this criticism and on 26 January 1924, at a special congress of the Party to pay tribute to Lenin, spoke in uncharacteristically emotional terms of the dead leader. Later, he was able to show that his policies of gradual change and 'Socialism in one country' were in the Leninist tradition. For example, when he sided with Bukharin against Kamenev's campaign for agrarian change, Stalin quoted Lenin's statement of 1919 that 'there is nothing more stupid than the idea of compulsion with reference to economic relations with average peasants'.

Time was to suggest that Stalin's use of Lenin's memory came from convenience rather than conviction.

The campaign for industrialisation was conducted as a war upon backwardness. *Gosplan*, the high command, sent out its orders for levels of production to specific areas and they in turn translated them into detailed requirements for each plant. On this local level, managers received the orders of the amount of production required, and had to achieve it as best they could. Plan requirements and achievements were published in the factories for all to see, and, as in wartime, constant propaganda urged the workers to ever-higher efforts. There were medals, literally, for the highest producers and penalties for those who failed to achieve.

Obviously, such constant supervision and threats put pressure on many managers to falsify figures and take short cuts in production. Quantity was more important than quality. Nevertheless, the battle had to be won and, especially in comparison with the achievements of Western Europe at the same time, it apparently was.

This battle mentality had other, less pleasant, implications. The conditions of work and, especially, of living were neglected to a point of near disaster. Factory workers newly arrived in an area lived in shanties that would have compared unfavourably with pre-revolutionary times. Consequently, a high degree of compulsion and suppression of complaint were required, although there were also examples of idealism, especially amongst the younger generation of Communists.

Again as in war, failures were rarely admitted and always underplayed, so it is difficult for the Western historian to truly assess the impact of the Plans. It is certain that the targets of the First Plan were not achieved in many areas, most notably in iron and steel production, where production reached about 60 per cent of what had been planned, but then the ambitions were so great that this is hardly surprising. Equally, however, a warlike sense of patriotism made many workers accept hardships and renew their efforts in a way that would never have normally been possible.

The planners learnt from their errors and in many respects the Second Plan was more successful than the First. *Gosplan* officials had been hoping for improved harvests, a greater share of world trade and a fall in military expenditure, none of which materialised, during the First Plan. However, the first year of the First Plan had proved so promising that it was decided to complete the Plan in four years instead of five and increase the targets.

See Table 45(B) on page 263

In fact, their optimism proved false and 1933–4 was regarded as a year of relaxation before a renewed effort. Consequently, the Second Plan was slightly less optimistic, involved less administrative shuffling, and was more successful. This was especially true of the years 1934–6, by which time many of the new plants were in operation and less machinery had to be imported. In 1932, 78 per cent of machine tools had to be imported; by 1937 only 38 per cent.

Equally, however, the Second Plan had to be adjusted to increase defence expenditure, which became the first priority of the Third Plan. In addition, after two good years, 1937 showed a considerable slowdown, especially in the metallurgical industries, partly as a result of the purges.

	1927–8	First Plan			Second Plan	
		Planned 1932–3 first version	*1932–3 optimal*	*1932–3 actual*	*Planned 1937*	*1937 actual*
Electricity (mKwh)	5.05	17.0	22.0	16.6	38.0	36.2
Coal (m. tons)	35.4	68.0	75.0	64.3	152.5	128.0
Oil (m. tons)	11.7	19.0	22.0	21.4	46.8	28.5
Pig iron (m. tons)	3.3	8.0	10.0	6.2	16.0	14.5
Steel (m. tons)	4.0	8.3	10.4	5.9	17.0	17.7
Employment	11.3	14.8	15.8	22.8	28.9	26.9

TABLE 45(B)   *The Five-Year Plans and their achievement (details)*

Nevertheless, not only were production figures increased, but also, to some extent, workers' conditions improved. Malafayev has calculated that while prices rose by some 80 per cent, wages more than doubled, and that goods and shops were more readily available to workers.

C *Political history*

The warlike atmosphere of Russia in the 1930s extended into the political sphere. There were three particular aspects to this:

- as with all nations in wartime, the leadership became increasingly identified in one person and he was regarded as more and more infallible
- any opposition was ruthlessly suppressed
- some constitutional alterations were made to facilitate rapid decision making.

STALIN'S LEADERSHIP

Stalin's portrait first appeared in *Pravda* in 1929. For the next 20 years, his speeches and pronouncements were given all the more familiar media treatment to show him as the great leader and to spur his people on to greater and greater achievements. Not for Stalin the 'fireside chat' approach, but rather the cultivation of a distant 'Big Brother' image whose pleasure was a reward and whose anger was to be avoided.

Other cult figures were drawn not from Stalin's entourage, whose anonymity was to be carefully preserved, but rather from the ordinary people, the workers who had achieved more than their norm and whose portraits appeared outside works canteens. Best known of these figures was Alexei Stakhanov, the miner who propaganda claimed could hew ten tons of coal in the time most men managed one. Thus the great worker was glorified and the great leader's distant magic preserved.

THE PURGES

The purges of the mid and late 1930s were the climax of suppressing real and potential opposition. As early as 1930 a group of technicians and managers was brought to trial for sabotage and mismanagement. After this, many managers and local officials were tried for their fail-

- between November 1941 and April 1942 the Soviets managed to dismantle over 1500 key enterprises and reassemble them in the East, beyond the range of German forces. In addition many new factories were built
- unlike the Nazis, the USSR adopted a policy of 'total war' from the start. Everything was geared to the war effort. Soon the USSR was able to massively outproduce the Germans, and the Soviet war effort was superior in quality and quantity. Once Hitler's gamble of a short war had failed, a Soviet victory was always likely
- after the initial shock of the German attack, the *Stavka* or new High Command was created, chaired by Stalin and ensuring that all necessary measures were co-ordinated from above – a much more efficient system than that operated by Hitler, whose regime was characterised by competing bureaucracies until late into the war.

KEY ISSUE

What impact did World War II have upon the USSR?

On the Soviet home front, the regime maintained its brutal control of all aspects of life. The *NKVD* continued to arrest real or imagined opponents and its powers were increased. Non-Russian nationalities suspected of hostility to the regime were deported wholesale to distant parts of the Soviet Empire. However, the power of the Communist Party itself declined:

- the Red Army was spared much of the political interference it had experienced before the war. Stalin accepted the need for a 'professional' approach to fighting
- industrial managers were likewise given more freedom from red tape, so long as they delivered the actual goods
- persecution of the Church was relaxed, so that it could support the war effort and provide reassurance for the many believers still in the USSR.

Nevertheless, by the end of the War, although victorious, the USSR had paid a terrible price in loss of life and physical destruction of the country. It took several years to return to pre-war levels of production, and much longer for the psychological scars to heal.

5 ⌁ BIBLIOGRAPHY

There is a wealth of material available on Russian and Soviet history, and only a few of the books can be mentioned. General histories abound: one of the more concise is *The Russian Revolution 1917–1932* by S Fitzpatrick (OUP, 1982). More detailed on the earlier period, but very readable is *A People's Tragedy* by O Figes (Jonathan Cape, 1996). Economic matters are dealt with thoroughly in *An Economic History of the USSR* by A Nove (Penguin, 1976). *Russia 1914–1941* by J Laver (Hodder and Stoughton, History at Source, 1991) contains written and visual sources, along with a commentary and advice on answering essays and sources questions on this topic. One of the best detailed biographies of a Soviet leader is the three-volume *Lenin: A Political Life* by R Service (Macmillan). Also useful are *Stalin As Revolutionary* and *Stalin In Power* by R Tucker (Chatto and

Windus, 1974 and 1990). Much shorter books are *Stalin and the Soviet Union* by S Lee (Routledge, 1999), *Russia 1917–1941* by M McCauley (Sempringham, 1997) and *The Stalin Years* by E Mawdsley (Manchester University Press, 1998). *Lenin: Liberator Or Oppressor?* and *Stalin: From Revolutionary To Despot*, both by J Laver (Hodder and Stoughton, 1994 and 1993) and *Reaction and Revolutions: Russia 1881–1924* and *Stalin and Khrushchev: the USSR, 1924–64* by Michael Lynch (Access to History series, Hodder and Stoughton, 1992 and 1990) are written for students at this level and contain narrative, analysis and a survey of historiographical interpretations.

6 ➰ STRUCTURED QUESTIONS AND ESSAYS

1. (a) In what ways did Russia prove itself ill-equipped to fight World War I? (10 marks)
    (b) What impact did the war have upon Russia down to the end of 1916? (15 marks)
2. (a) Explain briefly what the Soviet set up during the February/March Revolution was; (3 marks)
    (b) To what extent was the February/March Revolution a spontaneous affair? (7 marks)
    (c) How successfully did the Provisional Government deal with the problems facing Russia between the two Revolutions of 1917? (15 marks)
3. Why was the first Revolution in Russia in 1917 followed so soon afterwards by a second one? (25 marks)
4. (a) Explain briefly what Lenin's 'April Theses' were; (5 marks)
    (b) Assess the roles of (a) Trotsky; and (b) Lenin in bringing about a successful Revolution in Russia in October/November 1917. (2 × 10 marks)
5. (a) What was the Constituent Assembly, which met in January 1917? (3 marks)
    (b) Explain why the Bolsheviks closed the Assembly down; (7 marks)
    (c) How valid is the judgement that 'Lenin's greatest achievement was not taking power, but holding on to it'? (15 marks)
6. Why were the Bolsheviks victorious in the Civil War which followed the Revolution of 1917? (25 marks)
7. (a) What do you understand by the phrase 'War Communism'? (3 marks)
    (b) Explain the significance of the Kronstadt Revolt of 1921; (7 marks)
    (c) To what extent did Lenin's NEP solve the problems caused by War Communism before his death in 1924? (15 marks)
8. Why was Stalin able to defeat his opponents on both the Left and the Right in the struggle for leadership in the USSR in the 1920s? (25 marks)

9. (a) What do you understand by the phrase 'collectivisation' in the context of Soviet history between 1927 and 1933? (3 marks)

   (b) What impact did collectivisation have upon the USSR during this period? (7 marks)

   (c) To what extent did the Five-Year Plans transform the USSR in the 1930s? (15 marks)

10. 'Brutal but effective.' Comment on this assessment of Stalin's rule down to 1941. (25 marks)

11. How consistent and successful was Soviet foreign policy between 1921 and 1941? (25 marks)

12. (a) How prepared was the USSR for World War II?(10 marks)

    (b) Why was the USSR able to emerge victorious from the War? (15 marks)

7 ◦ AN ESSAY-WRITING EXERCISE

The four exercises below are intended to help you practice the skills required in essay writing by breaking them down into a number of parts, and by allowing you to work on a number of titles, rather than just one.

1. You might be asked to write an essay on the reasons for the Reds' victory in the Civil War. Below are listed three sentences that might form the first sentences of paragraphs in answer to this question. In each case, list four pieces of data – facts, statistics etc. – that might be used to support the assertion made by the opening sentence.

   (i) Trotsky's leadership was one of the Reds' greatest assets.

   (ii) The Reds' control of the industrial centres was also to their advantage.

   (iii) On the other hand, the divisions of the White leaders and armies seriously hampered their efforts to overcome the Bolsheviks.

2. Another essay might ask you to assess the character and abilities of Lenin as ruler of Russia. Construct four sentences that would serve as first sentences of paragraphs for such an essay. Make sure that each is an important point that can be supported by evidence, but do not include that evidence.

3. A third question might ask 'Was Stalinism necessary?' Below are listed three sets of data that might be used in paragraphs in answer to this question. In each case, write a first sentence that might accompany each of these sets of data and then write the paragraph concerned, utilising the data given here.

   (i) Russia's agricultural production before 1928
       Communication and collection difficulties in the Russian countryside
       The needs of the cities
       Ideological undesirability of the *kulak* class

   (ii) 'We are 50 to 100 years behind ...'

Production levels of Russian heavy industry in 1928
Heavy industry as the basis for all development
(iii) Treatment of opposition to collectivisation
The show trials
Labour camps
The number of deaths in the purges

4. A fourth essay might require you to examine the changes of direction of Soviet foreign policy, and the reasons that underlay such changes, in the inter-war period. Construct and write any three paragraphs for this essay. Make sure each contains an assertion and evidence to support it. They do not have to be successive paragraphs, and should not include an introduction or conclusion.

8 ～ SOURCE-BASED EXERCISE ON SOVIET PROPAGANDA

Propaganda was an important feature of life in the USSR, especially visual propaganda designed for a population which still contained millions of illiterate people. Study the examples of Soviet propaganda issued in the early years of the Soviet Union, which are shown on pages 273–8 and answer the questions which follow.

SOURCE A (PICTURE 26)
Year of the Proletarian
Dictatorship, *October
1917–October 1918*

SOURCE B (PICTURE 27)
The Priest and the Rich Man
on the Shoulders of the
Labouring People, *1918*

**SOURCE D
(PICTURE 29)** Retreating
Before the Red Army, *1919*

SOURCE E (PICTURE 30)
Death to World Imperialism,
1919

SOURCE J (PICTURE 35)
Comrade Lenin Cleans the
World of Filth, *1920*

Тов. Ленин ОЧИЩАЕТ землю от нечисти.

Q

1. *There are several themes in these propaganda sources.
Identify the main themes. (6 marks)*
2. *Select any four of Sources A–J and explain*
  (a) *what the exact message of the Sources is;*
  (b) *what techniques are used to put across the message;*
  (c) *what is the tone of the propaganda in each case. (18 marks)*
3. *Select another four of Sources A–J and explain*
  (a) *who the propaganda was probably aimed at;*
  (b) *how accurately they reflect what was happening in Russia at
  the time;*
  (c) *how effective you think they are as propaganda. (18 marks)*
4. *Select any three examples from Sources A–J and explain what their
uses and limitations might be to an historian of this period in Soviet
history. (8 marks)*

International Relations and Crises 1919–39

11

INTRODUCTION

International relations in the inter-war period were more complex than ever before. They can conveniently be broken down into a number of periods, as below, although these are obviously artificial in many respects. To assist your overall understanding, it may help to construct an outline date chart on which you can plot the major events of the period. This will especially demonstrate the coincidence of events in different parts of Europe (and the world); this was particularly important in 1936.

Secondly, to get some idea of the shifts in attitude between the different countries, it may help to construct four 'friendship/enemy charts' (one for each of the periods 1919–24, 1925–30, 1930–6 and 1936–9) on which the attitudes of the different Powers to each other can be charted below. Where two countries drew obviously closer to one another, for instance by signing an alliance, score +3 in the appropriate boxes (e.g. France and East Europe I). Where countries are clearly enemies, score –3 (e.g. East Europe I and East Europe II). Use the intervening numbers (–2, –1, 0, +1, +2) to record degrees of friendship. For instance, France and Italy, although both members of the League of Nations Council, were not friendly, especially after 1922. Obviously, this is a very crude device, but four completed charts will reveal some important trends.

1919–24	Fr.	Ru.	GB.	It.	Ger.	EE. I	EE.II
France				0		+3	
Russia							
Britain							
Italy	0						
Germany							
East Europe I (Poland, Cz., Yugo.)	+3						–3
East Europe II (Hungary, Austria)						–3	

The Spanish Civil War has been included in this chapter for several reasons. Its European significance is such that to have written a separate chapter on it would have led to considerable repetition within this chapter. Moreover, it coincided with a number of crucial events and trends elsewhere that together altered the whole complexion of international relations after 1936.

1 ⌐ 1919–24: THE SETTLEMENT OF THE PEACE TREATIES

A *Introduction*

Four issues dominated Europe in the immediate post-war period:

- the treaties signed at the end of the war had left a number of unresolved problems, chiefly concerning the boundaries of Eastern Europe. These were mainly settled by 1924, either peacefully or, in some cases, forcefully
- European security. Both France and the East European nations felt that the treaty settlements had left them vulnerable and sought ways of making themselves safer
- economic problems were inevitable in the aftermath of the war, and the early 1920s saw, for the first time, international efforts at co-operation to solve these
- there were efforts, some of them planned, others less so, to ensure that the disaster of a major war did not happen again and that peace was to stay.

Several factors hampered all the efforts of statesmen to deal with these problems. By a vote of 11 November 1919 the United States Senate had refused to ratify both the Treaty of Versailles and the agreement to guarantee France's security. Instead, the American Government embarked on a policy of isolation, involving itself in European and world affairs only rarely and when directly affected. The Senate vote also meant that the USA was not a member of the League of Nations, since membership was incorporated in signing the Treaty of Versailles.

The suspicion and hostility between France and Germany continued. Many Frenchmen believed that Germany would be keen to gain revenge and would attempt to win back at least Alsace and Lorraine. Equally, the peace settlement outraged the majority of the German people, and German determination to overthrow its terms, by force if necessary, became a prominent feature of the 1920s.

The situation in Russia added a new dimension to international relations. At first, its major influence was in involving the European powers in the Civil War. Even before it became clear that the Communist Government could survive and rule, the West European Powers sought ways of protecting themselves from the threatened Communist advance. Throughout the 1920s, and even the 1930s, the USSR's posi-

KEY ISSUE

What major problems in international relations faced statesmen after World War I?

See pages 240–4

tion was to be crucial since it added a third aspect to international relations. On the one hand were the Western Powers and their allies which had won the war and devised the treaties. On the other were the defeated powers of central Europe, eager to revise the treaties. The USSR seemed at some times to be on the one side, at others the other side. Each change, or possible change, brought international repercussions.

B *The settlement of border problems resulting from the treaties*

These problems have already been examined under the national histories of the countries concerned. Table 46 therefore only summarises the major issues and their resolutions.

C *The settlement of French and East European security*

After America's rejection of the guarantee to protect French security in November 1919, France sought alternative means of protection. As the newly created East European countries also felt vulnerable, surrounded as they were by powerful enemies, their interests coincided with those of France.

The result was the construction of the alliance system by which France's security was linked to that of Eastern Europe. The foundations of this system were laid by the treaty between Czechoslovakia and Yugoslavia of 14 August 1920. This was initially a defensive treaty against Hungary, but was to become the basis of the Little *Entente*.

See page 150

Chronologically, the next agreement was the treaty between France and Poland promising each other assistance in the event of either being attacked. This formed the northern arm of France's East European defences, which was always kept separate from its southern arm – the Little *Entente* – because of the mutual hostility and suspicion between Poland and its southern neighbours. During 1921 the Little *Entente* was completed by treaties between Romania and both Czechoslovakia and Yugoslavia.

See page 151

These agreements also survived their first test when the Little *Entente* successfully opposed, by mobilisation, the attempts of former King Karl to regain his throne in Budapest. The Little *Entente* was first linked to France by the Franco-Czech Treaty of January 1924 which provided for mutual aid if either country were attacked without provocation. Subsequent treaties between France and Romania (1926) and France and Yugoslavia (1927) tightened these ties and, on the face of it, secured both France and the East European Powers against possible attack.

These treaties were to be crucial to the future security of Europe and it was ultimately an agreement between Poland and the Western Powers that led to the outbreak of war in 1939. Consequently, they are worth assessing a little more closely. To what extent did France really believe that the military strength of Poland, or Czechoslovakia, would genuine-

See page 312

TABLE 46

Post-war problems in Europe

Dates	Countries involved	Issue and resolution
1919–22	Poland and Lithuania	Possession of the town of *Vilna*. Won by the Polish Army in 1919 but taken from Poland and won by the Red Army in June 1920. In August taken by Lithuania, then again by the Polish Army in October. A plebiscite in January 1922 decided on union with Poland. Lithuania rejected this settlement, but was powerless to revise it.
1919–20	Poland and Czechoslovakia	Both countries claimed the area around the town of *Teschen*. In January 1919 Czech forces seized the town and there were serious clashes in the area. In July 1920 the area was divided between the two countries by the Conference of Ambassadors. (This was a body consisting of the ambassadors of the Great Powers in Paris.)
1919–20	Poland and Russia	The efforts of the Polish Government to push the Polish frontier eastwards resulted in war between the two countries. This war fluctuated both ways and was eventually settled by the Treaty of Riga (March 1921) by which Poland made considerable gains.
1919–21	Austria and Hungary	Both countries claimed the area of *Burgenland*. By the peace treaties it had been given to Austria, as most of the people were German. However, Hungarian troops occupied it and only left after a plebiscite organised by the Italians in December 1921. By it, most of the area was assigned to Austria.
1919–24	Italy and Yugoslavia	Both countries claimed the town of *Fiume* which was occupied by Italian forces led by D'Annunzio in September 1919. The issue was initially resolved by the Treaty of Rapallo (November 1920) by which Fiume became independent and Italy was given a number of the Dalmatian islands. But in March 1922 the town was again taken over by irregular Italian forces and eventually, in July 1924, Yugoslavia gave up its claim to the city and received Port Barros in exchange.
1919–22	Poland and Germany	The mineral rich area of *Upper Silesia* had been left undecided by the peace treaties as it contained a mixed population. A plebiscite of March 1921 was indecisive and in August 1922 the Conference of Ambassadors referred the matter to the League of Nations, whose Council accepted a partition scheme that had been drawn up by a committee of experts. By this, Germany received a larger part of the area but Poland won the richer mineral areas.

ly cope with either a German or a Soviet (or, at worst, a combined Soviet-German) attack? Or did the French Government really undertake the negotiations, and the treaties, as a way of satisfying its own conscience, and the protests of its people, in the aftermath of the American letdown? For their part, did the East European powers hold out much hope for the French to come to their aid if and when the Communist advance began?

Italy in 1914 and the USA in 1919 had shown that formal treaty arrangements were open to interpretation and could be used to justify both involvement and non-involvement in disputes. The 1930s were to show the same thing with more devastating effects. Consequently, the treaty arrangements of the 1920s were, to some extent, a sham. As long as the prevailing mood in Europe was peaceful, such treaties gave the semblance of security. In the face of the very threats that they were designed to combat, they were to be shown to be only as powerful as their signatories.

KEY ISSUE

How significant were the treaty arrangements of the 1920s?

D *International economic issues*

Two closely related economic issues dominated the early 1920s:

- all the combatants had suffered, to a greater or lesser degree, economic dislocation and, both during the war and in the period of reconstruction that followed it, had incurred enormous debts, partly to each other, but chiefly to the USA
- all the victors hoped to repay their debts, and continue their plans for reconstruction, through the reparations they were to be paid by the defeated Powers.

See pages 146–7

When the payment of these monies was not immediately forthcoming, the economic plans of the victor states were redundant and alternatives had to be sought. It was to seek such alternatives, and to try to salvage something from the reparations, that a series of international conferences were held.

At the Peace Conference, the final sum of reparations had not been settled, and a Reparations Commission had been set up to finalise this. During 1920 and 1921 a number of conferences were held with this aim in view. At Spa, in July 1920, Germany submitted a series of suggestions relating to the extent and methods of payment, which included plans for payment in kind. At the same time, the Allies agreed to apportion the payments in the ratio France 52 per cent, British Empire 22 per cent, Italy 10 per cent and Belgium 8 per cent. Further conferences were held in Paris, in January 1921, and London, in February and March 1921, to examine more detailed proposals.

Germany was supposed to have begun payments, to the tune of five billion dollars, before the final sum was fixed, and in March 1921 was claimed to be behind with its payments, although, using different figures, this was denied. The arguments and negotiations were ended by the decision of the Reparations Commission reached on 27 April 1921. Germany was to pay a total of 132 000 million gold marks (£6600 million or

KEY ISSUE

*How successfully were
reparations issues
resolved in the 1920s?*

See page 251

$33 000 million). At the reconvened London Conference two days later, it was decided that the first 1000 million marks were to be received by the end of May. In the event, this sum was not received until the end of August, and only then after a threat to occupy the Ruhr area and a loan from London bankers.

By this time, it was clear that the economic reconstruction of the victor Powers, and the repayment of debts, were less simple than had been hoped. Consequently, there followed a number of conferences intended to examine Europe's economic problems in as wide a context as possible.

The first of these was held at Genoa between 10 April and 19 May 1922. Significantly, representatives of Germany and the USSR attended, indicating a willingness to forget the quarrels of the immediate postwar period in the search for a genuine and lasting answer to Europe's economic problems.

The Genoa Conference had unexpected consequences. The Western Powers refused to moderate their demands for reparations from Germany, while France insisted that the new Soviet Government should repay its predecessor's debts. Therefore, Germany and the USSR felt as isolated and rejected as before and on 16 April signed the Treaty of Rapallo. Nevertheless, there was one optimistic sign in the aftermath of the Conference: on 31 May the Reparations Commission postponed all further payments from Germany for the rest of the year in view of the serious financial problems in Germany.

A second international conference was held in London in August 1922. It followed a British proposal of 1 August to cancel all debts to itself, and end its demands for reparations, if a general economic settlement could be reached, including America cancelling its debts from the European Powers. If the USA would not do this, then Britain would have to insist on sufficient payments to repay the USA. The American Government stated that, in its view, the debts to America were quite a separate issue to reparations and that they still stood. At the conference, therefore, France still sought repayment. Poincaré said that the postponement of payments could only continue if France received 'productive guarantees', including the exploitation of German mines in the Ruhr area and 60 per cent of the profits of German dye factories on the left bank of the Rhine. This demand brought sharp disagreement with Britain and the Conference broke up.

A second London Conference met in December 1922. This time, the new British Prime Minister, Bonar Law, agreed to cancel France's debts to Britain, even if America continued to require repayment. However, this had no tangible effects as Poincaré still sought German reparations, and these, in total, far outweighed France's debts to Britain.

One final effort to alter France's attitude was made at the Paris Conference of 2–4 January 1923, when Britain and Italy proposed that Germany's repayments could be staggered by them being paid in government bonds. This too was rejected. The French Government, with the support of the French people, remained adamant in its demands for cash payments supported by tangible payments in kind, such as coal and timber.

Consequently, after Germany had been declared in default on coal deliveries by the Reparations Commission on 9 January 1923, French and Belgian forces occupied the Ruhr area and remained there until the autumn, faced by a policy of passive resistance from the local population.

The reparations issue was ultimately resolved only by the intervention of the United States when, in April 1924, the Dawes Plan provided for the stabilisation of the German currency and the issue of a loan of 800 million gold marks to Germany to enable it to reconstruct and repay reparations. Significantly, the European Powers had not been able to resolve their economic problems for themselves.

See page 201

See page 202

E *The maintenance of future peace*

The chief hopes that the deluge of 1914–18 would not be repeated lay in the League of Nations. The League had been proposed in Wilson's Fourteen Points and its constitution (the 'Covenant') formed an integral part of the Treaty of Versailles. By it, a structure and organisation was provided not only to ensure that peace would be kept, but also that glaring denials of human rights should be eradicated. The organisation of the League is summarised in Diagram 5.

The Assembly was to be the heart of the League's activities. All members – the 41 original members had risen to 50 by 1924 and 60 by 1934 – were represented in the Assembly, where each had an equal vote. For important decisions, such as the imposition of sanctions, the vote of the members had to be unanimous, thus ensuring that any important action was not controversial. The Assembly admitted new member states and decided on the financial contributions of the different members.

Technically, the Assembly met only once a year, so a Council was formed to remain in permanent session and to take immediate action in a crisis. It had to report on and explain its actions to the Assembly, and was therefore accountable to it. Originally, there were eight members of the Council. Four of them, the four great victor Powers – Britain, France, Japan and Italy – were to be permanent members of the Council, while the other four, to be elected by the Assembly, were to be temporary members. The number of temporary members was raised to six in 1922 and to nine in 1926.

The Secretariat, headed by a Secretary-General, was to service both the Assembly and Council, as well as the League's other departments, with information, records and accounts. It would provide the inter-

DIAGRAM 5
The organisation of the League of Nations

preters and civil servants needed to run the new organisation from its headquarters at Geneva. Under the authority of the Assembly and Council, an International Court of Justice was convened at the Hague to deal with purely legal disputes between member states.

Numerous other bodies, usually referred to collectively as 'Special Departments', dealt with particular problems or topics. The ILO (International Labour Organisation) was the largest of these, having its own separate organisational structure. Governments, workers and employers were all represented on the ILO, which endeavoured to improve and standardise working conditions and employer-worker relations throughout the member states. There was a Mandates Commission to supervise the control of the mandated territories, a Drugs Department to attempt to end drugs trafficking, a Health Department, a Slavery Commission and a Refugees Department, among others. Between them, these new bodies would hopefully bring the better world that was promised after the 'war to end all wars'.

See page 145

The League had a number of means of maintaining international peace. When they joined the League by signing the Covenant, the members agreed to Article 10 of the Covenant, which stated: 'The Members of the League undertake to respect and preserve against external aggression the territorial integrity and existing political independence of all Members of the League'. Further articles of the Covenant – articles 16 and 17 – committed the members to take action against any member regarded as an aggressor by the League. In the first place, they were to sever trade relations (i.e. impose economic sanctions) and, if required 'contribute to the armed forces to be used to protect the Covenants of the League'. The keynote, therefore, was to be collective action by all members against an aggressor power.

In its early years, the League appeared to fulfil some of its promises. Several minor international issues were successfully dealt with. In 1921 Yugoslav troops were forced to leave Albania. The disputed ownership of the Aaland islands between Sweden and Finland was resolved when the islands were given to Finland on condition that the Finns established an independent government there. Also in 1921 the issue of the ownership of Upper Silesia was ended by a League decision.

League officials took over the administration of several areas that had created problems during the peace process. The 'free cities' of Danzig and Memel and the disputed territory of the Saar all came under the administration of League personnel.

Equally, the Special Departments of the League seemed to be making progress. The Health Department worked on the control of epidemics in Eastern Europe. The Refugees Department, headed by the Norwegian explorer, Fridtjof Nansen, gave considerable assistance to Austrian refugees in Vienna and to Greeks in Thrace and Asia Minor. The ILO won action on child labour in Persia, where it had long been the practice to employ very young children in making carpets.

The League was also charged to organise the promised disarmament of the Great Powers. However, little was actually done before 1926, although there were some other steps towards disarmament. The chief

KEY ISSUE

How successful was the League of Nations in resolving international issues?

of these were taken at the Washington Conference, which met from 12 November 1921 until 6 February 1922. It was convened by the United States and had two main purposes – to consider naval armaments and to examine peace in the Far East.

A series of agreements resulted from it:

- by the 'Four-Power Pacific Treaty', the USA, Britain, France and Japan mutually guaranteed each other's rights in the Pacific islands and promised to consult with each other if these rights were in any way threatened
- by the Shantung Treaty Japan returned Kiaochow to China
- two Nine-Power Treaties, signed by the previous four plus Holland, Belgium, Italy, China and Portugal, guaranteed China's territorial integrity and administrative independence. They also repeated the 'Open Door' principle, by which all Powers had equal rights of access to China
- a Naval Armaments Treaty was signed. By it, the signatories agreed not to build any warships over 10 000 tons with guns over 8″ over the next ten years. It also established a 'naval ratio' by which the USA and Britain were allowed 525 000 tons of capital shipping to Japan's 315 000 and France's and Italy's 175 000 tons. These were the first tentative steps towards arms control.

Despite the optimism surrounding the foundation of the League and the first armaments treaty, there were several disquieting signs in the early 1920s. These particularly surrounded the political activities of the League of Nations. For example, the League Commissioners in the Saar, headed by a Frenchman, angered the German population in the area by calling in French troops to quell a strike in 1923 and by issuing a decree which included penalties for criticising the Commissioners or the peace treaties. Similarly, the settlements in Vilna and Upper Silesia were adequate but left a number of unresolved problems.

Most disturbing of all was the Corfu incident of 1923. Mussolini had clearly acted forcefully before the true criminals were known and had threatened to withdraw from the League when Greece appealed to it, and had still come out as the winner in the dispute. If such an important member of the League as Italy could treat it with such disdain, what were the prospects for the League in a really important case?

See page 182

Equally, some of the flaws of the League were already becoming apparent. Three major Powers were not members. The USA had opted out, and both Germany and the USSR had been barred from membership on the insistence of Clemenceau and Wilson. Yet the very essence of the League was the collective action of its members. Such action was inevitably hampered by the absence of these powerful countries. Not only might their forces be needed in a crisis, but also their actions were less controllable as long as they were outside the League. Since the United States still played an important role in European affairs, especially with regard to German reparations, League membership seemed to some extent irrelevant. Moreover, the absence of these three Great

force historians to focus as much on the actions of the other Powers as on Germany. It is now accepted for example that many of Hitler's actions were determined by the response, or lack of response, of the Western Powers to events in the 1930s. However, historians have also emphasised that the policy of appeasement should not be presented simplistically as deriving from British 'sympathy' for German claims or a fear of war. There were persuasive arguments behind such a policy in 1938: for example Britain's concern with the threat from Japan to its Empire in the East and a realisation that war against Germany and Japan simultaneously would be too risky. There was also a need to get Britain's air defences up to scratch.

Some historians continued to argue that Hitler was bent on European and even world domination – the argument for example of the German historians Hillgruber and Hildebrand in *The Foreign Policy of the Third Reich*, published in 1973. However, some well-established historians like Alan Bullock pursued a middle course, pointing out that it was quite possible to have a specific aim, such as establishing an empire in Eastern Europe, whilst being opportunistic in the tactics employed to reach this goal. One of the fundamental questions is this: did Hitler actually *want* war, and therefore welcome the events of September 1939? Or was he trying to win the fruits of victory, without necessarily expecting or wanting war, relying instead on diplomatic manoeuvres – although he was not unhappy to fight when it came to the crunch? Or indeed, was Hitler consistent at all?

7 ∽ BIBLIOGRAPHY

A useful short survey is *Origins of the Second World War 1933–1939* by R Henig (Routledge, 1985). Also useful is *The Origins of the Second World War* by R Overy (Longman, 1987).

One of the most readable and controversial works on the subject is *The Origins of the Second World War* by AJP Taylor (Hamish Hamilton, 1961). Much of the ensuing controversy was summarised in *The Origins of the Second World War: A Symposium* edited by EM Robertson (Macmillan, 1971); and *The Origins of the Second World War Reconsidered* edited by G Martel (Unwin Hyman 1986). *The Great Dictators: International Relations 1918–39* by EG Rayner (Hodder and Stoughton, 1992) contains a collection of relevant sources along with commentaries and exercises and advice for students. *War and Peace: International Relations 1914–45* by D Williamson (Hodder and Stoughton, 1994) is also a useful survey with advice for students. A useful study of the League of Nations is *The League of Nations, its Life and Times* by FS Northedge (Leicester University Press, 1986).

An authoritative book on Spain is *The Spanish Civil War* by H Thomas (Eyre & Spottiswoode, 1961), and since updated. *Spain's Civil War* by H Browne (Longman, 1983) is also useful.

8 ⌒ STRUCTURED QUESTIONS AND ESSAYS

1. (a) Explain the meaning of 'reparations' in the context of the peace settlement in Europe after World War I; (3 marks)
    (b) Explain how the Dawes and Young Plans attempted to solve the problems caused by reparations; (7 marks)
    (c) To what extent had Franco-German hostility been ended by 1933? (15 marks)

2. To what extent had the hopes of the peacemakers of 1918–19 been fulfilled in Europe by 1929? (25 marks)

3. (a) Briefly explain the functions of the main organisations which made up the League of Nations; (10 marks)
    (b) How successful was the League of Nations as a peacekeeping agency in the 1920s? (15 marks)

4. Why did the economic crisis of 1929–31 so change international relations? (25 marks)

5. (a) Briefly outline the causes of the Manchurian crisis of 1931; (3 marks)
    (b) Explain how the Manchurian crisis was resolved; (7 marks)
    (c) How valid is the judgement that 'the League of Nations was a complete failure in the 1930s'? (15 marks)

6. (a) Why did Hitler and Mussolini intervene in the Spanish Civil War? (10 marks)
    (b) How successful was the British and French policy of Non-Intervention? (10 marks)
    (c) To what extent was the Spanish Civil war a struggle between Communism and Fascism? (10 marks)

7. (a) What do you understand by the term 'appeasement' in the context of European affairs in the 1930s? (3 marks)
    (b) Why did the Western Powers practice a policy of appeasement? (7 marks)
    (c) To what extent was appeasement in 1938 'a sensible concept, but applied in the wrong place at the wrong time'? (15 marks)

8. (a) Briefly outline the terms of the Nazi-Soviet Pact of 1939; (5 marks)
    (b) Why did the USSR fail to make an anti-Hitler alliance with Britain and France? (10 marks)
    (c) To what extent do you agree with the judgement that the Nazi-Soviet Pact 'made World War II inevitable'? (10 marks)

9 ⌐ AN EXERCISE ON THE CAUSES OF WORLD WAR II

Below are six different interpretations of the causes of World War II. Examine each carefully and expand upon it for yourself. In particular, assess whether you consider each to be a root cause that really lay behind the start of the war, or a contributory cause, that may have encouraged the war or affected the timing of its outbreak, but was not a fundamental reason for it. Also, assess whether each interpretation presents the view that the war was inevitable and unavoidable or the view that it could have been prevented, and if so how. Having done this, rank the interpretations offered into what you consider their order of importance and assess whether, between them, they offer a valid and sufficient explanation of the outbreak of war.

(1) The policy of appeasement encouraged Hitler to continue his plans for the expansion of the *Reich*. In particular, the attitude of the Western Powers at Munich confirmed his opinion that they would not go to war with Germany in defence of an East European power.

(2) Nazism meant war: once Hitler had come to power in Germany, a European war was inevitable as the aims and creed of Nazism were bound to conflict with those of other countries. One or more of these would ultimately attempt to resist Hitler.

(3) The creation of a series of weak states in Eastern Europe, especially ones that could not even agree with each other, brought about the war as it meant there was no state, or 'bloc' of states, to oppose Hitler in the very area that he had stated he planned to conquer.

(4) The unavoidable failure of the League of Nations in Manchuria and Ethiopia meant the end of collective security and, consequently, a return to the principle 'might is right'.

(5) Agreement between Britain and France and the Soviet Union would have prevented the outbreak of war. This agreement proved impossible only because of the fear and suspicion of Communism in Government circles in Britain and France, who must, therefore, take responsibility.

(6) The origins of World War II lie in the Treaty of Versailles. The penal clauses of that Treaty inevitably meant a hostile Germany that would, given the opportunity, attempt to redress its grievances.

An Outline of World War II in Europe

12

INTRODUCTION

THIS chapter provides a brief outline of World War II in Europe. There is not the space for treatment of the war against Japan in the Far East, a detailed study of the European countries under Hitler's rule, nor of the role of the air forces and the navies.

Between 1938 and 1940, Germany (and the USSR) conquered one country after another. There followed an almost complete lull in the fighting in Europe between June 1940 and June 1941, after which the focus of attention shifted to the Eastern Front, with continued success at first for Germany against the Soviet Union.

Until 1942 the Axis forces (Germany, Italy and Japan) achieved many successes, although crucially:

- they failed to knock Britain or the United States out of the war or force them to make peace
- they failed to destroy the USSR in a lightning campaign
- they failed to win a decisive victory in North Africa and the Middle East.

The first two failures were to be particularly significant.

In 1942, the Axis Powers suffered three major setbacks at the hands of the Allies (USA, USSR and Britain). In the Far East, the Japanese advance was held for the first time at the battles of Coral Sea and Midway, in Russia the German army was defeated at Stalingrad, and in North Africa the German and Italian armies were defeated at El Alamein. Thereafter, the history of the war was almost exactly the reverse of the first two years, and 1943–5 saw a series of defeats for the Axis forces.

1 ⤳ THE RUSSO-GERMAN CONQUEST OF EUROPE

A *The First Attacks: Poland and Finland*

On 1 September 1939 Germany launched *Blitzkrieg* or 'lightning-war' against Poland: a massive aerial onslaught followed by tank thrusts and fast moving infantry. The cumbersome Polish army was overrun. Soon the USSR launched its own attack on Poland from the East. Warsaw was heavily bombarded, both by air and artillery. Although the fighting continued in some areas until 5 October, the Poles, with no direct assistance from their Western allies, were defeated.

Germany and the USSR then divided the spoils. Germany annexed Danzig and over 30 000 square miles between East Prussia and Silesia. A further area of 39 000 square miles was not taken directly under German rule, but was known as the *Gouvernement General*, and was administered by Poles under German control. The USSR took over some 77 000 square miles of eastern Poland and over 22 million people including many White Russians. The Nazi-Soviet Pact had borne fruit within little more than a month.

However, Stalin had little faith in Hitler's promises in the Pact, and was eager to build a buffer between himself and the enlarged Germany. He forced the Baltic States of Estonia, Latvia and Lithuania to allow Russian troops and ships to be stationed in their countries.

The Finnish Government refused more extensive Soviet demands, including cessation of the Karelian isthmus between Lake Ladoga and the Gulf of Finland and in November 1939 the Russians declared war. The League of Nations' last, pathetically defiant, act against an aggressor, was to expel the USSR from its organisation.

See Map 24 on page 319

The Soviets won the 'Winter War' against Finland with difficulty. As a result of the treaty signed in March 1940, the USSR acquired 70 miles of the Karelian Isthmus and an area to the north of Lake Ladoga. Leningrad seemed more secure.

B *The 'phoney' war and the defeat of Norway*

After his easy victory in Poland, Hitler was expected to turn his attentions to the West and attack France. But he had no direct interest in such an attack: it might be that the Western Allies would still agree to give him a free hand in Eastern and Central Europe, and there were no detailed plans for a westwards offensive. As a result, the winter of 1939–40 saw little military activity in Western Europe and was christened the 'phoney war'. In Britain and France, the Governments prepared for the type of war they expected to come. Industry and agriculture came under more direct government control; rationing was introduced; children were evacuated to the countryside so that they would avoid the expected bombing raids.

Only at sea was there any significant activity, as German U-boats immediately began a campaign of unrestricted attacks against combatant and neutral shipping. In the River Plate in South America, the German battleship the *Admiral Graf von Spee* was cornered and scuttled itself.

The Phoney War ended in the spring of 1940, with the German occupation of Denmark and Norway to secure them as bases against Britain and to protect shipments of iron ore from Sweden to Germany. Allied forces sent to resist the Germans in Norway had to be withdrawn.

In France, the Russian victory in Finland led to the downfall of Daladier. In Britain, Chamberlain was replaced as Prime Minister on 10 May by Winston Churchill, long-time opponent of appeasement.

KEY ISSUE

Why did the Germans have so much success with Blitzkrieg in 1939–40?

MAP 24
*The campaigns against Finland
and Norway 1939–40*

C *The Low Countries and France*

On 10 May 1940, German troops attacked both Holland and Belgium. Rotterdam was systematically bombed from the air, and a part of it almost completely destroyed. Within days Holland surrendered. On 14 May, the very day of the Dutch surrender, the Germans made a vital breakthrough in the South through the wooded Ardennes into France, using the *Blitzkrieg* tactics successfully tried out in Poland. German forces threatened to cut off the Allied troops in Belgium.

As British troops retreated towards the sea, Belgium surrendered to the Germans. Some 200 000 British and 140 000 French troops were evacuated by sea from Dunkirk, leaving their equipment in Belgium, and returned to Britain.

The Germans turned their attack southwards into France. Marshal Pétain took over the French Government, which accepted armistice terms from Germany:

MAP 25

The German conquest of the Low Countries and France 1940

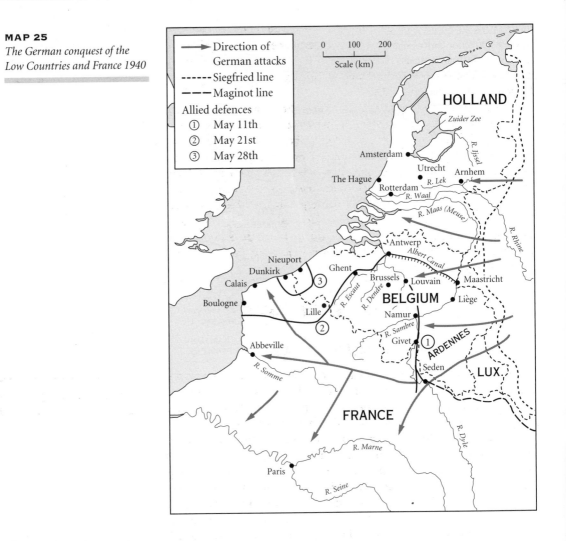

- Northern and Western France was to be occupied by the Germans. This meant that Germany took direct control of all the country's ports and of the northern industrial region
- the rest of the country was to continue under the rule of Pétain, whose Government was to be based at Vichy.

French troops were to be demobilised and the navy disarmed.

The French General Charles de Gaulle went to London when Pétain took over. He refused to accept surrender and announced the establishment of a Provisional National Committee to work for the liberation of France. The British sank the French fleet at Oran to prevent it falling into German hands.

D *The Battle of Britain*

The fall of France opened a new phase in the war. It left Britain alone against Germany, although Churchill rejected Hitler's offer of peace, which he made because he now wanted to focus his attention upon Eastern Europe. Hitler therefore pressed ahead with his plans for an attack on Britain. First the Royal Air Force would have to be destroyed. The result was the Battle of Britain, fought over Southern England in the summer of 1940.

In September the German attack shifted from the airfields to the major ports and cities, the start of the Blitz. Hitler was no longer preparing the ground for invasion, but rather attacking the civilian population in an effort to destroy morale. London, together with ports like Bristol and Southampton and cities like Birmingham and Coventry, all suffered heavily. Nonetheless, the invasion was postponed and the resolve of the British to go on fighting had not been destroyed. British resolve was boosted by aid from the USA acquired from March 1941 onwards under the Lend-Lease system, by which the President was permitted to supply any state 'whose defence the President deems vital to the defence of the USA'.

2 ✍ THE WIDENING WAR

A *Africa and the Balkans*

The Battle of Britain marked the end of the first phase of the war. Until September 1940 Germany had not been checked and had brought much of Europe under its control. Germany continued to make progress, but no longer in a single 'victory-by-victory' style in which each conquest was followed up by another. Instead, the war widened into a number of fronts, the most critical of which, to both sides, was the Russian. Because of its importance, this has been treated separately, but the other fronts have been summarised in the chart on pages 323–4.

See Map 26 on page 322

There was little fighting in Europe during the year from June 1940 to June 1941, since most of Western and Central Europe was under Hitler's control. There was fighting in Africa and Greece, areas in which Italy was seeking to expand its empire. Mussolini's decision to attack Egypt was to ultimately lead to his downfall.

See page 189

B *The invasion of Russia (1941–March 1943) and the entry of the USA*

Hitler had formally issued orders for the invasion of Russia in December 1940. It had always been a part of his plans to capture the south of European Russia and take its rich cornfields and raw materials. He and his advisers were convinced that the USSR would fall a relatively easy prey, an opinion shared by Western intelligence experts.

The German attack on the USSR was launched on three fronts in June 1941: one prong, assisted by Romanian forces, attacked through Southern Poland towards Kiev: its ultimate goals, when the Ukraine had been brought under German control, were the Don Basin and even the Caucasus oil fields. A second attack was launched through the Baltic

States and aimed to take the city of Leningrad (as Petrograd had been re-named). The third, central, prong of the attack was to go towards the capital, Moscow. The Germans were better equipped than the Russians and enjoyed air superiority.

MAP 26

Europe at the height of Axis expansion October 1942

Date	Balkans and east Mediterranean	Middle East	North Africa	East Africa	The War at Sea
1940					
26 June	USSR demanded and acquired Bessarabia and northern Bukovina from Romania.				
6 August				Italian forces occupied British Somaliland	
17 August					Germany declared total blockade of Britain
30 August	Under German and Russian pressure, Transylvania was ceded to Hungary.				
8 September	Romania forced to cede Southern Dobrudja to Bulgaria				
13 September			Italian attack on Egypt launched from Libya.		
8 October	German troops entered Romania				
28 October	Italian troops invaded Greece from Albania. British troops sent to Greece				
13 November					British aircraft sank three Italian battleships at Taranto
20 November	Hungary joined the Axis				
23 November	Romania joined the Axis				
3 December	Greek victory in Albania, pushing Italian forces back and forcing Germany to come to Italy's aid				
8 December			British counterattacked and moved into Libya		
1941					
15 January				British attack from Sudan and Kenya into Italian East Africa	
22 January		Capture of Tobruk by Allies			
7 February		Benghazi captured			
26 February				Mogadishu, capital of Italian Somaliland, captured	

(continued)

Date	Balkans and east Mediterranean	Middle East	North Africa	East Africa	The War at Sea
1 March	Bulgaria joined Axis and German troops occupied Sofia				
25 March	Yugoslavia signed Axis Pact but then Paul overthrown and new				
30 March	Government declared its neutrality				Battle of Cape Matapan—three Italian cruisers and two destroyers sunk
3 April			Italian forces, reinforced by German troops, re-entered Libya		
6 April				Addis Ababa fell to British and Haile Selassie reinstated	
17 April	Surrender of Yugoslavia				
23 April	Surrender of Greece				
20 May	German paratroopers invaded Crete				
27 May					German battleship *Bismarck* sunk
31 May		British forces entered Baghdad			
8 June		Combined Allied attack on Syria. German treaty with Turkey			
18 June					
22 June	German attack on Russia				
14 July		Armistice with Syria			
18 November			British counterattack launched into Libya, and Tobruk relieved		
7 December					Japanese attack on Pearl Harbour
1942 27 May			Axis attack launched: Tobruk taken and advance into Egypt halted at El Alamein		

The impact of the war on the home front

The scale of World War II was such that all the European countries were drastically affected not just by military operations but in terms of the impact on economies, political life, societies and attitudes. 'Total war' involved everybody, not just those in uniform but those civilians who endured bombing, rationing and other changes to their lives. Those populations living under the rigour of Nazi occupation were affected most. In the occupied countries of Western Europe, civilians got on with their lives as best they could, and generally survived, unless they took dangerous risks such as joining resistance movements, or were unlucky enough to be Jews deported to death camps in the East or as labourers to Germany. Occupation in the Eastern areas such as Poland was far more rigorous, with whole communities being forced to resettle and generally being treated as inferior races, and either being exterminated if they belonged to a particularly despised group such as the Jews, or made to work as slave labour for the German *Reich* if they were Slavs.

However, even populations which were not directly under German rule, such as the British, had to adjust to wartime conditions: whether it was rationing; joining the home guard, evacuation away from cities into the countryside, working in the Women's Land Army. All nations experienced an increase in control over their lives as Governments took on extraordinary powers in order to boost the war effort. In the USSR, where the State already controlled people's lives to an extraordinary degree, ordinary people would not have noticed much change in terms of individual freedom. Yet even here, those Soviet citizens living in areas not under German occupation would still have noticed considerable changes to their lives.

It is not possible to detail the impact of the war on every country involved, but the USSR will be taken as an example of the ways in which it could impact upon society, the economy and attitudes.

POPULAR INVOLVEMENT

Soon after the German attack in 1941, not only were all reservists called up into the armed forces, but emergency labour laws drafted all able-bodied man between 18 and 45, and women between 18 and 40, into work in defence industry or on defence construction. The upper age limits were later raised, people were tied to their jobs, and the whole nation was mobilised for the war effort.

GOVERNMENT CONTROLS AND PROPAGANDA

Government controls, already much in evidence, were further strengthened by the war. Censorship was tightened up; propaganda was increased, both to heighten fear and loathing of the enemy and to encourage greater unity and effort from the population; a People's Militia was formed to provide back up support for the army; the secret police became ever more active in rooting out possible 'defeatism', opposition or slackening.

LIVING CONDITIONS

The war caused a crisis in living standards for the Soviet people. Food rationing was implemented in the first months of the war. The rations were minimal, and people often did not get their entitlement. The majority of the population existed at subsistence level, and disease and starvation were common, reflecting the fact that the USSR's economy was severely disrupted by the German attack and the Government ruthlessly determined its priorities, transferring resources from consumption to production. In contrast to the Soviet experience, rationing in Britain actually succeeded in raising the standard of health by the end of the war.

SOCIAL AND ECONOMIC CHANGES

The employment of women, already a notable feature of the Five-Year Plans in the USSR, reached new heights in the war. Women soon formed the bulk of the civilian work force. The war saw an exodus of people from rural areas into the armed services or into cities. Disruption and lack of training led to a major decline in productivity, although overall production levels for the war sector increased considerably. The bureaucracy increased in size. Minority national groups such as the Volga Germans and the Crimean Tartars, whose loyalty was suspect to the regime, suffered harsh treatment such as wholesale deportation to new areas of the country.

Some features of the impact of the war on employment in the USSR can be deduced from the following tables, both adapted from *The Soviet Home Front 1941–1945* by J. Barber (1991). Reproduced by kind permission of Pearson Education Ltd (Longman).

TABLE 47

The composition of the Soviet Working Population 1940–5 (millions, annual average)

	1940	1941	1942	1943	1944	1945
Military personnel	4.2	7.5	10.9	11.1	11.2	11.6
Public Sector Employees	31.2	28.0	18.4	19.4	23.6	27.3
Collective Farmers	47.0	34.9	22.7	23.8	28.9	33.6
Working Population	85.1	72.8	53.3	55.6	65.3	74.6

	1940	1941	1942	1943	1944	1945
Public Sector	38	–	53	57	57	55
industry	41	–	52	53	53	51
construction	23	–	24	29	–	32
transport	21	–	35	42	45	40
farming	34	–	54	61	–	61
Collective farming	–	52	62	73	78	80

TABLE 48
The proportion of women in employment in the USSR 1940–5 (per cent). Extract *from* The Soviet Home Front 1941–1945 *by J. Barber (1991). Reproduced by kind permission of Pearson Education Ltd (Longman).*

Britain and the USSR signed an alliance, and the USA also extended its lend-lease arrangements to Moscow. However, the Germans made rapid progress on all fronts, getting to the outskirts of Leningrad and capturing the Ukraine. In the centre, a huge offensive was launched towards Moscow during October. There, however, it was held by the Soviet Army, and the offensive came to a halt in December.

Air power in World War II

ANALYSIS

Air power played a far more crucial role in World War II compared to World War I, although there were arguments at the time and since about its precise importance and how it should be used.

Many soldiers believed that the best use of air power was to provide tactical support for land operations. This was seen possibly at its most effective in the *Blitzkrieg* tactics used by Germany to achieve its rapid victories in Poland and Western Europe in 1939–40: the use of fighter aircraft and light bombers in conjunction with tanks and infantry to disrupt enemy defences and allow for rapid advances.

In contrast, most Western air experts before the war believed in the strategic primacy of the bomber: it could cause such damage to the enemy's industry and civilian morale that it could virtually win the war by itself, as an independent weapon. The failure of the German Blitz of 1940–1 appeared to disprove this theory, although the evidence was not conclusive because the German airforce had not developed heavy bombers and strategic bombing had never been an important part of its philosophy. The British and American air forces put much more faith in bombing of Germany, and their heavy bombers dropped much more tonnage of bombs on Germany between 1941 and 1945 than the Germans had dropped on Britain. Much damage was certainly done. However, bombing raids were very costly – the highest casualty rates in the war were among bomber crews – and there was controversy about how much damage conventional bombing could actually do. In order to seriously disrupt war production the same areas had to be bombed repeatedly, and precision bombing techniques were not accurate enough. German war production was maintained and even increased well into 1944. Moreover, although bombing affected civilian morale, it did not destroy it. However, supporters of strategic bombing claimed that other immeasurable effects could not be ignored: for example they calculated that the enemy, as a result of bombing, was forced to divert large quantities of resources into air defence and rebuilding damaged factories that otherwise would have gone into supporting front line ground operations.

What was indisputable was the fact that more sophisticated air weapons had changed the nature of warfare forever. No army or navy could now be safe without adequate air support. Air power played an important part in the German *Blitzkrieg* tactics in 1939–41. The cause of the Battle of Britain was German and British recognition that Hitler could not risk a seaborne invasion of Britain without destroying the Royal Air Force first, otherwise his naval forces would be destroyed. By the end of the war more sophisticated and deadly weapons of destruction from the air had been developed, such as jet aircraft, and the atom bombs dropped on Japan in 1945.

KEY ISSUE

Why did Germany fail to defeat the Soviet Union?

Despite its territorial gains, the German Army had not been as successful as it appeared. Although the Soviet frontline armies had crumbled, and thousands of Soviet soldiers were killed or captured, the Germans were increasingly met with fierce resistance. It was not for nothing that Russians referred to World War II as 'The Great Patriotic War'. Some Soviet civilians, in parts of the Ukraine for example, initially welcomed the Germans as liberators. But brutal Nazi treatment of Soviet soldiers and civilians alike – the Nazis treated the campaign as a war to enslave or exterminate inferior races – quickly lost them support. Rather, the civilians, often in company with any serviceable equipment and materials, were evacuated and the Germans forced to bring up their own equipment over enormous distances. Over 25 000 miles of railway track had to be either rebuilt or converted to German gauge in the central region alone. Moreover, the German troops suffered badly during the winter of 1941–2, having not been prepared for a long winter campaign. However, the Germans survived the winter and were once again ready to take the offensive in May.

The German failure to defeat the USSR in a *blitzkrieg* war in 1941 was a decisive turning point in the war. Once the USSR had survived the initial onslaught, it was always likely to defeat the Germans. Unlike Hitler, Stalin from the very beginning of the war put his country on a total war footing. The Soviets greatly outproduced the Nazis, apart from Western aid, and the unified Soviet command structure, which applied to both the military and the economy, worked much more efficiently than the German system. The latter was improved by Albert Speer later in the war, but by then it was too late.

See page 223

MAP 27
The Eastern Front 1939–43

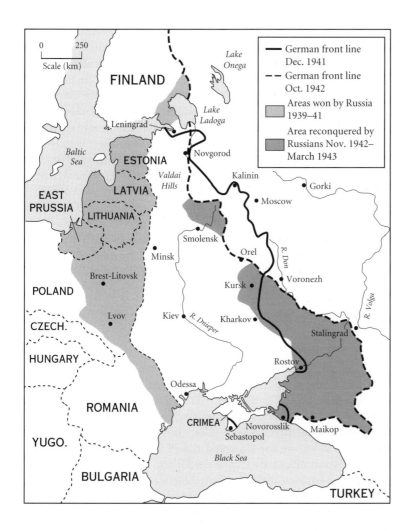

Legend:
- German front line Dec. 1941
- German front line Oct. 1942
- Areas won by Russia 1939–41
- Area reconquered by Russians Nov. 1942– March 1943

Sea power in World War II

The experience of World War I had been that the submarine had overtaken the surface ship as the most potent naval weapon, particularly as the combatants proved reluctant to risk their great warships in open battle at sea. In several respects World War II confirmed this trend, particularly as surface ships were now also vulnerable to attack from the air. Nevertheless, the war at sea was still crucial. In the Pacific campaign, covering a vast area, naval operations were very important, including the use of aircraft carriers to support air operations. For a country such as Britain control of the sea was vital, since the blocking off of trade, particularly vital imports, would have crippled its attempts to continue the war. Churchill recognised this when he declared that the 'Battle of the Atlantic', the long campaign involving German

U-boats preying on shipping, particularly between the USA and Britain, was ultimately of more significance to the outcome of the war than the Battle of Britain. Until 1943 the British were in danger of suffering unacceptable losses of shipping from convoys bringing vital supplies to Britain, and it was fortunate that Germany did not realise the full potential of submarine warfare and devote more resources to building up their U-boat fleet than they did. Whilst occasional naval engagements involving great warships, such as the sinking of the German battleship *Bismarck* in 1941 (which, significantly, could not have been achieved without the participation of aircraft) attracted great attention, the U-boat war was of more significance. However, sea power remained a vital part of operations overall: the Allied invasion of France in 1944 could never have taken place without command of the sea and sufficient resources to land the invasion force safely.

By the time of a new German offensive in the USSR in the spring of 1942, the whole balance of the war had been altered by the entry of Japan and the USA into the war following the Japanese raid on Pearl Harbour on 7 December 1941. The attack had the immediate effect of solidifying the alliances on both sides. On 11 December Germany and Italy declared war on the USA, and signed a full military alliance with Japan. This was ultimately to prove a decisive factor in the outcome of the war. The Japanese attack brought America into the war, and Hitler's declaration enabled the American President to get backing for the principle that the defeat of Germany was the first priority. Hitler certainly underestimated the power of the United States. Only the Soviet Union stayed out of the mutual declarations of war, having signed a mutual non-aggression pact with Japan earlier in 1941. However, it did join the United States and Britain in January 1942 in signing a joint declaration pledging an all-out war against all their enemies and agreeing not to make a separate peace.

In 1942, Hitler restricted his offensive against the USSR to the southern front: the south contained the rich industrial area of the Don Basin and the oilfields of the Caucasus. Ultimately, German forces might be able to take the Caucasus and march southwestwards to link up with Axis forces from North Africa to take the Middle East in a mighty pincer movement.

By mid-August they had made considerable advances over the Don and into the Caucasus, the first German forces reached the outskirts of Stalingrad. They were to remain outside the city until the end of January, having encountered some of the stiffest resistance of the war. Thomson has described the battle as 'a sort of Verdun in reverse – an objective so vital for Germany to win that she poured in her men and material extravagantly, only to lose both to no avail'. As the German Sixth Army fought snipers among the streets and ruins of the city, the Soviets attacked from the North-East in September and from the South in October. The German Army was trapped in a pincer, with the city in front of it and Russian armies in its rear. All efforts to extricate it from its dilemma were repulsed and in January 1943 the surviving 80 000 Germans surrendered. At the same time, the siege of Leningrad was relieved, and the Germans were driven back over 200 miles on a wide front in the South.

3 ‒ THE MEDITERRANEAN COUNTER ATTACK

A *The Allied conquest of North Africa*

In the summer of 1942 Axis forces were successful in North Africa. Tobruk was captured in June and German troops advanced along the coast to take Bardia. The British forces formed their defensive line at El Alamein, 70 miles west of Alexandria, and bounded on one side by the sea and on the other by the Qattara Depression. Following a German attack, the British launched a counter-attack in October, breaking through and taking some 30 000 prisoners, many of them Italian. The Germans began a long retreat. Anglo-American landings in the north-west took place in November 1942, at Casablanca, Oran and Algiers. As a result of the invasion, and ostensibly to guard against an attack on the southern coast, the Germans occupied southern France and removed Pétain's regime.

By May 1943 Allied forces had pushed Axis forces well back into Tunisia. In all the Axis Powers had lost nearly a million men, 8000 air-craft and two and a half million tons of shipping in the North African fighting. Mussolini's dreams of an Italian Empire in Africa were dead, as were Hitler's hopes for the domination of Egypt and the Middle East. Instead, the Allies had reopened the southern Mediterranean to shipping and had made possible attacks into Southern Europe.

B *The Invasion of Italy*

The Allied leaders had agreed at the Casablanca Conference in January 1943 that the invasion of Italy should follow victory in North Africa. They had accepted that any attempt to reconquer France should not be made before 1944. Such an attack was seen as the key to victory in Europe, and should therefore only be undertaken when enough men and materials had been prepared to ensure success. In the meantime, an attack was made on Italy in order to relieve pressure on the Red Army on the Eastern Front. In July 1943, Allied forces landed in Sicily, an event which prompted the overthrow of Mussolini. The new Italian Government secretly surrendered to the Allies on 3 September. American forces soon landed at Salerno. As expected, the Germans did not

See page 189

accept this all too easy surrender, but occupied much of Italy. The Allies made slow progress, not capturing Rome until June. The final conquest of Italy was not complete until 1 May 1945.

The conquest of Italy had brought the Allies several advantages:

● it eliminated Italian troops not only from Italy but also from other fronts
● it also occupied up to 26 divisions of German troops which might otherwise have been available in France or Russia at a crucial time
● it provided the Allies with bases for bombing raids into the Balkans, Southern France and Central Europe, which would otherwise have been out of their range.

4 ↪ THE DEFEAT OF GERMANY

A *The Eastern Front 1943–5*

After the Soviet successes of early 1943, a German counter-attack was expected. It came in July at Kursk, but petered out. Kursk was the largest tank battle of the war and marked the end of major German offensives in Russia. The Soviets launched their own offensive against the German salient around Orel.

See Map 28 on page 333

The success of the operation confirmed the Soviet generals in their belief that they could now move to the offensive and it was decided that this should be launched at various points in order to force the German defenders to move from one place to another to reinforce their line. These Soviet offensives, apart from minor setbacks, were almost entirely successful and not only drove the Germans out of the USSR but also provided a launching pad for a Soviet attack into Germany. In order to record this advance as simply and briefly as possible, it has been catalogued in the timeline below, which can be studied in conjunction with Map 28.

TIMELINE

1943	**August**	Soviet offensives launched. In the north, advance towards Smolensk (captured 5 September); in the South, reaching the river Dnieper on a 400-mile front by October.
	November	Kiev recaptured.
1944	**Jan–Feb**	In the north an offensive from Leningrad relieved the siege
	March–April	Soviet forces crossed the Dniester and entered (pre-war) Poland. In early May the Crimea was recaptured.
	10 June	Offensive in northern-central sector. Viborg taken.
	June–July	Offensives in northern-central sector liberated Vitbsk and Minsk.

July–October	In Poland, the advance from the South led to capture of Lvov, Brest-Litovsk and Lublin but the advance halted outside Warsaw. As a result, the Germans turned on the Polish supporters in Warsaw and crushed them; there was considerable political outcry at the failure of the Soviets to provide them with more aid. In the north, the Soviet advance through Latvia reached the Gulf of Riga. Soviet troops reached East Prussia.
August	Romania surrendered. Romania joined the Allies.
September	Bulgaria surrendered and Soviet troops entered Sofia.
October	Belgrade liberated by the Soviets.
1945 January	Three-pronged Soviet assault on Poland and East Prussia. Warsaw, Cracow and Lodz taken. The Red Army reached the Oder and by 20 February Soviet forces were within 30 miles of Berlin.
20 April	Soviet troops entered Berlin.

MAP 28

The Eastern Front 1943–5

Throughout the advance, the Soviets had concentrated on the Southern front although it was ultimately in the north – through East Prussia and Poland – that the decisive battles were to be fought. This concentration on the South was chiefly because it was easier to attack there and success was more assured. It was also the result of Stalin's determination to ensure that the East European states of Bulgaria, Romania, Yugoslavia and Hungary would be loyal to the Soviet Union after the war.

In view of the USSR's singular failure to successfully resist Germany's attacks in 1941, its spectacular successes in 1943–5 were remarkable. They were chiefly due to sheer courage and fortitude, highly effective and efficient artillery, improving administration of the Red Army, and the assistance of America and Britain.

B *D-Day and the reconquest of Europe*

The Allied leaders had always accepted that victory in Europe would finally be achieved by the reconquest of France and subsequent invasion of Europe. The landings were elaborately prepared and finally carried out in Normandy in June 1944. In the first 100 days of the operation, over two million men, 450 000 vehicles and four million tons of equipment had reached France. By August the Allied advance through France was supported by Franco-American landings at Toulon in the south of France, which then moved northwards to join the main attack. On 26 August the Allies reached Paris, and de Gaulle and the Free French forces marched into their capital.

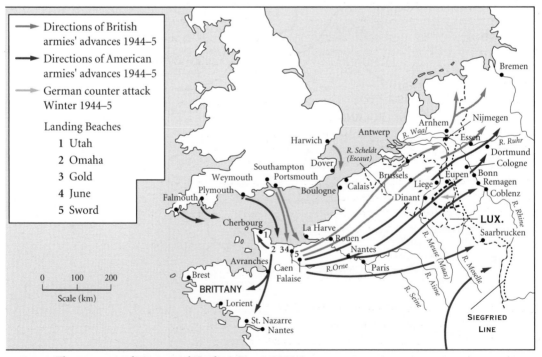

MAP 29 *The reconquest of Western and Northern Europe 1944–5*

In early September, the advance continued and Brussels and Antwerp were liberated. In order to secure crossings of the vital rivers of Holland, Allied paratroopers were landed at Arnhem but were isolated and had to be withdrawn without capturing the crossing. Following this, the Germans launched their last counter-offensive against Allied lines, but this 'Battle of the Bulge' failed. By March 1945 Germany was under attack from both sides. On 16 April the Soviets launched what proved to be the final attack on Berlin from the Oder. On 6 March American forces reached Cologne and were able to cross the Rhine.

On 25 April the fate of Germany was sealed: Berlin was surrounded, and Soviet and American troops met up at Torgau. On 1 May Hitler's death was broadcast to the German people: he had committed suicide in his bunker the night before. Admiral Dönitz took over and, on 7 May, the official surrender was signed. On 8 May President Truman and Prime Minister Churchill announced the victory in Europe (VE) to their people, and the next day Stalin told his people that their war was over.

Historians have argued at great length about the reasons for Germany's defeat in the war. Much criticism was directed at Hitler personally. He did make serious errors, such as his declaration of war against the United States, which made it easier for Roosevelt to persuade the American people that they had to fight Germany. But having got himself into war in 1939, many of Hitler's military decisions were quite rational, until his judgement and health deteriorated in the later stages of the war.

The defeat of Germany was brought about by many factors. Among them was the failure of the Germans to command both the sea and the air – something for which they had not planned, having counted upon a short war. But the chief reason for Germany's defeat lay in the overwhelming economic superiority of the United States and the USSR, in addition to the battlefield sacrifices of the Red Army. Once Hitler had failed to defeat Stalin in a *blitzkrieg* campaign in 1941, and the Americans were involved in the war, it was unlikely that the Axis Powers could win. The Germans did well in resisting the Grand Alliance for so long, but the war hastened the process by which Europe was losing its supremacy to the new Superpowers of the USA and the USSR. Even traditional Great Powers like Britain which had contributed to the Allied victory, and in Britain's case, had stood alone against Germany for several months, were bankrupted by their victory and saw their real power decline. The old dominance of Europe was over.

> **KEY ISSUE**
>
> *Why was Germany ultimately defeated in World War II?*

5 ⌐ BIBLIOGRAPHY

There are many hundreds of books on World War II. This is a very restricted list. All the books contain bibliographies which will refer you to more detailed works and to works on more specialist aspects.

One of the best introductory books on the war as a whole remains *World at War* by Mark Arnold Forster (Collins, 1973), which was originally the book accompanying a television series of the same name. It contains extensive illustrations and highlights all the important features of the War, illustrating them with personal memories that are often taken from interviews for the television series. Another readable history of the war is *A World in Flames: A Short History of the Second World War in Europe, 1939–1945* by M Kitchen (Longmans, 1990). Another work is *History of World War II* edited by AJP Taylor and compiled by SL Mayer (Octopus Books, 1974). This is adapted from the magazine series 'History of the Twentieth Century' and contains many colour pictures and diagrams and chapters by separate authors not only on military but also political and social aspects of the war. AJP Taylor also produced *The Second World War: An Illustrated History* (Hamish Hamilton, 1975, also published by Penguin). Another useful work, and one that includes documents, is *The Ordeal of Total War 1939–45* by G Wright (Harper Torchbooks, 1968). *War in Europe 1939–1945* by A Wood (Longmans Seminar Studies, 1987), contains some documents but is most useful for its lengthy introduction.

Some books that may help you with different aspects of the war include: Robert Aron, *The Vichy Regime* (Putnam, 1958); *Hitler's War Directives* (Sidgewick & Jackson, 1964); *To Lose a Battle* by A Horne (Macmillan, 1969); *The Russo-German War, 1941–1945* (Barker, 1971); *Six Armies in Normandy* by J Keegan (Penguin, 1983).

6 ∽ STRUCTURED QUESTIONS AND ESSAYS

1. (a) What do you understand by the term 'Blitzkrieg'? (3 marks)
    (b) Why did Germany achieve such rapid successes in the military campaigns of 1939–41? (11 marks)
    (c) Why did Germany fail to defeat Britain in this period? (11 marks)
2. Why was Germany successful in 1939–41, and ultimately defeated in 1945? (25 marks)
3. In what ways (a) was the war similar to; and (b) different from, the campaigns of World War I? (25 marks)

Europe and the Cold War 1945–62

13

INTRODUCTION

The nature of the Cold War

The Cold War is a term used to describe the tension which characterised relations between the two Superpowers, the USSR and USA. They emerged from World War II theoretically as allies, but in practice as the representatives of two incompatible political, economic and social systems – one representing the Socialist world, one the capitalist one.

Europe was weakened by the ravages of war. Even European states on the victors' side, notably Britain, had been bankrupted by the experience of total war. The USA and the USSR rapidly replaced Europe as the centres of world power, a process already begun before the war but accelerated by it. Yet, ironically many of the tensions of the Cold War were played out in Europe and particularly in Germany, without ever escalating into what would have been, in an era of nuclear weapons, a devastating 'hot' war. The respective leaders of the 'free' capitalist world and the Soviet-dominated *Bloc* of Central and Eastern Europe manoeuvred for influence in a divided Europe until the late 1980s and the eventual dissolution of the USSR. Although there were flashpoints and periods of heightened tension along the way – for example the Berlin Blockade, the building of the Berlin Wall and the invasions of Hungary and Czechoslovakia – it was also paradoxically a period of stability. The Cold War was played out according to certain implicit conventions, whilst many of the old enmities, particularly those which had existed between France and Germany, faded into virtual insignificance.

Soon after World War II Europe was divided into two armed camps, separated by the 'Iron Curtain', and with both sides confronting the other with propaganda or threats. Yet, despite the apparently all-pervasive nature of this confrontation, its end came suddenly in 1989, chiefly because Gorbachev's USSR gave up the unequal struggle to match American economic power and ceased to stand in the way of fundamental change in the previously Communist-dominated Central and Eastern European states. Without Soviet backing, the Communist regimes quickly fell apart, the process beginning even before the breaching of the Berlin Wall in late 1989 marked the symbolic end of Cold War Europe.

In this and the following chapter the impact of the Cold War on Europe will be analysed, with a focus on particular aspects and flashpoints. Whilst reference will be made to the impact of the Cold War

KEY ISSUE

How was the balance of world power changed by World War II?

world-wide, taking account for example of crises in areas such as Korea and Cuba, the focus will be on Europe itself.

1 ⌐ THE ORIGINS OF THE COLD WAR

In terms of its impact upon Europe, the Cold War really dates back to the Russian Revolution of 1917:

See page 251

● Communist Russia after 1917 appeared to threaten the liberal democracies of Western Europe. The Comintern, founded in 1919, was dedicated to working towards the overthrow of capitalism. In turn, Western Governments tried to crush Bolshevism in its cradle in the Russian Civil War of 1918–21
● the USSR was effectively isolated from the West. Although fear of Nazi Germany caused the USSR and the Western Powers to seek some form of alliance in the 1930s, mutual suspicion prevented effective collaboration – marked dramatically by the sudden signing of the Nazi-Soviet Pact in 1939, when Stalin realised that, at least in the short term, he had more to gain from allying with Hitler
● when Germany invaded the USSR in 1941, the USSR and the West perforce became allies against the greater enemy. However, mutual suspicion was never far below the surface: for example the Soviets suspected that the West was prepared to let the USSR do the bulk of the fighting against Germany; whilst many in the West were afraid that as the Red Army drove the Germans out of Central and Eastern Europe in 1944–5, they would establish Soviet power in those regions. Mutual suspicions were not resolved by the Great Power conferences at Yalta and Potsdam.

KEY ISSUE

To what extent were the seeds of the Cold War already in place before 1945?

ANALYSIS

The Yalta and Potsdam conferences

The Yalta Conference was the final summit held before the end of the war, and was attended by Stalin, Churchill and Roosevelt. Agreements at Yalta included the following:

● Germany would be occupied by the Allies
● The USSR would join in the war against Japan
● The Soviet-Polish border would be moved Westwards and Poland would be compensated by territory taken from Germany
● Stalin agreed to free elections in Poland.

Yalta was to be a controversial topic. Some historians and right-wing commentators came to see it as a betrayal of smaller Powers, especially Poland, which was essentially handed over to the USSR. Those hostile to Yalta saw it as a cynical manipulation of the Western leaders by Stalin, who skilfully played on the divisions between naïve Roosevelt and the more down-to-earth Churchill. Of course hindsight appeared to support this interpretation, with Poland soon after the war falling within the Soviet orbit.

However, there is an alternative interpretation. One is that a 'free election' meant something different to Stalin than to Western leaders (indeed, Stalin would never have experienced a 'free' election in the Western sense). Stalin did not automatically break his promises: for example he fulfilled his promise not to interfere in the Greek Civil War which was soon to break out. The most likely interpretation is that Stalin was acting pragmatically. Poland was vitally important to the USSR, both for historical reasons and because Stalin was determined to have friendly states on Russia's Western borders as security against attack – which is not the same as suggesting that Stalin was waiting for an opportunity to spread Communism Westwards. One consistent feature of later Soviet foreign policy under Stalin was that it put the USSR's national interests before ideological considerations.

Most leaders behave pragmatically. Churchill certainly did. In 1944 Churchill had met Stalin and suggested dividing Europe into spheres of interest. Churchill wrote his proposals on a scrap of paper, and Stalin agreed to them. The proposals gave the USSR 90 per cent influence in Romania and 70 per cent in Bulgaria in return for 90 per cent British influence in Greece, whilst influence in Yugoslavia and Hungary would be divided equally between them. There was no reference to the USA, and Churchill told an adviser that there was nothing he could do for Poland. If there was a Western 'sell-out' at Yalta, it was based on very practical considerations, and was made without the benefit of hindsight.

When the three Powers met again, at Potsdam in July and August 1945, the situation was different. The war in Europe was over, Truman was now the American President, and Clement Attlee replaced Churchill during the Conference. Truman took a much tougher line than Roosevelt, especially on Poland. Nevertheless the German frontier with Poland was finalised (the 'Oder–Neisse line') and arrangements were made for the occupation and control of Germany and Berlin. There was no general peace settlement agreed. What changed at Potsdam was not the Soviet position – Stalin was still concerned to consolidate Soviet power on the USSR's borders – but the American position, which hardened partly due to the confidence which possession of the Atom bomb now gave the USA.

2 ❧ THE DIVISION OF EUROPE 1945–55

A *The Truman Doctrine and the Marshall Plan*

World War II had the effect of bringing the USA out of isolation. American economic and military power had played a crucial role in the defeat of Germany, and the USA was now to be a key player in bolstering the West and determining the future of Europe. Europe had been seriously weakened by the war, and there were particular fears which determined American and British policy in the aftermath of war:

MAP 30

Central and Eastern Europe in 1945

Key:
1 Russian zone
2 British zone
3 US zone
4 French zone

Polish gains from Germany
Russian gains from Poland
Russian gains from Germany

0   200   400
Scale (km)

- Britain, weakened by its war efforts, began to withdraw from some areas of involvement such as Greece, where there was a civil war, and parts of its empire such as India and Palestine. There were fears that the USSR might seek to exploit any resulting power vacuum
- Communist parties were making headway in Central and Eastern Europe, mostly with Soviet backing or encouragement. Without the 'containment' of Communism, it might spread to Western Europe
- even in more established Powers such as France and Italy there were serious economic problems, industrial unrest and a growth in Communist support. Material help was needed to bolster democratic governments.

The result of these fears was the Truman Doctrine of March 1947 in which the American President made a public commitment to 'contain' the spread of Communism to the Free world. It was followed by the Marshall Plan which promised massive economic aid to countries recovering from the war. The West saw this as generosity. Some later commentators, and Soviet propaganda, pictured Marshall Aid as a deliberate attempt to bolster American influence in Western Europe and exclude the Soviet *Bloc*. The offer was originally made to all States, and the Czech Government expressed its interest. However, it was soon pressurised by Moscow into rejecting the offer, which in any case had certain strings attached.

The impact of Marshall Aid was considerable:

- billions of dollars of aid assisted Western European Governments in stabilising their economies and helped to reduce the threat of electoral success by Communist Parties, particularly in France and Italy, where they had considerable support

KEY ISSUE

What were the importance of the Truman Doctrine and the Marshall Plan in the development of the Cold War?

● the effect of this aid, by boosting the economies of Western Europe, increased the division between them and the economically far less prosperous regions of Central and Eastern Europe

● Soviet suspicions of American motives were increased. These suspicions were fuelled by incidents such as American interference in the 1947 Italian elections, in which the USA funded the main anti-Communist Party, and by the fact that the Americans gave aid to Franco in return for the use of air bases in Spain

● Marshall Aid led to the Soviet creation in September 1947 of the Communist Information Bureau or 'Cominform'. This body in effect replaced the old Comintern in its aim of supporting Communist movements in the West. For example, the Cominform supported strikes in France and Italy in 1947–8.

TABLE 49

Date chart of events in the Cold War 1945–62

1945	Feb	Yalta Conference
	July–Aug	Potsdam Conference
1946	Mar	Churchill referred to 'Iron Curtain' in Europe
	Oct	Fourth Republic created in France
1947	Jan	Bizonia created by Britain and US
	Mar	Truman Doctrine outlined
	June	Marshall Plan proposed
	Oct	Creation of Cominform
1948	Feb	Communist Government in power in Czechoslovakia
	April	OEEC set up to administer Marshall Aid
	June	Yugoslavia expelled from Cominform
		Soviet blockade of Berlin imposed
1949	April	Creation of NATO
	May	Federal Republic of Germany (West Germany) created
		Berlin Blockade lifted
	Oct	Chinese Communists in power
		German Democratic Republic (East Germany) created
1950	June	Beginning of Korean War
1951	September	Explosion of first Soviet atomic bomb
1953	Mar	Death of Stalin
	June	Risings in East Germany
	Aug	USSR exploded H-bomb
1954	May	French defeat at Dien Bien Phu
1955	May	Creation of Warsaw Pact
		West Germany joined NATO
1956	Feb	Khrushchev's 'secret speech' attacking Stalin
	Oct–Nov	Hungarian Rising
1957	Mar	Rome Treaties created EEC
1958	May	De Gaulle returned to power in France
1959	Jan	Castro took power in Cuba
1960	May	Shooting down of U-2 spy plane
1961	April	French Army revolt in Algeria
	Aug	Berlin Wall built
1962	Oct	Cuban Missile crisis

B *The Communist advance in Central and Eastern Europe*

The USA and Britain accepted that, because of the role of the USSR in defeating Germany, much of Central and Eastern Europe was within the Soviet sphere of influence. The problem for the West was that no one was sure of Stalin's intentions. It was recognised that at the very least Stalin wanted friendly Governments on the USSR's Western borders as a buffer against future attacks from the West. However, particularly as the Cold War developed, many in the West assumed that Stalin had a much more ambitious aim of consolidating Communist control in his sphere of influence and then seeking to extend Soviet influence into Western Europe itself.

The process of establishing Communist control in Central and Eastern Europe was more complex than was generally appreciated at the time:

- the first stage was straightforward: the power of pro-German *élites* in the occupied countries such as Hungary was quickly destroyed, for example by land seizures
- Communist parties increased their support in the region. This was not done by Soviet pressure alone. There was considerable popular support for Communists who had campaigned for radical reform before the war and who had been prominent in resistance against the Nazis. There was no wish to restore the old right-wing regimes
- the process of establishing new Governments was complicated by the fact that some countries, notably Poland, had Governments-in-exile in Britain with their own claims to power, even if they had less popular support
- as the Cold War intensified, the USSR did try to influence the region more, and imposed more discipline on the Communist Parties there, to ensure that not only did they come to power, but that they followed Moscow's line. In countries such as Czechoslovakia, Hungary, Bulgaria, Romania and Poland, the new Governments were usually coalitions of Communists, Socialists, Agrarian parties based on peasant support, and various democratic groups. The Communists usually won control of important ministries such as the Interior ministries, which controlled the police. Communist politicians who were experienced in political infighting, and who were assisted by Moscow and the ultimate threat of Soviet intervention, then eased other parties out of the coalition Governments, often forcibly united the Socialist parties with themselves, and took control of the Governments. Then those opponents who did not voluntarily go into foreign exile were usually arrested. Non-Communist Governments sometimes aided their own destruction.

By 1948 Communist control was reasonably secure in most countries of Central and Eastern Europe.

KEY ISSUE

How did Communist movements come to power in Central and Eastern Europe after the war?

ANALYSIS

The Communist takeover of Czechoslovakia

Western analyses of the Communist take-over in Czechoslovakia often presented it as a carefully conceived *coup*, probably engineered by Moscow, but this is to simplify a complex situation. After the war Stalin showed considerable caution in his dealings with Czechoslovakia. The Communists already had considerable popular support, winning 39 per cent of the vote in the May 1946 elections, but President Beneš was wary of Soviet influence and hoped that Czechoslovakia could be a bridge between East and West.

Czech Communists already controlled the army and the police, and won the peasants' support by giving them land confiscated from the German inhabitants who were expelled after the war. After the election Gottwald became head of a Coalition Government freely entered into by members of the wartime Government-in -Exile and the Communist Party. He soon ran into difficulties. Gottwald's willingness to accept Marshall Aid from the USA was opposed by Moscow, and Socialist members of the Government complained when several non-Communist police officials were sacked. An election was set for May 1948, but the Government was divided. Social Democrats remained in the Government, but members of other parties resigned in protest at Communist proposals to change the electoral system. It was probably a bluff which went wrong. The other parties hoped to force a showdown and push Beneš into refusing their resignations and calling an election. They claimed that they were trying to bolster Beneš in resisting the Communists, but they gave Beneš no practical support. There was no evidence of a Communist conspiracy, and the other parties had blundered by essentially removing themselves from the scene.

The Communists felt encouraged to press for further changes. Socialists who refused to join the Communists were arrested, and the Communists had a majority in parliament. Beneš agreed to a Communist-dominated Government. Communists held all the key posts and were in control, without having to call on Stalin's offer of help from the Red Army.

The Czech Communists had seized an opportunity. But they did not plan it beforehand. The distinguished British historian H Seton Watson wrote in the *Manchester Guardian* on 4 August 1949, 'The Communists conquered Czechoslovakia not by smashing the state machine but by taking it over from above after careful penetration.'

C *The Berlin crisis 1948–9*

GERMANY AFTER THE WAR

The Potsdam Conference had issued certain guidelines on the future of Germany:

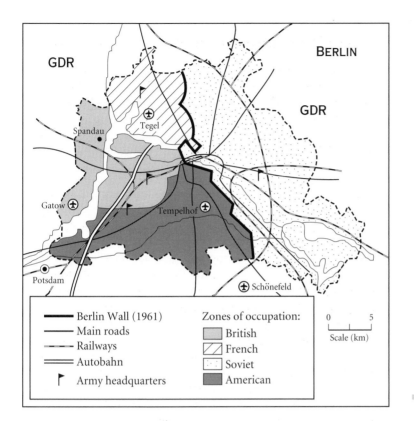

MAP 31
Divided Berlin

- along with Austria, Germany was divided into four military zones of occupation – American, Soviet, British and French
- Berlin, deep inside the Soviet zone, was itself divided into four zones. The three Western Powers had rights of access to Berlin across the Soviet zone of Germany
- Germany would pay $20 billion reparations, half going to the USSR
- the occupying Powers would carry out denazification, democratisation, demilitarisation and **decartelisation**
- however, there was no formal peace treaty signed, and no suggestion in 1945 that any geographical divisions in Germany would somehow become permanent.

decartelisation the breaking up of great industrial and business cartels which restricted competition

THE CAUSES OF THE 1948–9 CRISIS

Already in 1946 there were arguments between the West and the USSR about how and when German reparations should be paid. The West was keen to help German reconstruction in order to assist long-term stability, whereas the Soviets were anxious to extract payment from Germany and simply took what they wanted from their zone. A series of actions by both sides intensified distrust between them and impeded a proper settlement of what had already become the 'German problem':

- in January 1947 Britain and the USA combined their zones into the single economic unit of Bizonia. The British had already decided that the USSR would never agree to a united Germany that was not Communist and so pushed for an independent West German state. Such a decision was formally agreed at a six-Power London Conference in June 1948, followed soon afterwards by the introduction of a new West German currency, the *Deutsche Mark* (DM)

● the USSR responded to these unilateral actions by the West with its own initiatives: in June 1947 it created a German Economic Commission, with more economic powers in its zone; the Soviets mobilised popular opinion against a separate West German state; and in June 1948 they introduced the East *Mark* as a currency in their zone.

The stage was set for a crisis which no one really wanted. Both sides blamed the other for the hardening of positions.

THE BERLIN BLOCKADE AND AIRLIFT

On 24 June 1948 the Soviets imposed a blockade on Allied land access to West Berlin, in an attempt to stop the creation of a West German state, which in Soviet eyes would become a powerful part of the anti-Soviet Western alliance. Stalin probably hoped to force the West into renegotiating the arrangements for Berlin and Germany. With West Berlin effectively cut off from outside support, the expectation was that the city would be starved into surrender unless the West compromised.

The West responded with a massive airlift of supplies into West Berlin. The airlift lasted for eleven months until May 1949. It was an effective response by the West, both practically and psychologically, because despite the costs and effort involved, the West was calling

PICTURE 38

A Soviet cartoon satirising Nazi war plans

Stalin's bluff. It rightly calculated that the USSR would not shoot its planes down, the only possible means of stopping the airlift, but one which would have started a general war which the USSR could not win in face of the West's monopoly of atomic weapons. The Blockade was eventually lifted, and the whole affair had important consequences:

● the North Atlantic Treaty Organisation was set up in 1949, comprising several West European countries along with the USA and Canada. An attack on one member was to be regarded as an attack on all. NATO confirmed that the USA was committed to the defence of Western Europe

● there was far less uncertainty in relations between the two Superpowers. The rules of engagement were now much clearer, and in this paradoxical respect, the Berlin crisis had a stabilising effect upon international relations

● the division of Germany became more formalised. The West German Republic was created in 1949. Konrad Adenauer was elected first Chancellor and a Constitution was put together

● the response by the Soviets was the creation in October 1949 of the German Democratic Republic (GDR). The East German State was closely modelled on the system in the USSR, and the leading figure was

KEY ISSUE

What were the consequences for Europe of the 1948–9 Berlin crisis?

MAP 32
The Warsaw Pact confronting NATO

Party Secretary Walther Ulbricht (the equivalent of the Communist Party in the GDR was the Socialist Unity Party – SED). However, the USSR was not yet committed to the existence of this separate East German State, and for several years considered using its existence as bargaining tool in a possible general European settlement

● in 1955 the Warsaw Pact was set up as a counter to NATO. It consisted of the USSR and other Eastern *Bloc* countries, although Yugoslavia was never a member. The principal difference from NATO was that the USSR dominated the Warsaw Pact much more completely than the USA dominated NATO.

See pages 357–8

After 1949 the two Germanies to some extent went their separate ways, although Berlin remained as a potential flashpoint in the Cold War, and did become one again in 1961.

D *The widening of the Cold War*

In an age dominated by two Superpowers, the Cold War became a global phenomenon from which Europe could not be isolated. An area of several flashpoints was the Far East. Mao Zedong's Communists came to power in China in 1949. As a consequence, the USA became concerned about Communist expansion in the Far East, particularly in the former European colonies. The USA suspected a worldwide conspiracy to spread Communism – a fear which never materialised, because the Chinese and Soviets became bitter enemies despite both claiming Marxist credentials. However, a crisis in the Cold War exploded in 1950 when the Communist-led North Koreans, probably prompted by Stalin, invaded South Korea. The attack was pushed back by United Nations forces, containing some British troops but essentially an American operation. When UN forces invaded North Korea, China joined the war on North Korea's side. After two years of fighting an uneasy truce was declared, although no peace treaty was signed. 'Containment' of Communism by the USA seemed to have worked, and NATO was replicated in the Far East by SEATO (South East Asia Treaty Organisation), to which some European countries belonged. For much of the 1950s Western policy was determined by President Eisenhower and his Secretary of State John Foster Dulles. They believed in the 'Domino theory': if one country were allowed to fall to Communism, so the next country would, and so on. This philosophy led the USA into its costly involvement in Vietnam, once the French had failed to prevent the incursion into their former colony of Indo-China of the nationalist, and later Communist, forces of the *Viet Minh*.

3 ⌁ DEVELOPMENTS IN CENTRAL AND EASTERN EUROPE 1948–62

A *Stalin's USSR*

Stalin's rule in the USSR after World War II was very similar to before.

	1940	1945	1950 (Plan)	1950 (Actual)
National Income (index)	100	83	138	164
Gross Industrial Production	100	92	148	173
Producers'/capital goods	100	112	–	205
Consumer goods	100	59	–	123
Gross Agricultural Production	100	60	127	99
Coal (million tons)	165.9	149.3	250	261.1
Electricity (milliard kwhs)	48.3	43.2	82	91.2
Oil (million tons)	31.1	19.4	35.4	37.9
Steel (million tons)	18.3	12.3	25.4	27.3
Tractors (thousands)	66.2	14.7	112	242.5
Workers and Employees (millions)	31.2	27.3	33.5	39.2

TABLE 50
*The Fourth Five-Year Plan
(From Soviet sources)*

Purges were less extensive than in the 1930s, but just as arbitrary. In 1949 the Leningrad Party organisation was purged, despite its heroic work during the wartime siege, and just before his death Stalin launched a purge against Russian Jews, following an accusation that several Jewish doctors in Moscow were plotting to poison him. Stalin's rule after 1945 actually became more autocratic, if that were possible: he began to rule without the Central Committee and the *Politburo*, whilst Soviet citizens lived in fear of Lavrenti Beria's *NKVD* and must have been aware of the *gulags*, the extensive system of labour camps across the USSR.

The post-war years were mainly devoted to restoring the economic damage done by the war. Collectives or state farms were re-established in the once-occupied territories and the country's infrastructure was rebuilt. Although significant progress was made, as shown by Table 50, there were massive sacrifices made and not all targets could be reached.

KEY ISSUE

*How successfully did
the USSR recover from
World War II?*

B *Khrushchev's USSR*

At the time of Stalin's death in 1953 there was no obvious heir to take power. After a period of collective leadership and political manoeuvring, which also saw the arrest and execution of Beria, Nikita Khrushchev emerged as leader. He made his mark in 1956 with a speech to the Party Congress, supposedly secret but leaked to the West, in which he criticised Stalin for his 'excesses'. The speech was followed by a period of 'Destalinisation', meaning a relaxation of some of the harsher and more arbitrary aspects of Stalinism. Khrushchev boasted that the USSR would soon achieve Communism and overtake the West, but he more realistically recognised that there were urgently needed reforms, particularly as the Stalinist command economy and rigidly controlled society were not achieving significant economic progress. Consequently Khrushchev instituted a number of measures:

● many collective farms were changed into state farms, whilst the Virgin Lands scheme saw massive areas of previously uncultivated

KEY ISSUE

How successful were Khrushchev's reforms?

land turned over to agriculture. Peasants were given more incentives. However, food production did not significantly increase
● there were attempts to decentralise the command economy, giving more incentive to managers. There was more emphasis on producing consumer goods for ordinary people. However, Khrushchev's tinkering with the system never solved the fundamental problems of inefficiency and poor quality, and although living standards rose, they remained low by Western European standards
● attempts to also decentralise political controls involved reducing the authority of some of the powerful central ministries and sending bureaucrats away from Moscow and into the provinces – an unpopular development which was stifled by the bureaucrats themselves
● there was a limited relaxation of cultural controls, resulting in less censorship. However, no fundamental criticism of the regime was allowed, and there was renewed persecution of churches.

Khrushchev's reforms had relatively little success. This was partly due to the fact that the Party itself resisted reform, and if reform were to work, it would be Party members who would enforce the changes. Khrushchev was not trying to change the fundamentals of the one-party state as moulded by Stalin. Even so he upset powerful factions such as the military, he suffered a serious loss of face particularly over the Cuban missiles climbdown and his populist style of mixing with the people, in total contrast to Stalin's aloofness, did not endear him to conservative Party leaders. His policies of limited Destalinisation were also held to be responsible for unrest within the Socialist camp, particularly in Hungary. In October 1964 the *Politburo* voted him out of office. At least Khrushchev had achieved something: as he himself said, in Stalin's more ruthless era nobody who fell from office would have been allowed to survive in retirement as Khrushchev was until his death in 1971.

See pages 359–60

C *The Communist States of Central and Eastern Europe*

Once Communist parties were in control of the Soviet-dominated *Bloc*, by the end of the 1940s, they introduced Stalinist-style institutions and practices in most cases modelled on the Soviet model. This was scarcely surprising, since most of the leaders had come to power after years in the Communist underground: many were Stalinist by instinct, and in some cases had even received their political training in Moscow. Typical of the developments were:

● purges conducted against opponents of the Communists, and then, once they were established in power, conducted against various individuals and factions within the Communist Parties themselves
● the introduction of Stalinist economic measures, particularly centralised command economies with a priority on heavy industry, and the collectivisation of agriculture – although the latter was abandoned in Poland after 1956

See page 265

● the full panoply of political, social and cultural controls typical of Stalinism in the USSR.

CZECHOSLOVAKIA

After 1948 over 500 000 ordinary party members and bureaucrats were purged as the Communist leader Klement Gottwald established his authority. Czechoslovakia became a notoriously hard-line state under both Gottwald and his successor from 1953, Antonin Novotný. Novotný showed his ruthless credentials in two ways in particular:

● he showed contempt for the Slovak wing of the Party, doing away with many Slovak institutions
● he resisted calls for reform in the wake of Khrushchev's Destalinisation measures, for example refusing to rehabilitate the victims of earlier purges
● Novotný continued to resist change until he lost Soviet backing and was forced to resign as Party leader in 1968.

> ### KEY ISSUE
>
> *What features charac-terised the political and economic systems of the new Communist States of Central and Eastern Europe?*

POLAND

Communists and Socialists in the new Polish Government began to introduce radical reforms from 1946 onwards. However, the Communist leader Wladyslaw Gomulka tried to resist total Soviet domination, for example by resisting collectivisation of agriculture, and was ousted in 1948 in favour of Boleslaw Bierut, who followed the Moscow line. Following serious disturbances by workers protesting about their conditions in 1956, Gomulka was rehabilitated as First Secretary. At first Gomulka appeared to be offering a new approach, allowing contested elections, albeit between Party members, in 1957. However, by the 1960s there was a return to a hard-line approach, although Poland was unique in the Eastern *Bloc* in having avoided major collectivisation of agriculture and remaining a strongly Catholic state.

HUNGARY

Communists were part of a coalition Government which took power in Hungary after World War II. Following political infighting and manoeuvring, other parties were edged out of office or their leaders arrested. By 1948 the Hungarian Workers' Party (the Communists) were virtually in control and the purges began. Under Matyas Rakosi Hungary, like Czechoslovakia, became a hard-line state on the Stalinist model. However, following a poor economic performance, Rakosi was forced out of office in 1953. The new Prime Minister, Imre Nagy, was a reformer in the Khrushchev mould, and sought to raise the standard of living. More dangerously, he talked of genuine popular participation in the Party and a more open style of government, although he was assuming the continued dominance of one party. In 1955 Nagy was expelled from office and from the Party by worried colleagues. However, the USSR was alarmed by the divisions which it saw in Hungary. Nagy was rehabilitated in an attempt to stabilise the situation, but popular feeling against the presence of Soviet troops in Hungary led to protests

PICTURE 39
Soviet tanks in Budapest, 1956

KEY ISSUE

*What was the signifi-
cance of the 1956
Hungarian Rising?*

in Budapest and occupation of the capital by Soviet troops in October 1956. About 3000 Hungarians were killed during the rising – another 2000 were later executed and about 200 000 Hungarians fled to the West. The Soviets formed a new Government under János Kádár. Nagy, blamed for not preventing the Rising, was executed.

The Hungarian rising and the brutality of its suppression were significant events not just for Hungary but for the Cold War generally. The Rising confirmed Western impressions of the USSR as a dangerous, dogmatic force, not to be trusted. However, the Western Powers were involved in their own crisis in the Middle East, in conflict with Egypt over Nasser's nationalisation of the Suez Canal. In any case, they recognised Hungary as being within the USSR's sphere of influence, and Khrushchev made it clear that he would brook no Western interference. The rules of engagement implicitly drawn up at the time of the Berlin crisis were being observed.

ROMANIA

The Socialists and Communists took control of post-war Romania by 1946, and the Communist leader Gheorghe Gheorghiu-Dej at first followed the orthodox Stalinist line. However, after Stalin's death he followed an independent line of 'national Communism', requesting that Soviet troops leave Romania and objecting to Soviet proposals that Romania organise its economy around agriculture, in order to provide food exports for the USSR, rather than industrialise. Strangely, Moscow accepted this 'independent' line, probably because Romania was less powerful than States like Poland or Hungary, and the Communist Party in Romania stayed firmly in control of events.

BULGARIA

The Communist take-over in Bulgaria was a bloody affair. Over 30 000 representatives of the previous regime were shot and all other parties were banned by the time the Communists secured complete control in 1947. Thereafter Bulgaria loyally followed Moscow's line, under the leadership of Vulko Chervenkov from 1956, and Todor Zhivkov from 1956.

YUGOSLAVIA

Socialism in Yugoslavia followed a different course from the rest of the Eastern *Bloc*, partly because of the way in which the Yugoslav State emerged from the war. Yugoslav partisans played a major role in driving the Axis forces out of Yugoslavia, and the Communist leader Josip Tito secured Stalin's agreement that Soviet troops would leave the country after Belgrade was liberated in 1944. Therefore Yugoslavia was spared Soviet occupation. Nevertheless the consolidation of Tito's rule was marked by bloodshed. Although he joined a coalition Government in March 1945, domestic opposition was eliminated. This included thousands of non-Communist partisans, many of whom were supporters of the royalist partisan leader Draza Mihailović, who was captured in March 1946 and executed.

The new Federal Republic comprised six Republics and two autonomous regions, one of which was Kosovo, which had a predominantly Albanian population. The Yugoslavian situation was complicated by the fact that the Federation contained seven principal nationalities, the most numerous being Serbs and Croats. Religious and ethnic divisions were kept in check principally because Communist control papered over the cracks. The 1946 Constitution organised the Party on Stalinist lines, and there was a programme of industrialisation. However, there was a cumbersome bureaucracy, since as well as central ministries there were six separate regional bureaucracies. Even before Tito died in 1980, strains in the unity of the Republic were evident.

Yugoslavia played an important role in Cold War politics. Tito and Stalin fell out, principally because Stalin refused to back Tito's claims on Trieste or Tito's wish to set up a Balkan federation, whilst Tito would not support the Cominform. Yugoslavia was expelled from the Cominform in 1948. Therefore, although Tito's regime continued to promote Socialist policies such as collectivisation, it was courted by the West as a weak link in the Soviet *Bloc*. The USA provided considerable military and economic aid to Tito from 1950 onwards.

Although overt dissent was not tolerated, Yugoslavian Socialism was more relaxed than elsewhere in the Eastern *Bloc*, and a considerable degree of religious and cultural diversity was permitted.

> ### KEY ISSUE
>
> *Why did Yugoslavia follow a different course from the rest of the Eastern Bloc?*

EAST GERMANY

The East German Communist regime could not feel secure. It was in the front line of the Cold War, for many years its very existence was not recognised by the West, and there was not even a guarantee that the USSR would support its existence permanently. Possibly for these reasons the GDR was also one of the most hard-line states in the Eastern *Bloc*, and its leader Ulbricht was rigidly Stalinist in outlook.

Ulbricht's regime was not popular within the GDR. In June 1953 there were serious disturbances across the country, sparked by the discontent of farmers protesting at low prices and the threat of collectivisation, and industrial workers who resented state controls and the sacrifices expected of them in order to finance the Five-year Plan. Ulbricht was forced to show his dependence on the USSR by calling in Soviet troops to crush the revolt in Berlin and elsewhere. Moscow then insisted on concessions such as the production of more consumer goods. Nevertheless Ulbricht also increased the powers of the *Stasi* or secret police, buttressed by an army of private informers. Ulbricht managed to defeat his own rivals within the Party and felt secure in power by the late 1950s.

4 ∽ DEVELOPMENTS IN WESTERN EUROPE 1948–62

There was a gradual recognition amongst more far-sighted politicians in Western Europe after World War II that the pre-war world had disappeared for good. New realities had to be faced if their countries were to recover from the war without being totally dominated by the the USSR or the USA, although if complete independence were not possible, most people in the West far preferred the prospect of living under American influence. An awareness that countries could not go it alone if they wished to achieve either prosperity or security led to such initiatives as the Common Market, the precursor of the European Union, and involvement in defence initiatives such as NATO. The process was not smooth. France and West Germany early on recognised that their future prosperity depended on a level of co-operation between them unthinkable before the war. However, the French, particularly under de Gaulle, still harboured the ambition to be the leading force in Western Europe, and were reluctant for example to contribute fully to NATO since they saw it as an instrument of American domination as well as a means of defence. Many in Britain were reluctant to surrender what was perceived as their economic independence and would not commit themselves to the Treaty of Rome which established the Common Market. When the Market proved a successful economic venture, Britain applied to join in 1962, and again in 1967. However, the application was rejected mainly because of opposition from the French leader de Gaulle, who distrusted Britain for its links with its old Empire and with the USA. In one major respect at least De Gaulle was right: one of the most notable features of West European history in this period was the degree to which American influences, expressed particularly in areas such as the cinema and music, came to dominate popular culture, reinforcing the USA's economic dominance.

co
fro
lin
on
trc
the
fro
clc
of
Ca

Du
de
Ge
Eu

Kh
cat
pic
the
to
wo
●

WEST GERMANY – THE GERMAN FEDERAL REPUBLIC

The most remarkable feature of West German history in this period was the speed of its economic growth, which undoubtedly assisted its political stability and soon made it a valuable part of the Western anti-Communist alliance, despite initial misgivings from its neighbours, hardly surprising given its Nazi past.

The new state was ably led by Chancellor Konrad Adenauer, who united the Christian Democrats (CDU) and the Christian Socialists (CSU). Amongst Adenauer's achievements were:

● securing the recognition by the West of West Germany as a sovereign state in May 1955, its admission into NATO and its rearmament
● securing social harmony partly by promoting good labour relations. For example Adenauer secured trade union support for joining the European Coal and Steel community, the precursor of the Common Market. He also embarked on a rapid house-building programme
● securing good relations with neighbouring countries, particularly France.

Some historians dispute whether Adenauer succeeded in creating a 'new' liberal Germany, rather than resurrecting a traditional society in which there was still much latent respect for the Nazis and a reluctance to take the blame for the war. However, there is no doubt that the resurgence of Germany was one of the great 'success stories' of post-war Europe.

FRANCE

In several respects the history of post-war France was also one of success, given the crisis of confidence before the war and the turmoil of the war years, including the experience of occupation and the Vichy regime. Like West Germany, France achieved considerable economic prosperity, based initially on central economic planning. Paradoxically the Fourth Republic down to 1958 was marked by political instability and changes of government, hardly a new phenomenon in French history. Although Charles de Gaulle was elected head of a Provisional Government in November 1945, he resigned the following January through a reluctance to indulge in coalition politics, particularly with Communist ministers. French politics for much of the next decade were based around an alliance of moderate centrist parties, an alliance which became known as the 'Third Force'.

The Fourth Republic faced major challenges which contributed to political instability:

pre
Bei
A
cor

● between 1946 and 1954 France fought a long war to maintain its Empire in Indo-China against the nationalist movement for Vietnamese independence, the *Viet Minh*, led by Ho Chi Minh. A crushing defeat at Dien Bien Phu in May 1954 finally forced France to concede defeat and accept that its days as a great imperial Power were over. Tunisia was granted independence in 1956

KEY ISSUE

To what extent, and why, did West Germany become a major state in post-war Europe?

KEY ISSUE

What problems faced the Fourth French Republic?

seemed a real danger of confrontation between the Superpowers when the USSR threatened to intervene directly to save Egypt from defeat. The USA placed its air bases in Europe on full nuclear alert, without consulting its NATO allies, even though such an act would have placed them directly in the firing line. The crisis led Western leaders to doubt the wisdom of over-dependence on the USA.

B *Britain and the Cold War*

Britain had an ambivalent attitude towards the USA. The British were very proud of their perceived 'special relationship' with the USA. It was a relationship which had been forged in World War II, and despite coming under strain in 1956 when the USA refused to support Britain during the Suez crisis, solidarity had been demonstrated during the Cuban Missiles crisis. British Prime Minister Harold Macmillan had got on well with Kennedy and had secured the *Polaris* missile from the Americans. This missile was the key part of Britain's independent nuclear deterrent. However, relations cooled after 1963. President Johnson and British Prime Minister Harold Wilson did not get on well, and Britain would not provide the support for American policy in Vietnam which the USA expected. Britain further annoyed the Americans by reducing its own military commitment in the Far East, mainly for economic reasons. Such actions convinced many Americans that their Allies acted unreasonably, expecting the USA to provide the bulk of Western Europe's defence against the Eastern *Bloc*, whilst not contributing enough themselves nor providing committed support to America's own interests. On the other hand, Britain's relationship with the USA caused problems within Europe itself, particularly with de Gaulle's France, which felt that Britain was tied to the USA and could not be trusted to pursue a policy which was in Europe's genuine interest, or just as bad, might challenge French pretensions to be the leading influence in Western Europe.

C *France and the Cold War*

Under de Gaulle, France from 1958 pursued an independent foreign policy, although it technically remained part of the Western alliance. Such a stance was bound to create difficulties in Europe:

- de Gaulle was determined to limit American influence in Europe, and particularly resented American dominance in NATO. He was determined that France should have its own nuclear deterrence force
- France pursued a policy of close friendship with West Germany. De Gaulle saw these two countries as the arbiters of the new Europe, but French policy created tensions with America and also isolated Britain, which was essentially kept out of the EEC by de Gaulle's opposition. De Gaulle thought that Britain would be a channel through which the USA would increase its influence in Europe

● France strongly opposed American policy in Vietnam.

France's independent line was demonstrated in various actions:

● in 1963 France and West Germany signed a treaty outside NATO and vetoed Britain's application to join the EEC
● de Gaulle refused to sign the Test-Ban Treaty, opposed American proposals for a multilateral nuclear force, and insisted on France having its own nuclear deterrent
● In 1966 France withdrew its forces from NATO, which in turn transferred its headquarters from Paris to Brussels
● de Gaulle made his own independent initiatives in Cold War politics, for example negotiating with the USSR, an action seen by the USA as destabilising the Western Alliance.

It was clear by the early 1970s that whilst the Western Alliance was integral to the defence of Western Europe, the leading Powers in Europe were also pursuing independent policies. Although the USA still exercised enormous influence by virtue of its economic and military strength, and American culture was still very influential in Europe, Western Europe had come a long way from 1945 when the USA was clearly calling all the shots and countries emerging from World War II seemed dependent on Washington for recovery and for protection of their independence.

KEY ISSUE
What were the principles of French foreign policy during the period of the Cold War?

THE ERA OF DÉTENTE 1973–80

Although the Cold War continued to dominate much of international relations, particularly when crises focused attention on the rivalries of the Superpowers and the dangers of nuclear war, there was also a change in those relations which had important implications for Europe. This was the period of *Détente*, or relaxation of tension: the various Powers sought ways of defusing tension, and in particular sought agreement on arms control, limiting the growth in arsenals of nuclear and conventional weapons. The ultimate objective was actual disarmament. *Détente* was marked by a series of long-drawn out negotiations. These did not mean that either side had given up its fundamental objections to the political and economic system of the other. The USA was still convinced of the superiority of capitalism and saw the USSR as a dangerous threat both to its way of life and to world peace. Likewise the USSR still professed belief in the ultimate triumph of Socialism and the warlike intentions of the West. However, there seemed good reasons to limit the growth of weapons and reduce the risk of a devastating war:

1964			1974	
USA	*USSR*		*USA*	*USSR*
834	200	ICBM	1054	1575
416	120	SLBM	656	720
630	190	Long-range bombers	437	140

ICBM = Intercontinental ballistic missile
SLBM = Submarine-launched ballistic missile

TABLE 52
The nuclear balance between 1964 and 1974

KEY ISSUE

How significant was the Solidarity movement in Poland?

there was further unrest in 1976 following a new announcement of price rises, and further strikes and protests in 1980. An organised opposition began to form in Poland in the late 1970s, despite harassment and arrests, with the main focus being the Lenin shipyard in Gdansk (formerly Danzig). Here the strikes were led by the union activist Lech Walęsa.

The Government began negotiations with *Solidarity*, the first independent trade union in the Communist world, because it was afraid of the prospect of a general strike and massive social unrest, with possible Soviet intervention. Stanislaw Kania replaced Gierek as Party leader in 1980. The following year General Wojcieck Jaruzelski was appointed Prime Minister, and soon afterwards replaced Kania as Party leader. *Solidarity* won concessions, but was soon divided within itself as members argued about the extent to which it should engage in political activities or remain essentially a trade union organisation. Jaruzelski was under considerable pressure from the Kremlin to act decisively. In December 1981 martial law was declared, *Solidarity*'s leaders arrested and trade union activity suspended. The threat of Soviet intervention was lifted, at least for the time being, but although martial law was abolished in 1983, other repressive laws remained. Jaruzelski was appointed President in 1985. The Polish economy was in decline, the population remained passive, and *Solidarity* continued to operate underground although it had been formally banned. Polish prospects were not promising.

HUNGARY

Under the leadership of János Kádár, Hungary appeared to achieve considerable stability following the crushing of the Hungarian Rising in 1956. Kádár felt secure enough in 1962 to declare 'Whereas the Rakosites used to say that those who are not with us are against us, we say, those who are not against us are with us. By Eastern *Bloc* standards, Hungary's regime was relatively relaxed. There was less censorship and more tolerance of 'foreign' influences than elsewhere in the Eastern *Bloc*. The USSR tolerated this approach because it was satisfied that the Hungarian Communist Party was firmly in control and was loyal to the basic tenets of the Kremlin.

The key to Hungary's apparent success was its New Economic Mechanism, introduced in 1968. It was a novel approach to managing the economy within a one-party state: central planning and allocation of resources, one of the basic tenets of the Stalinist system, was abolished. Individual enterprises were given some autonomy and were expected to make profits. The State allowed supply and demand to determine priorities. Some control was retained over the production of consumer goods, and a complex system of price controls was designed to allow for some flexibility. The early results were promising, with output in agriculture and consumer goods increasing significantly and real wages doubling. Hungarians appeared better off than many of their counterparts in the Eastern *Bloc*. During the 1970s the economy experienced a slowdown in growth, and the Government felt forced to intervene more in the economy. Nevertheless, the Hungarian economic experiment provoked considerable interest, not least in the USSR where it influenced some of the thinking behind the reforms of *perestroika* in the 1980s.

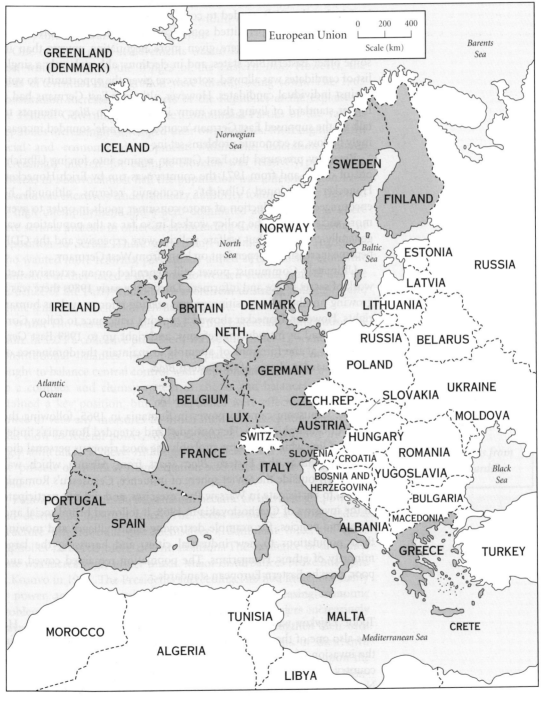

MAP 33 *Post-1991 Europe*

dealt with in *The Khrushchev Era 1953–64* by M McCauley (Longman Seminar Studies, 1995). Also useful on the USSR since 1945 is *Last of Empires* by J Keep (OUP, 1996). A good biography is *Gorbachev* by M McCauley (Longman, 1998).

Germany's post-war history is dealt with in *Germany Since 1945* by L Kettenacker (Oxford, 1997). Useful material on East Germany will be found in *Anatomy of a Dictatorship: Inside the GDR, 1949–89* by M Fulbrook (Oxford, 1995). A readable account of the end of divided Germany is *The Rush to German Unity* by K Jarausch (Oxford, 1994). For France, useful accounts are *France Since 1945* by R Gildea (OPUS, 1996) and the later parts of *France, the Three Republics 1914–69* by P Neville (Hodder and Stoughton, 1993).

For Central and Eastern Europe, a book written for 16–19-year-olds is *The Eastern and Central European States 1945–1992* by J Laver (Hodder and Stoughton, 1999). More detailed accounts are *Eastern Europe since 1945* by G and N Swain (Macmillan, 1993) and *Central Europe Since 1945* by P Lewis (Longman, 1994). The dramatic events of 1989–92 are analysed in *Revolution in East-Central Europe* by D Mason (Westview Press, 1992). A vivid journalistic account is *We The People-The Revolution of 1990* by T Ash (Penguin, 1990). Yugoslavia before its break-up is covered in *Yugoslavia: Politics, Economics and Society* by B McFarlane (Pinter, 1988), whilst *Yugoslavia: Tracking the Break-up, 1980–92* by B Magas (Verso, 1993) is also useful.

7 ⌐ STRUCTURED QUESTIONS AND ESSAYS

1. (a) Explain briefly why Germany and Berlin were divided into zones of occupation at the end of World War II; (5 marks)
   (b) Explain why Berlin became the centre of an international crisis in 1948–9; (10 marks)
   (c) What were the consequences of the 1948 crisis for Germany and for Europe? (10 marks)

2. (a) Explain briefly the purpose of the Marshall Plan; (3 marks)
   (b) Why did the 'Iron Curtain' come into existence in Europe in the period 1945–8? (7 marks)
   (c) How justified is the statement that 'Germany was the key to the Cold War'? (15 marks)

3. Which Power was more responsible for causing the Cold War, the USA or the USSR? (25 marks)

4. (a) Explain briefly what was meant by 'Peaceful Coexistence'; (3 marks)
   (b) To what extent did Khrushchev carry out a policy of Peaceful Coexistence between 1956 and 1962? (7 marks)
   (c) To what extent did Soviet foreign policy change under Brezhnev? (15 marks)

5. Why did Communist regimes come to power in Central and Eastern Europe in the period 1945–8? (25 marks)

6. (a) Why was the Berlin Wall built in 1961? (3 marks)
   (b) Why did West and East Germany develop in different ways after 1961? (7 marks)
   (c) Why was Germany reunified in the early 1990s? (15 marks)
7. (a) What was meant by *Détente*? (10 marks)
   (b) How successful was the policy of *Détente* in securing better international relations in Europe in the 1970s? (15 marks)
8. How important was de Gaulle in French and European politics between 1945 and 1968? (25 marks)
9. (a) What was meant by *perestroika*? (3 marks)
   (b) Why did Gorbachev introduce *perestroika* into the USSR? (7 marks)
   (c) How successful was *perestroika*? (15 marks)
10. Why were the Communist regimes of Central and Eastern Europe dismantled so quickly in the late 1980s? (25 marks)
11. Why did the Cold War never become a hot war in the period 1945–91? (25 marks)

8 ᴄ⟩ SOURCE-BASED EXERCISE ON SOVIET FOREIGN POLICY

Study Sources A–D and answer the questions which follow

There is no doubt that the peoples of the Socialist countries and the Communist Parties have and must have freedom to determine their country's path to development. However, any decision of theirs must damage neither Socialism in their own country nor the fundamental interests of other Socialist countries ... This means that every Communist Party is responsible not only to its own people but also to all the Socialist countries and the entire Communist movement. Whoever forgets this is placing sole emphasis on the autonomy and independence of Communist Parties, lapses into one-sidedness, shirking his internationalist obligations.

SOURCE A
The Brezhnev Doctrine (from S Kovalev, Sovereignty and the International Obligations of Communist Countries in Pravda, *26 September 1968)*

The USSR and USA ... have agreed as follows:
First: They will proceed from the common determination that in the nuclear age there is no alternative to conducting their mutual relations on the basis of peaceful coexistence ...

Second: The USSR and USA ... will always exercise restraint in their mutual relations, and will be prepared to negotiate and settle differences by peaceful means.

Third: The USSR and USA have a special responsibility to do everything in their power so that conflicts or situations will not arise which would serve to increase international tensions. Accordingly, they will seek to promote conditions in which all countries will live in peace and security and will not be subject to outside interference in their internal affairs.

SOURCE B
Détente, Basic Principles of Relations between the USSR and The USA *signed in Moscow, 29 May 1972*

SOURCE C

Détente runs into problems.
V Nekrasov The Roots of
European Security *(Moscow,*
1984)

In the late 1970s and early 1980s international relations once more became complicated and dangerously aggravated. Increasingly active were circles [which] resented the improvement in international relations in the preceding decade and systematically attacked the process of *Détente*. In the vanguard of the forces striving to direct world developments along a dangerous path ... was the Republican Administration led by Ronald Reagan ... Washington has in effect wrecked the 1979 Soviet-US treaty on limiting strategic armaments (SALT II), a treaty which took years of hard work to prepare.

SOURCE D

A new approach? An article
by Soviet Foreign Minister
E Shevardnadze in Pravda, *June*
1990

The policy of using military power to underpin diplomacy always drove states to political bankruptcy or catastrophe ... Foreign policy can only achieve limited objectives ... Foreign policy, like domestic policy, cannot defend and protect the indefensible ... When we talk about ridding inter-state relations from ideological confrontation we have in mind the need to liberate foreign policies from deformed ideology, and from ideological extremism ... What reply is there for those who challenge us to explain why we permitted changes in Eastern Europe, or why we have agreed to withdraw our troops from there? These critics seem to imply that we should have used tanks to 'bring about order'. Can anyone seriously believe that the problem can be solved by such methods? ...

It is time we understood that neither Socialism, nor friendship, nor good neighbourliness, nor respect can rely on bayonets, tanks and bloodshed. Relations with any country must be built on mutual interests, mutual advantage, on the principle of free choice.

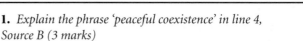

1. *Explain the phrase 'peaceful coexistence' in line 4,*
Source B (3 marks)
2. *Using your own knowledge and Source A, explain why the USSR issued the Brezhnev Doctrine in 1968 (6 marks)*
3. *(a) What changes in attitude towards international relations can you detect in these Sources? (8 marks)*
    (b) Using your own knowledge, account for these changes. (15 marks)
4. *Take any two of these Sources and assess their usefulness and reliability as evidence of the thinking behind Soviet foreign policy in the period 1968–90 (8 marks)*

Glossary